Social Networks in Language Learning and Language Teaching

Also available from Bloomsbury

Essentials for Successful English Language Teaching, by Thomas S. C. Farrell and George M. Jacobs
Foreign Language Learning and Use: Interaction in Informal Social Networks, by Naomi Kurata
Study Abroad and the Second Language Learner, edited by Martin Howard
Teaching Pragmatics and Instructed Second Language Learning, by Nicola Halenko
The Interactional Feedback Dimension in Instructed Second Language Learning, by Hossein Nassaji
The Production-Comprehension Interface in Second Language Acquisition, by Anke Lenzing

Social Networks in Language Learning and Language Teaching

Edited by Avary Carhill-Poza
and Naomi Kurata

BLOOMSBURY ACADEMIC
LONDON • NEW YORK • OXFORD • NEW DELHI • SYDNEY

BLOOMSBURY ACADEMIC
Bloomsbury Publishing Plc
50 Bedford Square, London, WC1B 3DP, UK
1385 Broadway, New York, NY 10018, USA
29 Earlsfort Terrace, Dublin 2, Ireland

BLOOMSBURY, BLOOMSBURY ACADEMIC and the Diana logo
are trademarks of Bloomsbury Publishing Plc

First published in Great Britain 2021
This paperback edition published in 2022

Copyright © Avary Carhill-Poza, Naomi Kurata and Contributors, 2021

Avary Carhill-Poza and Naomi Kurata have asserted their right under the Copyright,
Designs and Patents Act, 1988, to be identified as Editors of this work.

For legal purposes the Acknowledgments on p. ix constitute
an extension of this copyright page.

All rights reserved. No part of this publication may be reproduced or
transmitted in any form or by any means, electronic or mechanical,
including photocopying, recording, or any information storage or retrieval
system, without prior permission in writing from the publishers.

Bloomsbury Publishing Plc does not have any control over, or responsibility for,
any third-party websites referred to or in this book. All internet addresses given
in this book were correct at the time of going to press. The author and publisher
regret any inconvenience caused if addresses have changed or sites have
ceased to exist, but can accept no responsibility for any such changes.

A catalogue record for this book is available from the British Library.

Library of Congress Cataloging-in-Publication Data

Names: Carhill-Poza, Avary, editor. | Kurata, Naomi, editor.
Title: Social networks in language learning and language teaching / edited
by Avary Carhill-Poza, Naomi Kurata.
Description: New York, NY: Bloomsbury Academic, 2021. |
Includes bibliographical references and index.
Identifiers: LCCN 2020034760 (print) | LCCN 2020034761 (ebook) |
ISBN 9781350114258 (hardback) | ISBN 9781350200432 (paperback) |
ISBN 9781350114265 (ePDF) | ISBN 9781350114272 (eBook)
Subjects: LCSH: Language and languages–Study and teaching–Technological
innovations. | Language and languages–Computer network resources. |
Language and languages–Computer-assisted instruction. |
Social networks.
Classification: LCC P53.855.S625 2021 (print) | LCC P53.855 (ebook) |
DDC 418.0071–dc23
LC record available at https://lccn.loc.gov/2020034760
LC ebook record available at https://lccn.loc.gov/2020034761

ISBN: HB: 978-1-3501-1425-8
PB: 978-1-3502-0043-2
ePDF: 978-1-3501-1426-5
eBook: 978-1-3501-1427-2

Typeset by Deanta Global Publishing Services, Chennai, India

To find out more about our authors and books visit
www.bloomsbury.com and sign up for our newsletters.

Contents

List of Illustration		vii
Acknowledgments		ix
1	Social Network Analysis and its Application in Applied Linguistics *Avary Carhill-Poza and Naomi Kurata*	1
Part I	Immigrant Children and Adolescents' Social Networks in School Settings	13
2	The Social Networks of Adolescent Emergent Bilinguals in High School *Avary Carhill-Poza*	15
3	Social Networks and Patterns of Participation in Linguistically Heterogeneous Classrooms *Amanda Kibler, Lauren Molloy Elreda, Vonna Hemmler, Alexis Rutt, Sydney Cadogan, and Betina Fuentes*	37
4	Social Networks with Purpose: Heritage Language Networks of Practice among Transnational and Transcultural Japanese Youth in Sydney *Kaya Oriyama*	64
Part II	Out-of-Class Social Networks of University Students in Home-Country Settings	87
5	The Effects of Social Networks on L2 Experiences and Motivation: A Longitudinal Case Study of a University Student of Japanese in Australia *Naomi Kurata*	89
6	Changing Informal Language Learning Networks in a Gulf Arab Community *David M. Palfreyman*	113
7	How Do Social Networks Facilitate Out-of-Class L2 Learning Activities?: Case Studies of Australian and Swedish University Students of Japanese *Miho Inaba*	138

Part III Social Networks in Study Abroad Contexts ... 159

8 Implementing Mental Contrasting to Improve English Language Learner Social Networks *Hannah Trimble-Brown, Dan P. Dewey, Vashti Lee, and Dennis L. Eggett* ... 161

9 Developing Friendship or Practicing Japanese?: Differential Impacts of Language Pledge on Study Abroad Students *Atsushi Hasegawa* ... 184

10 Social Network Development and Language Learning in Multilingual Study Abroad Contexts: Case Studies of Japanese Adolescents *Levi Durbidge* ... 209

Concluding Discussion ... 235

11 A Social Network Perspective on Language Teaching *Avary Carhill-Poza and Naomi Kurata* ... 237

List of Contributors ... 249
Author Index ... 250
Subject Index ... 252

Illustration

Figures

2.1	Social networks by role, language, and academic support (N=102)	23
2.2	Peer social networks	27
4.1	Transnational Japanese youths' HLNoPs	72
5.1	Emily's motivational profiles	95
5.2	Emily's L2-related social networks	98
7.1	Melissa's social network for out-of-class language learning	147
7.2	Fredrik's social network for out-of-class language learning	148
9.1	Student housing	188
9.2	Whole program network in Week 1	191
9.3	Program network in Week 8	193
9.4	Program network in Week 8 (only "very close" ties)	194
9.5	Lily's egocentric network in Week 8 (only "very close" ties)	197
9.6	Rose's egocentric network in Week 8 (only "very close" ties)	200
9.7	Joey's egocentric network in Week 8 (only "very close" ties)	203
11.1	Language learners' social networks	242

Tables

2.1	School Descriptors as a Percentage of Total Students 2007–8	20
3.1	Classroom Demographics	44
3.2	Task Types in Study Classrooms, by Integration Level	45
3.3	Key Patterns of Active Participation	47
3.4	Level of Focal Student Participation in High and Low Integration Classrooms	48
3.5	Similarities and Differences in Types of Active Participation	49
4.1	Transnational Japanese Youths' Demographics	71
6.1	Sampling Strategies and Respondent Demographics for the Two Years	119

6.2	Core Respondents (Sample 2) and their Recruited Contacts (Sample 3)	121
6.3	Frequency of English Use (Scale: 1 (Rarely)—2 (Once a Week)—3 (A Few Times a Week)—4 (Every Day); Mann-Whitney U-Test)	122
6.4	Family Members Living with the Respondent (% of Respondents; Mann-Whitney U-Test)	124
6.5	Family Members' English-Related Experience (% of Respondents as Applicable; Mann-Whitney U-test)	125
6.6	Time Spent with Family Members Weekly (as Applicable; Scale: 1 (Once or Twice a Week)—2 (a Little Time Every Day)—3 (a Lot of Time Every Day); Mann-Whitney U-Test)	126
6.7	Frequency of Contact (Scale: 1 (Rarely)—2 (Once a Week)—3 (a Few Times a Week)—4 (Every Day); Mann-Whitney U-Test)	126
6.8	Mean Frequency of Help with English at Home (Scale: 1 (Never)—2 (Rarely)—3 (Sometimes)—4 (Often); Mann-Whitney U-Test)	127
6.9	Cited First Source of Help with English (as Applicable; Scoring: 0 (Not Mentioned)—1 (Second Resort)—2 (First Resort); Ranked for 2018; Mann-Whitney U-Test)	128
6.10	Cited main Source of Help with English at Home (% of Applicable Respondents, Ranked for 2018; Mann-Whitney U-Test)	128
6.11	Usefulness of Resources for English Learning (Scale: 1 (Not Useful)—2 (a Bit Useful)—3 (Useful)—4 (Very Useful); Ranked for 2018; Mann-Whitney U-Test)	129
6.12	Cited Main Recipient of Help with English at Home (% of Applicable Respondents, Ranked for 2018; Mann-Whitney U-Test)	131
7.1	Background of the Participants	145
8.1	Participant Demographics	165
8.2	Estimated Differences from Pre- to Post-SASIQ: Control vs. Experimental (MCII)	170
8.3	Estimated Differences from Pre- to Post-SASIQ: MCII New vs. Returning Students	171
8.4	Percentage of MCII Students Indicating Degree of Agreement to MCII Survey Questions	172
10.1	Demographic, Background, and Study Abroad Data	216
10.2	Support Offered by Informants' Social Contacts at Different Stages of their Sojourn	226

Acknowledgments

We want to first thank the learners and students who have generously shared their experiences inside and outside class with us and allowed us to relate aspects of that experience to a wider audience. We have learned so much from you.

We would like to express our gratitude to the authors who have contributed to this book for their hard work on their chapters and their patience in dealing with our suggestions and questions. Bringing together research from so many different learning contexts in this book has been challenging and exhilarating, and we are proud of this collaboration.

We are thankful to Andrew Wardell and the other professionals at Bloomsbury. They have been receptive to our ideas, accommodating of our questions, and unflagging in moving the publication of this book forward.

We thank our students for their support of this project—Julia and Jesse in particular. And we thank the reviewers who provided feedback on each chapter.

Finally, we offer heartfelt gratitude to our own multilingual families for inspiring us and supporting us in developing these ideas. This journey began long before Naomi and Avary met at the American Association of Applied Linguistics annual conference to present a panel about social network analysis in applied linguistics. In our daily lives, as mothers, mentors, language learners, and language teachers, as we tugged at the threads of theory and practice, we have been grounded by you.

Avary is particularly grateful that Naomi asked, "What do you think about an edited book?"

Avary Carhill-Poza
Naomi Kurata

1

Social Network Analysis and its Application in Applied Linguistics

Avary Carhill-Poza and Naomi Kurata

As the influential linguist and pioneer in Japanese language education Jiří V. Neustupný rightly pointed out over thirty years ago, "Unless they [learners of Japanese] can find Japanese who agree to speak to them, there will be no practice and no learning" (Neustupný, 1987: 7). Sociocultural research in language learning has long recognized social interaction as the primary source of language development. But current theories of language learning often assume that social interactions are a given in the classroom and a natural outcome of learners' interest in a second language (L2). Our understanding of the role of relationships in language learning is, to date, insufficient to support our students within and beyond the classroom. How important are families, friends, acquaintances, and teachers for language learning and developing one's identity as an L2 user? What qualities in a relationship matter most for learning a new language and becoming a member of an L2 community? How do relationships change over time and how do these changing webs of relations affect language learning or language attitudes? These questions and many others should be asked by language teachers and language learners. By asking these questions, we are asserting the unacknowledged reality of using and learning a new language—that language development requires sustained interpersonal connections.

The current volume presents cutting-edge research on social networks and their applications in language teaching and language learning in order to describe and theorize the relationships that mediate language learning in and out of classrooms. By documenting the social networks of language learners from different linguistic and learning contexts, we can better understand language development. In this chapter, we first review the use of social networks from an interdisciplinary perspective—not only in language learning but also in sociolinguistics and in education more broadly—and situate our collected work in that landscape. Then, we outline our theoretical and methodological approach to social network analysis, noting similarities and differences across the chapters in this volume. In closing, we provide a brief overview of the empirical studies presented in this volume.

Social Network Research from an Interdisciplinary Perspective

Social network analysis is becoming increasingly interdisciplinary as it takes root in academic fields far from its inception in sociology at the turn of the century (Wasserman & Faust, 1994). In the past thirty years, social network analysis has attracted significant interest in education, public health, anthropology, sociology, and applied linguistics, among other fields, resulting in a near-exponential increase in publications within the social sciences (Carolan, 2013). Sociolinguistic research took up social network analysis forty years ago, defining a social network as "the informal social relationships contracted by an individual" (Milroy, 1987: 178) and engaging the concept to understand how individuals utilize linguistic resources. Numerous sociolinguistic studies have focused on the effect of speakers' social networks on linguistic variation and language change (e.g., Dodsworth & Benton, 2020; Wei, 1994; Milroy, 1987; Sharma, 2017).

Social network analysis in language learning is relatively new in applied linguistics. Most studies in this area are directly concerned with the relationships between characteristics of language learners' networks and their L2 learning (e.g., Bernstein, 2018; Carhill-Poza, 2015; Dewey, Bown, & Eggett, 2012; Hasegawa, 2019; Isabelli-García, 2006; Kurata, 2004; Smith, 2002; Wiklund, 2002; Zappa-Hollman & Duff, 2015). Smith (2002) and Wiklund (2002), for example, have found that the frequency of interaction within the network and the percentage of L2 users in the network are positively related to communicative competence and L2 proficiency. Research has primarily shown the benefits of participants' close and multiplex ties (a tie with multiple roles) with their peers for language learning. Peers—including bilingual and multilingual peers—have been shown to be an important source of linguistic and academic support for adolescents (Carhill-Poza, 2016; Kibler et al., 2018; Wiklund, 2002) through reciprocal provisions of scaffolding as well as social and affective support. These studies have highlighted peers as "very powerful agents of (co-) socialization and identity work" (Zappa-Hollman & Duff, 2015: 358).

Social network analysis has also been used to examine the interconnections among L2 learners' social networks, motivation, and attitudes. Researchers have found evidence that motivation depends on integration (the degree to which students incorporate themselves into social networks), dispersion (number of social groups in which a learner participates), and the strength of relationships with L2 speakers in those social networks (Dewey et al., 2012; Isabelli-García, 2006). This research shows that interaction in social networks is a conduit or mediator between motivation and language development. Dewey et al. (2012), for example, analyzed the links between the social network development, language use, and speaking development of American learners of Japanese who studied abroad in Japan, demonstrating an interdependent relationship between the development of networks and language development.

Research has also shown that a number of learner characteristics—such as the learners' multiple social roles, network members' experiences, genders, and perceived expertise—were related to their language learning, including linguistic awareness (Kurata, 2004, 2007, 2011; Palfreyman, 2006). Viewing social networks as a key concept in understanding the ecology of social resources, for example, Palfreyman (2006) claimed that gender and perceived expertise in English of female university students in the United Arab Emirates affected their use of these resources.

Not all contexts of language learning have received the same amount of scrutiny using a social networks lens. Study abroad contexts, with their explicit focus on building cross-linguistic relationships (between L1 and L2 speakers), have been particularly productive (Bown, Dewey, & Belnap, 2015; Isabelli-García, 2006; Kinginger, 2008; Mitchell, Tracy-Ventura, & McManus, 2017). Compared with studies of L2 learners' social networks in host-country contexts, there is a very limited number exploring foreign/second language learning in home-country settings (cf. Ferenz, 2005; Kurata, 2004, 2007, 2011; Palfreyman, 2006). Similarly, research on immigrant students learning a new language at the same time as they are learning academic content in school is a new area of exploration in social network research (Bernstein, 2018; Carhill-Poza, 2016; Kibler et al., 2018; Wiklund, 2002). In home-country contexts, a focus on L2 teaching and instruction has dominated the research agenda. As those classroom teaching methods have become more collaborative, relationships have gradually become a more compelling concern.

Research that describes social networks in the classroom has received less attention than in out-of-school contexts. Although few in number, L2 classroom-based social network studies have uniquely contributed to our understanding of how the quality of interactions with network members relates to language learning outcomes. Carhill-Poza (2016) documented the role of teaching practices and school policies in structuring peer social networks in secondary schools. Kibler et al. (2018, 2019) demonstrated the power of teaching practice to shape peer social networks in middle school classrooms. Classroom-based research has by necessity confronted the relative roles of individual agency and structural inequity in the development of social networks that tend to be segregated by language. And research conducted outside the classroom has also contributed to our understanding of classroom practice. Examining the perceptions of undergraduate students' language learning experiences inside and outside class, for example, Lai (2015) found that the students acted on the affordances of these two contexts to create complementary and synergetic learning experiences across the two.

The extant literature provides insights into the relationships between some important features of social networks and certain aspects of L2 learning and teaching, but there is far more to learn. We know that well-developed social networks including monolingual and multilingual L2 speakers can have a positive influence on L2 learning—specifically, oral language development, academic L2 socialization, and linguistic awareness—but we do not yet know how these relationships vary across contexts and time, nor do we fully understand factors that can mediate social network development. We have seen that the social support captured by social network analyses relates to classroom, school, and program policies, but research is needed to connect these structural factors to students' understanding and use of social resources. Researchers in applied linguistics have noted the need for a more holistic picture of learners' experiences in order to understand the complex relationships between learners' social networks and L2 learning and the myriad factors—including learners' L2 motivation and identities—that mediate these relationships.

In this volume, we explore these links in diverse multilingual settings. The research presented here allows us to analyze the complex and dynamic nature of social network construction, how networks affect language learning, and how they can be effectively leveraged in language teaching.

Our Theoretical Approach to Language Learners' Social Networks

The chapters of this volume are grounded broadly in sociocultural perspectives that regard L2 learning as socially constructed in and through interaction in situated activities (Lantolf & Thorne, 2006; van Lier, 2004). Building on the principles of sociocultural theory and constructivist models of human activity, van Lier (2004, 2008) developed an ecological approach to language learning and teaching. This approach views language learning processes as part of the dynamic interrelationship between learners and their environment. Van Lier (2004) also suggests that the notion of input can be replaced by the ecological notion of affordance, which is defined as the relationship between properties of the environment and the active learner. He further claims that if language learners are active and engaged, they will perceive linguistic affordances and use them for linguistic action. In his previous work, van Lier (1998: 133) also points out, "since the person is a social being, relations and experiences with fellow-persons form the core and the engine of the construction of consciousness." An ecological approach thus connects cognitive processes with social processes and provides a window into how language is acquired through collaborative interaction. The majority of the contributors to this volume adopt an ecological approach and many use the concept of affordance (cf. Carhill-Poza, Durbidge, Kibler et al., Kurata, and Palfreyman). We believe that these perspectives allow for a nuanced accounting of the influences of social context on language learning and offer fertile ground for exploring classroom applications.

The idea that social contexts, including social relations, shape learning (and the concomitant focus on the social nature of learning) is shared by sociologists of education (Bourdieu, 1986; Coleman, 1988; Lin, 2001) who stress the importance of social capital, or resources obtained through social interactions, for educational outcomes. Bourdieu (1986) defines social capital as an intrinsic part of an individual's social networks, both real and virtual, and the potential benefits that one can accrue from being a part of that particular group. Social capital, or "the connections between individuals" includes "the norms of reciprocity and trustworthiness that arise from them" (Putnam, 2000: 19). This idea has been integrated into research in education, second language acquisition (SLA), and applied linguistics when we consider learning outcomes. Social network analysis creates a snapshot of the patterns of social relationships that shape actions and behaviors (Coleman, 1988). The chapters in this volume utilize social network analysis to understand how social contexts affect individual learning by drawing on the idea that networks provide language learners with access to social capital, including language-rich environments in which to use and learn a new language, often in combination with other linguistic resources.

A particular consideration in the research featured in this volume is how language learners accrue and access social resources in multilingual and complex learning contexts. Social network analysis in these chapters foregrounds language use and language learning situated in K-12 immigrant education, when learning a foreign/second language in one's home country, and when studying abroad. We highlight the importance of social network analysis for capturing a variety of supports which are conducive to language learning and exploitable in language teaching.

Methods of Social Network Analysis

Measurement of social networks can occur at four different levels: the egocentric network, the dyad, the triad, and the complete network (Carolan, 2013). An egocentric network consists of individual actors (ego) and all other actors (alters) that the ego identifies as members of her personal networks. More specifically, egocentric networks include the relationships that each ego has with her alters as well as the relationships among alters. Each ego can be analyzed by the number, frequency, density, and other characteristics of her relations. The social network as an analytic unit draws on attribute-based social science (such as gender and age) as well as relational research. Egocentric network analysis can incorporate or connect to a range of data collection and analytical techniques (Borgatti & Ofem, 2010) including surveys of respondents who are not likely to know each other (Carolan, 2013). An egocentric approach to social network analysis has been most commonly applied in language learning research as it allows us to analyze individual learner networks in depth while also examining the impact of relationships on the learner's language use and learning outcomes. In this current volume, Carhill-Poza (Chapter 2), Oriyama (Chapter 4), Kurata (Chapter 5), Palfreyman (Chapter 6), Inaba (Chapter 7), Trimble-Brown et al. (Chapter 8), Hasegawa (Chapter 9), and Durbidge (Chapter 10), all employ this approach. Moreover, the majority of the contributors analyze some changes in their participants' social networks over time and the relevance of these changes to language learning and/or learners' identities (cf. Trimble-Brown et al., Durbidge, Hasegawa, Inaba, Kurata, and Palfreyman). Kurata's chapter in particular leverages the affordances of egocentric social network analysis to build a longitudinal case study tracing a learner's journey through several stages of social relationships and their implications for her own identity as a language learner. She describes the opportunities her social network provided for language learning across time.

In contrast to egocentric social network analysis, dyadic network analysis is composed of a pair of actors. A typical analysis at the dyad level could help us to explain change in relationships as a function of a pair of learners' characteristics (Carolan, 2013). Although none of the contributors of this volume specifically adopt dyadic (or triadic) approaches to social network analysis, many of them focus on a particular dyadic relationship that their participants (egos) have with important network members (cf. Durbidge, Chapter 10; Hasegawa, Chapter 9; Inaba, Chapter 7; Kurata, Chapter 5; Oriyama, Chapter 4) and we can see the potential of this level of social network analysis for classroom-based and longitudinal research.

The complete network focuses on a set of actors in a bounded sample and the relationships among them (Carolan, 2013). A setting such as a classroom, school, or study abroad program is chosen to serve as the population for the study and ties between each pair (dyad) of participants in the population are measured. Analysis at this level allows us to examine individual actors, groups of actors, and the whole network, providing us with detailed contextual information that is unavailable in other forms of social network analysis. In this volume, Kibler et al. (Chapter 3) and Hasegawa (Chapter 9) analyze complete network data, namely the networks in middle school classrooms and in a study abroad program, respectively.

Depending on the aims, types of data, and settings of the inquiry, social networks can be analyzed in depth using interactional criteria and structural criteria (Boissevain, 1974). Interactional criteria include *Multiplexity* (a tie with multiple roles), *Transactional content* (material and nonmaterial elements that are exchanged between two people), *Directional flow* (the direction in which the exchanged elements move), and *Frequency and duration of interactions*. Structural criteria, on the other hand, consist of *Size* (the total number of links in the network), *Density* (the degree to which the members of a network are in touch with each other independently of the ego), *Degree of connection* (the average number of relations each person has with others), *Centrality* (an index of the degree to which a tie is accessible to others in their network), and *Clusters* (segments of networks which have a relatively high density). The contributors of this book utilize a combination of network variables in their studies in accordance with the specific aims of the research.

In addition to the network approaches and variables outlined here, the contributors of this book employ a variety of qualitative and quantitative approaches to data collection and analysis. For example, Carhill-Poza (Chapter 2), Hasegawa (Chapter 9), and Kibler et al. (Chapter 3) utilize a mixed-methods approach that includes quantitative social network analysis of student interview or survey data as well as qualitative analysis of ethnographic observation. Trimble-Brown et al. (Chapter 8) also use diary entries and surveys. Inaba (Chapter 7) and Kurata (Chapter 5) interpret their participants' diary entries together with in-depth analysis of interview data. Durbidge (Chapter 10) analyzes individual questionnaire responses, interview, and the Instagram data. Oriyama (Chapter 4), on the other hand, utilizes both survey and interview data in qualitative analyses. Palfreyman (Chapter 6) mainly analyzes survey data supplemented by some analysis of short open responses in the survey.

An Overview of this Book

This volume captures the experiences of learners from a wide range of linguistic backgrounds and age groups as well as a variety of language learning contexts. Because of these differences in the learners' background and setting, we divide the book into three parts. Each chapter explicitly lays out the theoretical constructs guiding the application of social network theory and concludes with pedagogical implications.

Part I consists of three chapters that examine school-aged immigrant children's social networks in classroom and family settings in the United States and Australia. Carhill-Poza (Chapter 2) explores how the linguistic resources of peers, families, and school adults are engaged by newcomer immigrant adolescents for language learning in US high schools. She describes how emergent bilingual students create, access, and build on social resources from peers, teachers, and families for language development. Kibler et al. (Chapter 3) examine peer social networks in the classroom with a particular focus on patterns of participation among sixteen English learner-classified students in eight heterogeneous middle school classrooms that varied in terms of high or low peer network linguistic integration. The following chapter, by Oriyama (Chapter 4), explores how transnational Japanese youths' social networks contributed to heritage language development and maintenance as well as cultural identity construction in Sydney, Australia.

In Part II, attention shifts from immigrant students to the social networks of university students in home-country settings in Australia, Sweden, and the United Arab Emirates. In her longitudinal case study, Kurata (Chapter 5) examines how one learner of Japanese constructs her social networks over time and how these experiences relate to her L2 motivation. The study follows changes in the student's social networks and corresponding changes in her identity as an L2 user and learner for three and half years. In Chapter 6, Palfreyman reframes social network data collected fifteen years ago from female university students in Dubai (Palfreyman, 2006). Data from the same context shows that a changing opportunity structure for women has led to different network members providing support for language learning. Inaba (Chapter 7) describes the social networks of Japanese language learners in Australia and Sweden and how relationships with specific network members ("significant others") facilitate language learning activities outside of the classroom.

The studies reported in Part III examine high school and university students' friendships and language learning in study abroad contexts. Trimble-Brown et al. (Chapter 8) describe the use of mental contrasting with implementation intentions (a form of self-regulation) and its impact on the social networks of English language learners in the United States. The authors also examine students' perception of this self-regulation strategy as part of an in-class teaching activity. In the next chapter, Hasegawa (Chapter 9) uses visualizations of social networks to describe a whole network of participants in a short-term study abroad program in Japan, noting changes over the eight-week period. He further examines the peer socialization processes of three focal students vis-à-vis their engagement with a language pledge over the program period. In the last chapter in this section, Durbidge (Chapter 10) looks at how the social networks of Japanese adolescents were formed and developed during a year abroad in nominally non-English language (multilingual) contexts. He also describes the role of relationships in supporting the linguistic development and social integration of participants during their time abroad.

In the concluding chapter (Chapter 11), we describe the pedagogical implications of social network research with language learners, drawing on the rich variety of contexts presented in the chapters of this volume. We present ideas that can transform classroom teaching practice with examples from the data presented here. We then theorize the importance of social network analysis for establishing links between learners' social resources and language learning. Finally, we point the way to a research agenda for social network analysis that can clearly and persuasively inform language teaching.

References

Bernstein, K. A. (2018). The perks of being peripheral: English learning and participation in a preschool classroom network of practice. *TESOL Quarterly*, 52(4), 798–844.
Borgatti, S. P., & Ofem, B. (2010). Overview: Social network theory and analysis. In A. Daly (Ed.), *Social network theory and educational change* (pp. 17–30). Cambridge, MA: Harvard Education Press.

Boissevain, J. (1974). *Friends of friends*. Oxford: Basil Blackwell.

Bourdieu, P. (1986). The forms of capital. In J. G. Richardson (Ed.), *Handbook of theory and research for the sociology of education* (pp. 241–58). New York: Greenwood.

Bown, J., Dewey, D. P., & Belnap, R. K. (2015). Student interactions during study abroad in Jordan. In R.F. Mitchell, K. McManus, & N. T. Ventura (Eds.), *Social interaction, identity and language learning during residence abroad* (pp. 199–222). Essex: Eurosla Monograph Series Four.

Carhill-Poza, A. (2015). Opportunities and outcomes: The role of peers in developing the academic English proficiency of adolescent English learners. *The Modern Language Journal*, 99(4), 678–95.

Carhill-Poza, A. (2016). "If you don't find a friend in here, it's gonna be hard for you": Structuring bilingual peer support in urban high schools. *Linguistics & Education*, 37, 63–72.

Carolan, B. (2013). *Social network analysis and education: Theory, methods & applications*. Thousand Oaks, CA: Sage Publications.

Coleman, J. S. (1988). Social capital in the creation of human capital. *American Journal of Sociology*, 94, S95–S120.

Dewey, D. P., Bown, J., & Eggett, D. (2012). Japanese language proficiency, social networking, and language use during study abroad: Learners' perspectives. *The Canadian Modern Language Review*, 68(2), 111–37.

Dodsworth, R., & Benton, R. (2020). *Language variation and change in social networks*. New York: Routledge.

Ferenz, O. (2005). EFL writers' social networks: Impact on advanced academic literacy development. *Journal of English for Academic Purposes*, 4, 339–51.

Hasegawa, A. (2019). *The social lives of study abroad: Understanding second language learners' experiences through social network analysis and conversation analysis*. New York: Routledge.

Isabelli-García, C. (2006). Study abroad social networks, motivation and attitudes: Implications for second language acquisition. In E. Churchill & M. DuFon (Eds.), *Language learners in study abroad contexts* (pp. 231–58). Clevedon: Multilingual Matters.

Kibler, A. K., Karam, F. J., Futch Ehrlich, V. A., Bergey, R., Wang, C., & Molloy Elreda, L. (2018). Who are "long-term English learners"? Using classroom interactions to deconstruct a manufactured learner label. *Applied Linguistics*, 39(5), 741–65.

Kibler, A. K., Molloy Elreda, L., Hemmler, V., Arbeit, M., Beeson, R., & Johnson, H. (2019). Building linguistically integrated classroom communities: The role of teacher practices. *American Educational Research Journal*, 56(3), 676–715.

Kinginger, C. (2008). Language learning in study abroad: Case studies of Americans in France. *The Modern Language Journal*, 92(s1), 1–124.

Kurata, N. (2004). Communication networks of Japanese language learners in their home country. *Journal of Asian Pacific Communication*, 14(1), 153–78.

Kurata, N. (2007). Language choice and second language learning opportunities in learners' social networks: A case study of an Australian learner of Japanese. *Australian Review of Applied Linguistics, 30*(1), 05.01–05.18.

Kurata, N. (2011). *Foreign language use and learning: Interaction in informal social networks*. London: Continuum.

Lai, C. (2015). Perceiving and traversing in-class and out-of-class learning: Accounts from foreign language learners in Hong Kong. *Innovation in Language Learning and Teaching, 9*(3), 265–84.

Lantolf, J. P., & Thorne, S. L. (2006). *Sociocultural theory and the genesis of second language development*. Oxford: Oxford University Press.

Lin, N. (2001). *Social capital: A theory of social structure and action*. New York: Cambridge University Press.

Milroy, L. (1987). *Language and social networks*. Oxford: Basil Blackwell.

Mitchell, R., Tracy-Ventura, N., & McManus, K. (2017). *Anglophone students abroad: Identity, social relationships and language learning*. Abingdon: Routledge.

Neustupný, J. V. (1987). *Communicating with the Japanese*. Tokyo: The Japan Times.

Palfreyman, D. (2006). Social context and resources for language learning. *System, 34*, 352–70.

Putnam, R. (2000). *Bowling alone: The collapse and revival of American community*. New York: Simon and Schuster.

Sharma, D. (2017). Scalar effects of social networks on language variation. *Language Variation and Change, 29*(3), 393–418.

Smith, L. R. (2002). The social architecture of communicative competence: A methodology for social-network research in sociolinguistics. *International Journal of the Sociology of Language, 153*, 133–60.

van Lier, L. (1998). The relationship between consciousness, interaction and language learning. *Language Awareness, 7*(2 & 3), 128–45.

van Lier, L. (2004). *The ecology and semiotics of language learning: A sociocultural perspective*. Boston, MA: Springer.

van Lier, L. (2008). The ecology of language learning and sociocultural theory. In A. Creese, P. Martin, & N. H. Hornberger (Eds.), *Encyclopedia of language and education, vol. 9: Ecology of language* (pp. 53–65). New York: Springer.

Wasserman, S., & Faust, K. (1994). *Social network analysis: Methods and applications*. New York: Cambridge University Press.

Wei, L. (1994). *Three generations, two languages, one family: Language choice and language shift in a Chinese Community in Britain*. Clevedon: Multilingual Matters.

Wiklund, I. (2002). Social networks from a sociolinguistic perspective: The relationship between characteristics of the social networks of bilingual adolescents and their language proficiency. *International Journal of the Sociology of Language, 153*, 53–92.

Zappa-Hollman, S., & Duff, P. A. (2015). Academic English socialization through individual networks of practice. *TESOL Quarterly, 49*(2), 333–68.

Part I

Immigrant Children and Adolescents' Social Networks in School Settings

2

The Social Networks of Adolescent Emergent Bilinguals in High School

Avary Carhill-Poza

Adolescent emergent bilinguals are aiming for a moving target as they acquire English at the secondary level, a challenge made more difficult by classroom pedagogies that can marginalize the least fluent speakers of English and stigmatize the use of other languages in the classroom (Carhill-Poza, 2018; Gutiérrez, Baquedano-López, & Tejeda, 1999). Many immigrant youth who are still learning English struggle to reach their academic potential under such unfavorable conditions. In contrast, research presented in this chapter takes an asset-based approach to learning in order to understand how peers, family members, and school adults—including those who are bilingual—can be leveraged to support language development. Valuing the knowledge and perspectives of immigrant youth is important not only because it supports language learning but also because it combats subtractive school climates.

Understanding the role of social relationships in language learning is particularly important in the current policy context because it raises awareness of factors beyond the individual that can support the academic success of immigrant youth who are still learning English. The relationships that emergent bilinguals draw on in their everyday language learning activities are shaped by both individual agency and social structures beyond the control of immigrant youth who were still learning English in schools and classrooms across the United States. Social network analysis can also be used to help teachers reframe their "English learner" students as bilingual peers who are assets for learning. To do so, teachers need to know more about the relationships that support language development and their relevance for classroom language teaching. In this chapter, social network analysis is used to describe how emergent bilingual students create, access, and build on social resources for language development within the constraints of school policies and classroom practices that structure their relationships.

Theoretical Frame and Literature Review

The Role of Social Resources in English Language Development

Schools serve as the entry point for most immigrant youth into new social, cultural, and linguistic worlds. While instruction has been the focus of much research about the academic achievement and language development of this diverse group, schools impact learning outcomes through much more than the classes taught. Research grounded in conceptions of social capital (Bourdieu & Passeron, 1977) has been used to understand how immigrant students' experiences in school lead them to accumulate and access resources via their relationships that over time differentiate their academic outcomes (Stanton-Salazar, 2001). The significance of relationships has been established through both qualitative and quantitative descriptions of immigrant students' social networks (e.g., Suárez-Orozco, Suárez-Orozco, & Todorova, 2008; Valdés, 2001). Social networks—an individual's web of relationships—can be used to describe the peers, family, and teachers who are the mediators of learning (Coleman, 1988) and can serve as a lens to understand the role of education policy and practice in fostering social support for English learners.

Research with multilingual individuals has shown that social networks consisting of many close relationships (a multiplex network of strong ties) are good predictors of language maintenance, whereas social networks with fewer or weaker ties or a lack of density (people in the network knowing each other) are related to language shift (Bortoni-Ricardo, 1985; Milroy, 1987). People that one feels close to exert the most influence on language choice and ultimately on the linguistic repertoire that an individual develops over time (Milroy & Wei, 1995; Zentella, 1997). Social networks can also shed light on the context of language learning by capturing the interpersonal landscape that affords learners opportunities to use and learn language in different ways (Kurata, 2010; Wiklund, 2002). The qualities of relationships (e.g., the interlocutor's role, type, and frequency of interaction) are indicators of both real and perceived opportunities for language learning (Smith, 2002). Social network measures in the current research were constructed to reflect a bilingual use of language across contexts to best capture the qualities in the close relationships of adolescent immigrant students that most affected their language development.

For adolescents, peers form a significant learning environment within and beyond the classroom. Immigrant youth, in particular, actively navigate social ties and social contexts to learn both a new language and academic content (Carhill-Poza, 2015, 2018). Most immigrant adolescents are strongly oriented to their peers and many lack significant concrete academic support from the adults in their lives (Suárez-Orozco et al., 2008). New research demonstrates that peer relationships are doubly important for adolescent English learners because academically engaged and more proficient conversational partners (bilingual or monolingual) afford them essential opportunities to use and learn academic language (Carhill-Poza, 2015, 2018; Carhill-Poza, Suárez-Orozco, & Páez, 2008; Kibler et al., 2019; Kibler et al., Chapter 3, this volume). Research on second-language learning has long established the importance of peers and peer scaffolding for language development (Lantolf & Appel, 1994). Sociocultural theories of language development (Vygotsky, 1978) conceptualize language learning and content learning as occurring at the same time so that as English learners engage in academic tasks at school with others and alone, they also acquire the specialized vocabulary, syntax, and discourse structures that are required for school success (Bailey, 2007).

The Role of Schools in Social Network Development

Examining the web of social relations that support adolescent English learners in school is particularly useful in the face of the widespread linguistic, ethnic, and racial segregation students encounter in US schools (Palardy, Rumberger, & Butler, 2015). Adolescent immigrant students who are still learning English are concentrated in schools that often do not have the systematic resources to support their learning. At the same time, immigrant parents are often ill-equipped to help their children navigate a new school system given their lack of familiarity with schools in the United States, work schedules that can make attending school events challenging, and the linguistic demands of communicating effectively with school personnel. In such contexts, bilingual peers play an especially important role in the transmission of academic knowledge and skills (Gándara & Contreras, 2009; Lee & Madyun, 2012; Suárez-Orozco et al., 2008) and for language development (Carhill-Poza, 2015, 2018). Social network analysis is able to capture a nuanced picture of the resources that immigrant students have and differentiate opportunity structures in a seemingly homogenous group.

Language teachers believe that peers with strong English language skills can support English language learning in structured activities, a view that is substantiated by sociocultural research (Donato, 1994; Watanabe & Swain, 2007).

However, positive attitudes toward peer interaction are not necessarily reflected in classroom teaching (Carhill-Poza, 2018; Zwiers, 2008). Often, teachers do not engage emergent bilinguals in the types of activities that best leverage peer resources. Well-intentioned school policies and teaching practices can suppress the development of important social resources including relationships with peers, family adults, and school adults.

Social support does not occur at random: schools structure peer support for immigrant youth still learning English by creating boundaries that either isolate English learners from mainstream peers (Callahan, 2005; Kanno & Kangas, 2014) and bilingual peers (Carhill-Poza, 2016; Wiklund, 2002) or apprentice English learners into relationships with mainstream and English learner peers (Kibler, Atteberry, Hardigree, & Salerno, 2015). A lack of peer support is often the result of well-meaning school policies seeking to ensure that English learners receive appropriate language support services or pass high-stakes tests (Carhill-Poza, 2016). Raising awareness of the social support available to English learners through their peers—inclusive of bilingual peers—is an important step in addressing policies and practices that do not serve emergent bilinguals well. Peer support is an area where school policy and classroom teaching can be adjusted to leverage a readily available resource for the success of adolescent immigrant students who are still learning English.

The Current Study

Guided by an ecological perspective (Bronfenbrenner, 1977; van Lier, 2004) as well as sociocultural theories of language development (Lantolf & Thorne, 2006; Vygotsky, 1978), this chapter describes the linguistic resources of newcomer immigrant adolescents—including peers, families, and school adults—and how they were engaged for language learning in US high schools. This study focuses on the following research questions:

1. What are the features of newcomer immigrant adolescents' social networks?
2. How do these social resources relate to language development outcomes?

Research Methods

A mixed-methods approach to social network analysis was used to describe the relationships that mediate language learning in and out of classrooms, highlighting the potential of peers, teachers, and families to support, transform, and augment classroom language teaching. The larger study drew on social network analysis to document that having bilingual peers who collaborated on academic tasks with participants in English or Spanish contributed to academic English proficiency beyond individual predictors of second language acquisition (Carhill-Poza, 2015). These data also linked social networks to classroom discourse structures and school policies, showing that at the school and the classroom level, policies and practices designed to support language development often isolated immigrant students learning English from their mainstream and more proficient bilingual peers (Carhill-Poza, 2016, 2018). Both qualitative and quantitative analyses that are part of the larger study are referenced where these connections help to present a more complete or nuanced picture of the role of social networks in the language development of adolescent emergent bilinguals in this sample, but previously published analyses are not presented in full. The analysis in this chapter integrates ideas that have hitherto been presented separately.

Study Background

The data consist of interviews with 102 Spanish-speaking immigrant students classified as English learners at their schools, their individual school records, and more than 600 ethnographic classroom observations conducted at their schools. Participants were closely equated by gender (48.5 percent female), and had on average been in the United States for 3.5 years ($SD = 2.03$) and were 16.5 years old ($SD = 1.26$). All participants spoke Spanish as their first language and were born in the Dominican Republic (62.6 percent), Ecuador (15.2 percent), Mexico (10.1 percent), and other Central American countries (12.1 percent).

Students were recruited from four public high schools in New York City typical of the secondary schools attended by Spanish-speaking immigrant youth (Table 2.1). Participating schools exemplified average quality learning environments compared to New York City averages for graduation (55 percent; New York City Department of Education, 2005). The schools employed an array of language program models so that adolescent English learners took a mix of English as a Second Language (ESL), bilingual content, and sheltered content courses in a ratio determined by school policies and state mandates corresponding to students' English proficiency level such that most beginning students took three to four periods of ESL each day, those who were intermediate took two to three periods of ESL, and those who were advanced had only one period. None of the schools offered dual-language or newcomer programs.

Table 2.1 School Descriptors as a Percentage of Total Students 2007–8

	NYC Average	West Side High School	New Riverside High School	East Side High School	Edgar Allen Poe HS
Total enrollment	1,876	2,026	3,352	2,920	2,432
Eligible for free or reduced lunch	49	69	72	70	70
Students classified as ELLs	12	26	15	13	22
Race					
Latino	39	60	57	49	62
Black	32	27	14	30	33
White	14	2	13	3	2
Asian	15	11	16	18	3
Graduation rate					
All students	55	38	59	62	49
ELLs and former-ELLs	55	38	43	39	45

Generally, classroom instruction could be described as traditional with students most often seated in rows with teacher-led discussion and activities.

Data Collection and Analysis

Data for this study were collected using mixed methods to document the relationship between the social networks and academic English proficiency of newcomer immigrant youth in a nuanced way. With the help of teachers and staff, all Spanish-speaking students taking Global History at the four school research sites were offered the opportunity to participate in the study.

Quantitative data collection and analysis. Students were individually interviewed in Spanish and English by a bilingual and bicultural researcher. Interviews centered on a description of the participant's social network and took between thirty-five and seventy-five minutes ($M = 44$ minutes) to complete. Students were asked to name the important people in their lives, those that they spent time with or felt close to. After generating an initial list, students were prompted to nominate additional members of their family, adults from school, friends from school, and friends and adults from other places (including work, church, after-school clubs, and the neighborhood).

Students were then asked how much of the time they spoke English and Spanish with each of the persons in their social network (100 percent

English, 75 percent English and 25 percent Spanish, 50 percent English and 50 percent Spanish, 25 percent English and 75 percent Spanish, or 100 percent Spanish). Members speaking English with the participant 50 percent of the time or more were coded as bilingual, and those speaking Spanish 75 percent of the time or more (and English 25 percent of the time or less) were coded as Spanish. Students were then asked which of the persons in their social network had done any of the following four activities with them and how frequently: (a) helped with homework, (b) helped find some information needed for schoolwork, (c) explained something a teacher said that they didn't understand, or (d) studied for a test with them. Social network members who engaged almost every day or a few times a week in one or more academic support activities with participants were coded as academic, while those who engaged infrequently (a few times a month or a few times a year) or not at all were coded as nonacademic.

A standardized test of oral academic English proficiency—the redesigned Idea Proficiency Test (IPT) for K–12 students (Ballard & Tighe, 2006)—was also individually administered to participants. The test measured oral academic English proficiency through tasks including describing a chart, explaining a scientific process, and reading math problems. Total raw scores range from 5 to 32 points and correspond to standardized percentile scores for high school English learners.

Descriptive statistical analyses were performed including calculating the mean, standard deviation, and range of social network size by role, academic support, and language support. Correlational analyses were conducted to show how each factor related to academic English proficiency.

Qualitative data collection and analysis. I conducted participant observation with newcomer immigrant youth and their teachers, counselors, and administrators over a three-year period. In order to understand the role of social relationships in language learning, I alternated more active engagement in classrooms and meetings with more passive observation in settings where I did not want to disrupt interactions. Students and teachers were informally interviewed throughout fieldwork, and I draw on these fifty-eight interviews (four minutes on average) in conjunction with ethnographic field notes to contextualize and explain patterns of social network attributes in this chapter.

Preliminary coding of qualitative data was documented in analytic memos over several months during data collection. Initial codes included student relationships with teachers, counselors, and other students as well as school policies articulated by staff, students, and school documents. Themes were developed through discussion with participants and additional data collection.

Coding was formalized using ATLAS.ti software through extensive rereading. Validity was ensured by using multiple sources of evidence, actively seeking disconfirmation of emerging themes, and through member checking drafts of the research (Yin, 2003). To describe patterns of newcomer immigrant adolescents' social networks and their relationship to language proficiency, findings are presented thematically with quantitative analyses folded in, first, describing the peripheral role of parents and teachers in students' networks, then looking at the central role of peers in students' lives, and, finally, detailing the role of schools in developing and engaging social networks.

Findings

The Peripheral Role of Family and School Adults

Although adolescent immigrant students in this sample reported a robust number of adults in their social networks (3.1 on average, with a range of 1 to 8), only a small number of adults provided them with academic language or English language support. On average, 1.8 family adults, 0.8 school adults including teachers and counselors, and 0.4 adults from other places including church, work, and youth groups spoke English with participants and 0.2 family adults, 0.4 school adults, and 0.2 adults from the community provided academic language support. Figure 2.1 describes social network characteristics for this sample. In total, only 13 percent of the sample had one or more adults who provided academic language support or English language support.

When asked about the family adults in their lives, newcomer immigrant youth were quick to point out the importance of aunts and uncles, grandparents, older siblings, stepsiblings, cousins, and parents. Family adults provided encouragement to do well in school and talked about the importance of education and learning English. Newcomer immigrant students had access to an abundance of aspirational support from the adults in their lives, but when asked to name people in their social network who provided help with homework or studying for a test, very few family adults were named—only 0.2 family adults on average (ranging from 0 to 1). More family adults used English with participants at least half the time (1.8 on average, ranging from 1 to 8), but the linguistic resources of family members did not significantly relate to English proficiency among participants in this study. Although family members were important to

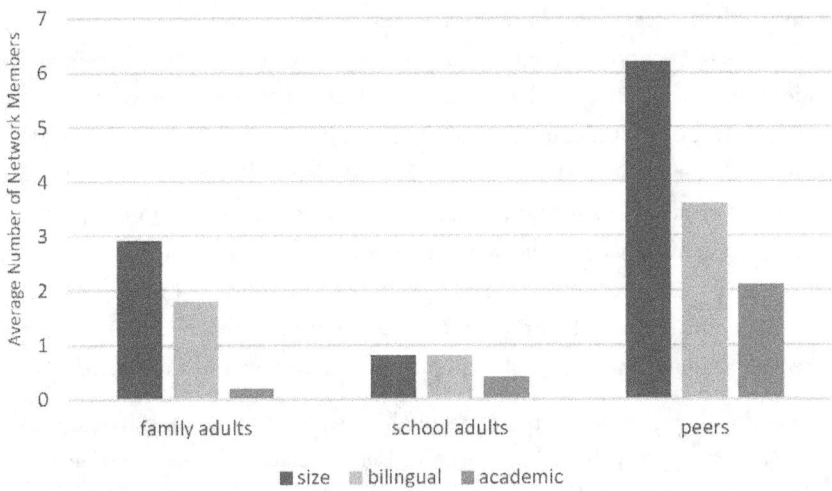

Figure 2.1 Social networks by role, language, and academic support (N=102).

youth in this study, many spent only modest amounts of time with them over the course of a week.

Teachers, counselors, and other school adults were even less central in the social networks of adolescent immigrant students. As described in Figure 2.1, on average, students reported less than one school adult who was important to them (0.8 on average, ranging from 0 to 2). Most of these school adults were bilingual and of immigrant origins themselves. Data show that the school adults in students' networks most often provided emotional support rather than academic support. Students reported that about half of the teachers or counselors in their networks (0.4 on average) explained things they did not understand or helped them to complete homework.

When asked about their relationships with the adults in their schools, students reported generally positive perceptions of teachers in the classroom but also tensions around teachers' ability to communicate with and trust Spanish-speaking immigrant students. For example, Juan, a sophomore at the time we talked, explained:

> "Me gustan las clases, todos mis maestros, y me gusta la atención que le prestan a uno aquí. No me gusta que a veces uno hace algo y sin escucharte ya toman algo y eso es y ya, pero no te escuchan."
>
> [I like my classes, my teachers, and I like that they pay attention to students here. I don't like that sometimes you get blamed for something you didn't do and they won't listen to you. They make a judgement and that's it, you are not even given a chance to explain.]

Many students described difficulties communicating with their teachers and other adults at school. Students pointed out that with as many as twenty-five students in each class, teachers did not always have time for each student individually. Some students referred to the adults in their school as racist or as being unfair to Spanish speakers. Many students described wanting more teachers to speak Spanish, arguing that bilingual teachers were more supportive of their academic success. The sense of bias coupled with a linguistic distance between Spanish-speaking immigrant students and their English-speaking teachers, counselors, and administrators had consequences for students' ability to recruit academic and linguistic support. A school social worker noted that

> Language is a barrier. There are people here who can do all of those things [academic support]. There is a college adviser, there are many, many resources, but if you feel out of place, then you're not going to know what is there for you.

For those few immigrant students who had relationships with adults at school, both teachers and students viewed them as important. A bilingual teacher reflected on the strength of emergent bilingual youth's relationships to school adults who spoke their language:

> I think that the school draws the students closer to us because they absolutely have no one else. ESL students have no one else to give them direction, like guidance. Or even just information like, 'What's the deal with going to college?' So I see them get really close to their [bilingual] teachers.

Findings show that while teachers provided less of a direct context for language learning than expected, they played an exceptionally important role in shaping students' social networks development, particularly their connections with bilingual peers. Adolescent emergent bilinguals in this study reported that teachers and counselors connected them to ethnic clubs, extracurricular activities, and service activities where they met other students who became friends and even peer mentors. One assistant principal described the process of recruiting "talented students" into an academic club as "a marathon" where she repeatedly reached out to parents and talked with the selected students to make club membership happen. She and other administrators explicitly described their criteria for selecting students to join these activities—that they were learning English rapidly and were serious about their studies. Administrators clearly enumerated the social and academic benefits for students, citing this as the reason they worked so hard to recruit promising students to academically aligned activities.

In sum, although family adults and school adults were infrequently represented in the social networks of adolescent immigrant students in this sample, this need not be the case. Their limited presence was a result of both overt school policy and individual agency in recruiting family and school adults into one's network. Subtle evidence of the value of bilingual teachers and parents for emergent bilinguals is found in their strong desire for more bilingual teachers to support their academic success while at the same time also describing the need for more teachers to speak only in English so that they could learn English more rapidly. Students' perceptions of teachers' support for language learning were constructed around conflicting ideas—that teachers should be modeling English for them and that using Spanish was more helpful. These beliefs similarly affected emergent bilinguals' understanding and recruitment of family adults— as parents and adult cousins were expected to provide aspirational support, these expectations were met and social capital was reproduced in kind, but familial adults were not tapped for help with academic tasks (cf. Palfreyman, Chapter 6, this volume).

The Centrality of Bilingual Peers in Adolescent Immigrant Students' Networks

Adolescent immigrant students reported large peer social networks ranging in size from 0 to 22 peers and averaging 6.2 peers. On average, most peers were from school (55.6 percent), but many were also kin (29.4 percent) and friends from church, work, or the neighborhood (15 percent). Many students nominated family members close to their age (including cousins, siblings, aunts and uncles, and stepsiblings) as friends. Because kin frequently attended the same school, family-peers were distinguished from the older generation of family adults and were counted as peers if they were within five years of the participant's age. Figure 2.1 describes the average number of peers in each student's social network and whether they were academic peers or bilingual peers.

Very few newcomer youth in this sample had made monolingual English-speaking friends. Only six students nominated one or more peers that they spoke only English with. In nearly all cases, this peer was from outside of school, usually from church or work. Some students mentioned wanting to become friends with monolingual English-speaking peers to accelerate their language development. Their reflections showed that adolescent emergent bilinguals saw themselves as agents of their own socialization and thought about monolingual English-speaking peers as a social resource. The segregation of English learners from mainstreamed students in their high schools generally precluded a great deal of interaction between students classified as English learners and their monolingual peers, however, as will be discussed in greater detail further.

While the total number of peers was not significantly related to academic English proficiency, both the number of bilingual peers (those who spoke English with participants at least half the time) and the number of academic peers (those who collaborated on academic tasks with participants) were strongly positively related to students' academic English proficiency ($r = .35$, $p < .001$, and $r = .41$, $p < .001$, respectively). The networks of most adolescent English learners consisted of peers with whom they spoke both Spanish and English in different ratios. Students reported using English as much as or more than Spanish with the most peers (3.6 peers on average) and speaking mostly Spanish with fewer peers on average (2.6 peers). The number of Spanish peers in a students' social network was negatively related to their academic English proficiency ($r = -.28$, $p < .001$).

On average, students had 2.1 academic peers but there was significant variance between individuals, ranging from 0 to 8 academic peers. More than a quarter of the sample did not have any academic peers. In the larger study, hierarchical regression analysis demonstrated that both having bilingual peers and having academic peers explained unique variation in academic English proficiency when controlling for age, time in the United States, gender, and maternal education (Carhill-Poza, 2015). According to that analysis, having academic peers (regardless of their use of English or Spanish) was more important for English proficiency than having peers that spoke English with participants (including bilingual and monolingual English-speaking peers). This finding underscores the importance of bilingual peers in academically and cognitively challenging tasks for English language development and undermines the popular conceptualization of monolingual English speakers as the most advantageous relationships for emergent bilinguals to develop.

To analyze how language use and participation in academic tasks with peers overlap in supporting the development of academic English, groups were constructed that combined the academic and linguistic characteristics of adolescent immigrant students' social networks to show high and low levels of bilingual peers and high and low levels of academic peers. Figure 2.2 shows an example of each of the four types of networks: *Academic Bilingual, Academic Spanish, Nonacademic Bilingual,* and *Nonacademic Spanish.*

As can be seen from the visual representations of student's peer social networks, the linguistic resources newcomer immigrant students had access

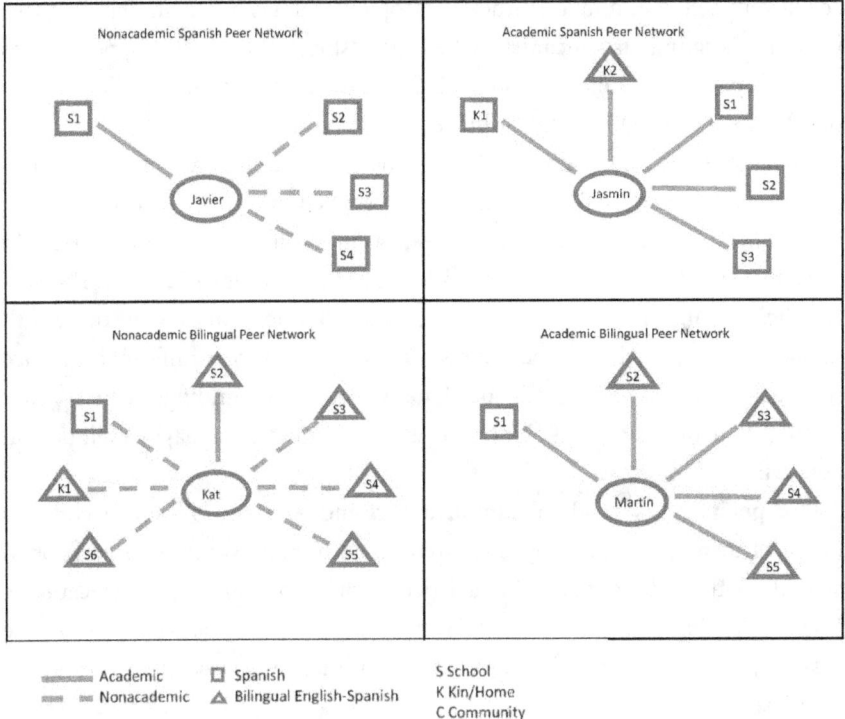

Figure 2.2 Peer social networks.

to varied significantly. Javier's network (a nonacademic Spanish peer network) was comprised of bilingual friends from school who spoke with him exclusively in Spanish. Only one peer participated in academic tasks with Javier. Although Kat had a larger peer network with six bilingual friends from home and school who spoke English with her regularly, like Javier she did not have access to academically rich interactions with her peers. Students like Kat with nonacademic bilingual peer networks used English frequently for social purposes but rarely for academic tasks.

Both Jasmin and Martín had networks of five academic peers, Jasmin's peers using mostly Spanish with her, while Martín's peers used English with him at least half of the time. For both Jasmin and Martín, their friends helped them to do homework, study for tests, and find information that they needed for school projects including websites, books, and people. Martín's academic bilingual network in particular indexed accrued social resources that afforded him consistent opportunities for learning academic language and content. Although Jasmin predominantly spoke Spanish in her academic Spanish peer network, consistent collaboration on academic topics and tasks—including English-medium assignments—meant that her friendships afforded her opportunities to develop her academic English. Detailed case studies of each of the students profiled here can be found in Carhill-Poza (2016).

What are the implications of these network configurations for English proficiency? As expected, when the groups were compared statistically, analysis of variance yielded significant between-group differences (summarized in Carhill-Poza, 2015). Students with academic bilingual peer social networks were significantly higher in English proficiency than all other groups while those with nonacademic Spanish peer social networks trended toward significant difference with academic bilingual peer social networks. These findings, which again highlight the importance of bilingual peers for academic language development, are surprising to many.

The perspectives of school administrators and teachers, focusing exclusively on the issue of how much English newcomer immigrant youth used, were often at odds with findings that bilingual peers could mutually support academic English development. Speaking Spanish with their peers was seen as evidence that they did not have a strong desire to learn English. For example, one school principal commented:

> The issue with many of our Latino kids is—and most of our Latino kids are from the Dominican Republic—is that they are a gregarious, very culturally tight community, and so they gravitate to their own community and I think this holds them back in terms of their acquiring English because they don't have to speak English with their friends.

He and most of the administrators and teachers we talked to valued teachers and monolingual peers as models of English for emergent bilinguals. They wanted immigrant students who were still learning English to spend as much time as possible hearing and using only English. For them, bilingual peers represented an obstacle to language learning rather than a potential source of support.

School Policies and Social Networks

School policies designed to support the language development of newcomer immigrant students often isolated them from more proficient bilingual and mainstream peers. The numbers tell a striking story: none of the 102 participant's peer social networks included monolingual English-speaking peers who supported them academically. Other school policies systematically excluded family adults from students' school lives and failed to connect school adults with immigrant youth, policies that were indexed by the low number of family and school adults who collaborated with participants on academic tasks. These features of schooling had profound repercussions for the immigrant youth in this study, particularly their access to opportunities to use and learn academic English. I refer to the effect of these policies as *hyper-segregation* (Carhill-Poza, 2016). In addition to the concentration of Spanish-speaking immigrant youth in poorly resourced schools based on their socioeconomic status, race, and home language, emergent bilinguals were further segregated in a hierarchical system of course-taking and tutoring regimens. In a purposeful choreography of course selection, scheduling, and physical separation within their school buildings, emergent bilinguals were effectively cut off from the majority of their peers. Hyper-segregation restricted the development of peer social networks, concentrating social and material resources at the top of an English development hierarchy. Students who had higher proficiency in English were offered more opportunities to develop academically focused peer social networks that included similarly proficient bilingual peers, greater access to teachers, more advanced coursework. As one student bluntly stated, "In this school, if you don't know English, you're dead."

Ethnographic data showed that peer social networks were shaped by the beliefs of teachers and school leaders about how academic English should be learned by newcomer immigrant youth. Educators believed that mastery of academic English was a prerequisite to learning grade-level academic content alongside English-proficient peers. A school principal explained the linear language development trajectory woven throughout school policies at all four public high schools in this study:

> A Spanish-speaking ELL who comes in the ninth grade, we'd like to graduate that person in the twelfth grade four years later. What we'd like is a student moved through the beginning levels of ESL through the first and second years, so we go through the beginning to low-intermediate in the first three years, the third year to be in the upper-intermediate or transitional [ESL] and then to move into an environment where they need as little language support as possible. That's the goal.

To support the development of academic English, school policies emphasized after-school tutoring, retaking courses, and large blocks of ESL coursework. Students complained about schedules that were longer than their English-proficient peers and keenly noted the physical and social isolation that these schedules created. Students who were classified as English learners described feeling frustrated by their inability to participate in aspects of school life such as extracurricular activities and specialized coursework. One student described his initial excitement over the arts curriculum at his school, "Cuando llegue aquí yo sabía que había arte pero el grado que yo tenía todavía no estaba disponible, no podía estar en clases de arte." [When I arrived here, I knew they had an arts program but it wasn't available to me in the grade I was in. I couldn't be in art classes.] School policies that required students to take preparatory coursework and tutoring until they passed the standardized tests in several subject areas (the Regents Exams) precluded enrolling in courses seen as nonessential, such as art.

Students also noted that they found great value in collaborating with bilingual peers in a mix of Spanish and English, something that teachers discouraged. While ethnographic observation provided numerous examples of academically focused interactions in which emergent bilingual youth used their full linguistic repertoire to solve math problems, write essays, and correct homework, teachers worried that translanguaging deprived students of time that could be spent using English. Bilingual peer talk and teachers' responses to it are documented in detail in Carhill-Poza (2018). Teachers and administrators expressed a consistent belief that students' first task was to learn English. As one assistant principal explained:

> At a minimum, we want the kids to be able to speak English to enable that kid to function in an English-speaking society, at a very bare minimum. And we'd like to do that in the time we have that kid here, because the truth of the matter is—I don't care if it's politically incorrect—every kid that comes to us is not going to go to college immediately after high school, they're just not. So we want to prepare kids for the possibility that they won't go to college and they'll just go into the work world. So I think that's the big picture.

Immigrant students who were still learning English understood school priorities. Angel, a sophomore, summed up school language policy saying, "If you don't know English you don't pass, you don't graduate from high school." He and many of his bilingual peers struggled to articulate a bilingual future for themselves that was successful in school and in life after school. "I don't think Spanish will help me much," he said. If Spanish was not going to help him do well in school, it was difficult to conceptualize the work that he routinely did with bilingual peers in Spanish as supporting his academic and linguistic development. And yet, in his academic Spanish peer social network, he interacted frequently with his peers around English texts using multiple turns at talk to solve complex academic problems. Angel's example highlights the tension between the agentive use of bilingual peer support and the expectation that only using English mattered most for academic language development.

Social Networks in Practice

In this study, social network analysis frames the relationships that coalesce around everyday interactions and serve as pathways to social capital (Coleman, 1988) for adolescent immigrant students who are still learning English. It is important to recognize students' individual agency in creating, maintaining, and accessing the capital available through their relationships and to notice the ways that they prioritize and cultivate relationships that support their L2 learning. Complementing these descriptions, ethnographic data show that emergent bilinguals are not solely responsible for the quantity and quality of their relationships—and therefore the social capital that they have access to via their interpersonal relationships—since many possible relationships are precluded or mandated by their family life, neighborhood, and school policy (Lee, 2014).

To support adolescents who are still learning academic English, teachers need to understand the important role that social resources play in language learning and language teaching, and how those social resources are created through individual agency within classroom and school structures. When language development is thought of as a linear and individual cognitive process, resulting policies and practices focus on the tasks each student completes and the gains they make in their annual language proficiency tests without considering the long-term and collaborative social processes that enable language development, that is, the relationships that sustain academic language development. Social network analysis brings into focus the relationships that are the context for language development and reframes language development as driven by sustained interaction.

Social network analysis showed that the most important people for language development in an adolescent language learner's life were not her family or her teachers, but her friends. These are surprising findings for many teachers and emergent bilingual students who view instruction as the essential means of learning a new language. Conceptualizing teaching practice as a way to foster and engage supportive relationships shifts many commonsense policies and teaching practices. Teachers are central to the development of supportive, academically focused social networks through the classroom environment and activities that they create as well as by providing access to networks beyond the classroom. In many cases, moving toward a more student-centered approach to teaching and intentionally scaffolding interactions around academic content supports the development of academic language resources in social networks.

In this chapter, analysis showed that bilingual peers were capable of supporting their own learning and that of their peers using their first language as well as English. This finding underscores the pedagogical importance of recognizing and facilitating the development of supportive bilingual peer relationships as well as knowing how to leverage these relationships for language learning within and beyond the classroom. Studies set in classrooms where developing cross-linguistic relationships was an explicit aim of the teaching have shown the beneficial effects of relationships with monolingual English-speaking peers for emergent bilinguals (Kibler et al., 2019), but participants in this study attended traditional high schools where such relationships were not consciously fostered. The absence of monolingual English speakers in participants' networks is an indicator of school policies and should not be taken as proof that monolingual peers are not desirable relationships to develop. Rather, these findings should be understood to show that monolingual peers are not essential for the development of academic English—bilingual peers who collaborated on academic tasks with participants using both Spanish and English were the most important resources for language development.

This analysis and others have shown that the importance of bilingual peers for learning inversely related to the ways they were engaged by teaching practices in many classrooms (e.g., Gutiérrez, 1992; Zwiers, 2008). In the current political climate, it is urgent that teachers build ecologies of learning that value bilingual peers in classrooms and bring bilingual peer talk out of the margins. Bilingual peers are one of the most powerful and underutilized scaffolds available in multilingual classrooms (Walqui & van Lier, 2010). Valuing peer knowledge and perspectives by bringing them to the forefront of teaching and learning activities is important because it not only supports learning but also challenges subtly subtractive school climate (García & Sylvan, 2011). In contrast to viewing students as isolated individuals—a view that reinforces a dominant ideology of emergent bilinguals as deficient and needing to linguistically pace their English-speaking peers in order to contribute to their own learning—social network analysis shines the light on the strengths of emergent bilinguals when purposefully engaged for classroom learning.

Family adults were not statistically associated with the language development of adolescent immigrant students in this study. This finding is not surprising given the limited role that immigrant parents and other family adults often play in their children's education. Many immigrant parents do not connect with schools or schoolwork in the ways that the parents of mainstream children and youth can. Research on parental and community involvement frames these missed opportunities as issues of equity where school structures and expectations exclude immigrant adults (Baquedano-López, Alexander, & Hernandez, 2013). The small number of academic family adults in this sample is not a given; we can imagine adolescent immigrant students' social networks filled with family adults and community members who support their bilingual academic success. Teachers can support the inclusion of family adults in academic activities as mundane as commenting on a completed homework assignment, providing an example or story as background for an activity, or advising teachers about the culture, geography, history, and language of their home country. Efforts to include family adults in the academic success of adolescent immigrant youth could change the role of family adults in their children's language development from one of peripheral involvement to central importance.

The balance between individual agency and structural forces is an important consideration in social network research, and it is especially important in considering the scarcity of family and school adults who provided academic and linguistic support to emergent bilingual youth. The expectation that parents and other family adults were peripheral to schooling and language learning was born out in the roles of these adults in the social networks that youth in this sample developed, highlighting the potential of expectations, or endogenous externalities, to regulate social capital (Coleman, 1988). The same can be said of teachers and other school adults who viewed their role as one of teaching students the language they didn't yet know rather than as providing stable, academically focused support as part of a relationship with students. It was not only direct access to social resources that social networks provided but also a set of latent expectations that permeated relationship norms (Lee & Madyun, 2012).

This chapter explored how the linguistic resources of peers, families, and school adults that were available to newcomer immigrant adolescents related to their English language development. The analysis of the relationships that framed emergent bilinguals' everyday activities strove to balance individual agency and social structures in describing how these pathways to social capital were understood and accessed by immigrant youth who were still learning English.

References

Bailey, A. (2007). *The language demands of school: Putting academic English to the test.* New Haven, CT: Yale University Press.

Ballard & Tighe. (2006). *IDEA proficiency tests technical manual: Grades 9–12.* Bree, CA: Author.

Baquedano-López, P., Alexander, R., & Hernandez, S. (2013). Equity issues in parental and community involvement in schools: What teacher educators need to know. *Review of Research in Education, 37,* 149–82.

Bortoni-Ricardo, S. (1985). *The urbanisation of rural dialect speakers: A sociolinguistic study in Brazil.* Cambridge: Cambridge University Press.

Bourdieu, P., & Passeron, J. (1977). *Reproduction in education, society and culture.* Beverly Hills, CA: Sage.

Bronfenbrenner, U. (1977). Towards an experimental ecology of human development. *American Psychologist, 32,* 513–31.

Callahan, R. (2005). Tracking high school English learners: Limiting opportunity to learn. *American Educational Research Journal, 42*(2), 305–28.

Carhill, A., Suárez-Orozco, C., & Páez, M. (2008). Explaining English language proficiency among adolescent immigrant students. *American Educational Research Journal, 45*(4), 1155–79.

Carhill-Poza, A. (2015). Opportunities and outcomes: The role of peers in developing the academic English proficiency of adolescent English learners. *The Modern Language Journal, 99*(4), 678–95.

Carhill-Poza, A. (2016). "If you don't find a friend in here, it's gonna be hard for you": Structuring bilingual peer support in urban high schools. *Linguistics & Education, 37,* 63–72.

Carhill-Poza, A. (2018). Silenced partners: The role of bilingual peers in secondary school contexts. *Teachers College Record, 120*(11), 1–28.

Coleman, J. (1988). Social capital in the creation of human capital. *American Journal of Sociology, 94*(Suppl.), 95–120.

Donato, R. (1994). A sociocultural perspective on language learning strategies: The role of mediation. *The Modern Language Journal, 78,* 453–64.

Gándara, P., & Contreras, F. (2009). *The Latino education crisis: The consequences of failed policies.* Cambridge, MA: Harvard University Press.

García, O., & Sylvan, C. (2011). Pedagogies and practices in multilingual classrooms: Singularities in pluralities. *The Modern Language Journal, 95*(3), 385–400.

Gutiérrez, K. (1992). A comparison of instructional contexts in writing process classrooms with Latino children. *Education in Urban Society, 24,* 244–52.

Gutiérrez, K., Baquendano-López, P., & Tejeda, C. (1999). Rethinking diversity: Hybridity and hybrid language practices in the third space. *Mind, Culture, and Activity, 6*(4), 286–303.

Kanno, Y., & Kangas, S. (2014). "I'm not going to be, like, for the AP": English language learners limited access to advanced college-preparatory courses in high school. *American Educational Research Journal, 51*(5), 848–78.

Kibler, A., Atteberry, A., Hardigree, C., & Salerno, A. (2015). Language across borders: Social network development in an adolescent two-way language program. *Teachers College Record, 117*, 1–48.

Kibler, A. K., Molloy Elreda, L., Hemmler, V., Arbeit, M., Beeson, R., & Johnson, H. (2019). Building linguistically integrated classroom communities: The role of teacher practices. *American Educational Research Journal, 56*(3), 676–715.

Kurata, N. (2010). Opportunities for foreign language learning and use within a learner's informal social networks. *Mind, Culture, and Activity, 17*, 382–96.

Lantolf, J., & Appel, G. (1994). *Vygotskian approaches to second language research.* Norwood, NJ: Ablex.

Lantolf, J., & Thorne, S. (2006). *Sociocultural theory and the genesis of second language development.* Oxford: Oxford University Press.

Lee, M. (2014). Bringing the best of two worlds together for social capital research in education: Social network analysis and symbolic interactionism. *Educational Researcher, 43*(9), 454–64.

Lee, M., & Madyun, N. (2012). Decoding Somali immigrant adolescents' navigation and interpretation of resources embedded in social relationships. In Z. Bekerman & T. Geisen (Eds.), *International handbook of migration, minorities and education: Understanding cultural and social differences in processes of learning* (pp. 659–76). Dordrecht: Springer.

Milroy, L. (1987). *Language and social networks* (2nd ed.). Oxford: Blackwell.

Milroy, L., & Wei, L. (1995). A social network approach to code-switching. In L. Milroy & P. Muysken (Eds.), *One speaker, two languages* (pp. 136–57). Cambridge: Cambridge University Press.

New York City Department of Education. (2005). *Annual school reports.* New York: Division of Assessment and Accountability, New York City Department of Education.

Palardy, G., Rumberger, R., & Butler, T. (2015). The effect of high school socioeconomic, racial, and linguistic segregation on academic performance and school behaviors. *Teachers College Record, 117*(12), 1999–2045.

Smith, L. (2002). The social architecture of communicative competence: A methodology for social network research in sociolinguistics. *International Journal of the Sociology of Language, 153*, 133–60.

Stanton-Salazar, R. (2001). *Manufacturing hope and despair: The school and kin support networks of U.S. Mexican youth.* New York: Teachers College Press.

Suárez-Orozco, C., Suárez-Orozco, M., & Todorova, I. (2008). *Learning a new land: Educational pathways of immigrant youth.* Cambridge, MA: Harvard University Press.

Valdés, G. (2001). *Learning and not learning English: Latino students in American schools*. New York: TC Press.

van Lier, L. (2004). *The ecology and semiotics of language learning: A sociocultural perspective*. Boston, MA: Kluwer.

Vygotsky, L. (1978). *Mind in society*. (Trans. M. Cole). Cambridge, MA: Harvard University Press.

Walqui, A., & van Lier, L. (2010). *Scaffolding the academic success of adolescent English language learners*. San Francisco, CA: WestEd.

Watanabe, Y., & Swain, M. (2007). Effects of proficiency differences and patterns of pair interaction on second language learning: Collaborative dialogue between adult ESL learners. *Language Teaching Research, 11*, 121–42.

Wiklund, I. (2002). Social networks from a sociolinguistic perspective: The relationship between characteristics of the social networks of bilingual adolescents and their language proficiency. *International Journal of the Sociology of Language, 153*, 53–92.

Yin, R. (2003). *Case study research: Design and methods* (3rd ed.). Thousand Oaks, CA: Sage.

Zentella, A. (1997). *Growing up bilingual*. Malden, MA: Blackwell.

Zwiers, J. (2008). *Building academic language: Essential practices for content classrooms, grades 5–12*. San Francisco, CA: John Wiley & Sons.

Social Networks and Patterns of Participation in Linguistically Heterogeneous Classrooms

Amanda Kibler, Lauren Molloy Elreda, Vonna Hemmler, Alexis Rutt, Sydney Cadogan, and Betina Fuentes

Introduction

Understanding and supporting the development of equitable learning environments for students who are traditionally underserved in formal schooling is a long-standing concern in applied linguistics. Within this area of inquiry, there are a number of provocative questions that remain unaddressed regarding the ways in which peer relationships found within linguistically diverse classrooms can serve as ecological affordances, particularly for children from multilingual immigrant or indigenous homes and communities. With social network research in these contexts persuasively arguing for the importance of peers as resources that can help support the English language development of immigrant adolescents (Carhill-Poza, 2015, 2017), it is vital to better understand the relationships between peer networks and students' participation in classroom settings.

In the present study, we define a *classroom peer network* as the network of relationships among all the students in a given classroom, and use a social network analytic approach to characterize the patterns of relationships within those networks. Social networks can be conceptualized in several different ways, with a focus on one person's connections to others (known as egocentric networks), the nature of individual pairs of relationships (dyadic networks), or the entire web of relationships that comprise a group of individuals (sociocentric networks) (Wasserman & Faust, 1994). We use a sociocentric approach to understand the relationships that comprise a classroom community, in keeping with an ecological perspective that considers classrooms to be an important context for language development (van Lier 2000, 2004, 2008). In this sense, we are exploring relationships between learners and their classroom ecologies, asking: "What is it in this environment that makes things happen the way they do?" (van Lier, 2004: 11).

Participants in classroom environments include both teachers and students, but in this chapter we focus in particular on students and their relationships with each other. We do so because we work under the assumption (supported by research, described further) that peer relationships are particularly important for adolescents, and that those classrooms in which students have relationships with a linguistically diverse network of peers can support the learning of both language and academic content. When these integrated (rather than segregated) networks of relationships exist in a classroom, it is assumed that they in turn create a sense of classroom community that offers new opportunities for students to participate in the learning environment. This occurs not just because of their individual relationships with other people, but because the classroom setting as a whole is more supportive.

Although it is important to understand that each classroom's network of peer relationships is unique, like a fingerprint, there are ways to quantify and compare networks to each other. In this chapter, we look at one particular quantifiable feature—the extent to which peers in a classroom report academic helping relationships with peers of a different language proficiency classification—and its connection to the level and types of participation in which English learner (EL)-classified students[1] engage.

In this study, we asked students to identify the classmates to whom they go for academic help, and used social network analysis to examine the extent to which the academic helping *peer nominations* made by students in a given classroom tend to be segregated by EL-classification status or integrated across language-status boundaries. In other words, do the EL students in a given classroom report going to their EL classmates for help (rather than their classmates who are not EL-classified, labeled here as non-ELs) more often than would be expected by chance, if EL status had no bearing on who interacted with whom in the classroom? (And are non-EL students similarly more likely to go to their non-EL classmates for help than would be expected by chance?) In a fully linguistically segregated classroom peer network, we would only see academic helping relationships *within* language-status groups (ELs nominating ELs only, non-ELs nominating non-ELs only), whereas in a fully linguistically integrated classroom peer network, rates of cross-group (EL/non-EL) academic helping nominations in the classroom would be just as high as rates of same-group (EL/EL, or non-EL/non-EL) academic helping relationships (relative to the number of possible cross- and same-group relationships in the classroom). As described further under "Methodology," by using peer nominations of academic helping relationships from all students in a given classroom, a social network statistic can be computed that represents the degree of *peer network linguistic integration* in that classroom's peer network.

Our current study uses observational data to examine classroom participation, in order to understand the links between (1) the level of peer network linguistic integration in a classroom (as defined earlier) and (2) the ways in which EL-classified students take up opportunities for participation in these settings. Specifically, this chapter explores the following questions, in relation to sixteen EL-classified youth across eight different middle school English language arts (ELA) or math classrooms:

1. How did EL-classified students' levels of participation vary according to the level of peer network linguistic integration in their classrooms?
2. When EL-classified students were actively participating, how was the nature of that participation similar and different across more and less integrated classrooms?

Theoretical Framework: Social Networks as Classroom Ecologies

In classroom settings, individuals' actions are embedded in social contexts; as such, we view classrooms as interconnected *social networks* rather than as collections of individuals (Coleman, 1988; Tseng & Seidman, 2007). We further conceptualize our study using a language-focused ecological perspective, in which "the active learner hears and sees things most effectively and by virtue of engaging with the linguistic environment in which he or she moves [. . .] thus providing the conditions for emergent learning" (van Lier, 2008: 55). In other words, ecological theories of language development recognize that dynamic interactions occur among language, language users, and their environments— each of which is diverse and composed of important elements that do not exist as separate entities (Creese & Martin, 2003; Kramsch, 2002; van Lier, 2008). In this sense, interactions are "full of potential meanings [. . .] that become available gradually" as the learner engages in them (van Lier, 2000: 246). Thus, from an ecological perspective, learning is made possible through affordances provided by an individual's interaction with the environment and the various actors and tools in it (van Lier, 2000). Understanding features of EL-classified students' participation in classrooms that vary by level of linguistic integration is important within an ecological perspective because such a view acknowledges the impact that peer networks (among other factors) can have on EL-classified students' classroom participation and, in turn, on their academic and linguistic development.

Relevant Literature

Our primary focus is on one aspect of classroom ecologies that might mediate EL-classified students' participation: the extent to which students in a classroom report connections to peers of a different language proficiency status. In the following sections, we explore the importance of this concept based on recent research on peer networks in school contexts and their potential impacts on EL-classified students. We then describe extant research on patterns of EL-classified students' participation in linguistically heterogeneous classrooms and factors that may influence it.

Impacts of Peer Network Linguistic Integration in School Contexts

Peer relations play important roles in adolescents' school-based experiences. Their individual connections with others, in terms of having friends and feeling accepted, have been shown to promote feelings of belonging in school, which in turn support academic engagement and performance (Bellmore, 2011; Ryan & Deci, 2009). For immigrant youth, school friendships can play a particularly important role in combating the linguistic or cultural isolation that can put them at risk for academic disengagement (Tsai, 2006). The literature on academic connections with peers—such as giving or receiving academic help or advice—likewise suggests these interactions' positive influence for both K-12 (Bowman-Perrott et al., 2013; Gest, Rulison, Davidson, & Welsh, 2008; Greenwood et al., 1984) and college (Smith & Peterson, 2007) students, including EL-classified youth (Molloy Elreda, Kibler, Johnson, & Karam, 2018).

While insights into students' individual peer helping relationships are useful, they do not capture a different and vitally important aspect of the ecological contexts in which students learn: the classroom setting as a whole. At the classroom network level, integration across group differences has been shown to reduce prejudice, support access to social and educational resources for all students, and promote classroom norms of inclusion, cooperation, and academic success (e.g., Goza & Ryabov, 2009; Tezanos-Pinto, Bratt, & Brown, 2010). In our own research, we have documented the impact of classroom-level peer network integration, and in particular, integration across EL-classification status. Specifically, our previous research on middle school EL-classified students and their non-EL-classified peers has found that students from both groups benefit from academically focused classroom peer networks within and across these groups. Of particular relevance to the focus of this chapter, analysis of our quantitative survey data has shown relatively greater across-year growth in teacher ratings of students' classroom participation when students have relatively higher rates of *cross*-group academic helping relationships (Molloy Elreda et al., 2018). Such findings suggest that being a member of a classroom peer network that is integrated across language proficiency status may facilitate students' interest in and comfort with engaging in classroom activities and discussions.

Patterns of EL-classified Student Participation in Heterogeneous Classrooms

Teacher practices play a fundamental role in creating opportunities for EL-classified students to engage in the classroom (Kibler et al., 2019), but the nature of students' participation is what determines the extent to which these practices can support learning and development. In the following section, we review research that has explored EL-classified students' patterns of participation in varied interactional contexts.

Task-related Teacher-student and Peer Interactions

Whole-class, group, and dyadic interactions have received notable attention by scholars, and it is clear that EL-classified students' participation in these contexts is mediated by several factors. Duff (2002), for example, found that students at earlier levels of language development were hesitant to participate in whole-class discussions out of fear of criticism during class discussions, although they did occasionally ask for clarification or acknowledge other students' comments. Patterns of more active whole-class participation have also been noted, typically occurring when teachers connect discussions to EL-classified students' personal lives (Zuengler, 2004) and carefully structure opportunities for their participation in discussions (Harklau, 1994; Li, 2011;

Szpara & Ahmad, 2007). In relation to group and dyadic peer interactions, researchers investigating collaborative learning in linguistically heterogeneous classrooms have also found robust and active EL-classified student participation when appropriate curricular and pedagogical planning and facilitation are implemented (Bunch, Lotan, Valdés, & Cohen, 2005; Cohen & Lotan, 1995; Cohen, Lotan, Abram, Scarloss, & Schultz, 2002; Daniel, Martin-Beltran, Peercy, & Silverman, 2016; Lotan, 2008).

Non-task-related Teacher-student Interactions

Luk (2004) has most clearly documented the ways in which EL-classified students' participation can extend to interactions with the teacher outside of the context of instructional tasks or activities, defined by the author as the "informal interactions between teachers and students that are not intended for formal pedagogical purposes" (118). Luk (2004) found that when students engaged in this *small talk* with the teacher, they were motivated to initiate participation, engaged in an egalitarian relationship with the teacher, and actively directed conversations as they developed comfort with this type of communication. Braden, Wassell, Scantlebury, and Grover (2016) have also argued for the importance of non-task-related teacher-student interactions because they provide avenues for understanding how students connect their out-of-school experiences with the content they are learning. In a previous analysis of a small subset of relatively higher-proficiency EL-classified students (Kibler et al., 2018), we found that such conversations were far less common than those focusing on academics, and when they were begun by students, they were often met with teacher redirection toward more academic topics.

Non-task-related Peer Interactions

Aside from ways in which it can reveal nuanced ethnolinguistic identity negotiation (e.g., Martínez & Morales, 2014) and peer conflict (e.g., Talmy, 2010), surprisingly little is known about the prevalence or nature of adolescent EL-classified students' non-task-related peer talk in linguistically heterogeneous classrooms. In our previous work with EL-classified students referenced earlier (Kibler et al., 2018), we found that many of them—but not all—engaged frequently with EL- and non-EL-classified peers about non-task-related topics during liminal moments such as transitions. They also often inserted conversations with peers about varied topics as they participated in teacher-assigned group or individual activities.

Summary

Research has established the importance of adolescents' and immigrant students' individual relationships with peers (i.e., egocentric networks), including the positive roles that academic peer networks can play. From a sociocentric perspective, classroom-level integration across group differences, including EL-classification status, has also been shown to promote positive social and educational outcomes. Our work builds on this foundation to better understand the classroom ecologies created by linguistically integrated peer networks, and in particular the processes through with EL-classified students take up opportunities for participation in more or less integrated classroom environments. Studies of EL-classified students' participation in linguistically diverse secondary classrooms suggest the importance of looking at both teacher- and peer-led interactions, task- and non-task-related, to understand these processes, and such considerations guided our focus on these varied dimensions in our analysis.

Methodology

In this mixed-methods study, we used social network analysis to identify two sets of classrooms: those with high peer network linguistic integration (HI, for high integration) and those with low peer network linguistic integration (LI, for low integration) at the end of the school year. We then used qualitative analyses to identify patterns of participation among EL-classified students in both HI and LI classrooms.

Research Context and Participants

The present study is part of a larger mixed-methods project in two middle schools in the South-Atlantic United States. Both schools placed EL-classified students in linguistically heterogeneous classrooms for core subject areas like ELA and mathematics and had levels of ethnic/racial diversity and economic disadvantage that were generally reflective of state and national averages (Kibler et al., 2019). Information related to the linguistic composition of classrooms in the study, as well as other demographics, is included in Table 3.1.[2]

Classrooms for the current analysis were chosen from those included in the larger study via social network surveys and maximum variation sampling

Table 3.1 Classroom Demographics

	% EL-Classified	Avg ELP Score (Range)	Languages Spoken by Students in Addition to English	Grade	Subject	Track[1]	Integration Level
Full sample	26	4.18 (1.8–5.7)	Spanish (269), Arabic (16), Dari (10), Mandarin (9), + 25 more				
Ms. Bayley[2] (WF)[3]	23	3.45 (2.8–4.9)	Spanish (8)	8	Math	S	Low
Mr. Brown (WM)	40	4.58 (4.2–5.1)	Spanish (5), Arabic (1)	6	ELA	S	High
Ms. Gibson (WF)	32	4.42 (4.0–5.7)	Spanish (7), French (1), Mandarin (1), Burmese (1)	8	ELA	B	High
Mr. Hansen (WM)	42	4.54 (3.8–5.1)	Spanish (8)	7	ELA	B	High
Ms. Husk (WF)	17	4.35 (3.8–4.9)	Spanish (4), French (2), Bangla (1), Nepali (1), Korean (1)	7	Math	H	Low
Dr. King-Porter (AAF)	17	4.23 (4.2–4.3)	Spanish (8)	6	Math	B	High
Ms. Lane (WF)	67	3.46 (2.2–4.8)	Spanish (6), Dari (3), Arabic (2), Turkish (2), Kachin (1)	7	Math	S	Low
Ms. Miller (WF)	61	3.84 (2.9–5.1)	Spanish (6), Arabic (1), Mandarin (1)	6	Math	S	Low

Notes: All data but WIDA™ English language proficiency (ELP) scores rounded to nearest whole number. [1]There were three academic tracks with placement through teacher recommendations and assessments: Basic (B, lowest track, often enrolling special education students via an inclusion model), Standard (S, middle track), and Honors (H, most advanced track). [2]All names are pseudonyms. [3]Abbreviations are AA = African American, W = White, F = Female, M = Male, ELA = English language arts.

(Patton, 2015; see Kibler et al., 2018 for more information on methodology). We identified eight classrooms as being either HI or LI in the spring of each study year and qualitatively analyzed observations conducted in them throughout that year.[3] In each of the eight classrooms, we had selected two EL-classified focal students based on a range of factors (see Kibler et al., 2018). This process led to observation of sixteen EL-classified students across the eight HI and LI classrooms. Notably, we found that classrooms were similar in terms of pedagogical structures (see Table 3.2). Instructional tasks did not vary notably by integration level, although HI classrooms were slightly more likely to feature teacher-led, group/whole-class instruction and student-led collaborative projects, and LI classrooms were slightly more likely to feature individual activities that focused on students independently applying what they had learned.

Table 3.2 Task Types in Study Classrooms, by Integration Level

Task	High Integration Classrooms (%)	Low Integration Classrooms (%)
Teacher-led group/whole-class instruction	47	39.2
Individual activities to apply learning	25.43	37.64
Student-led collaborative projects	8.07	2.03
Other	19.54	21.14
Total	100	100

Social Network Data Collection and Analysis

Broadly, social network analysis refers to a set of measurement and statistical tools designed to operationalize particular group dynamics (e.g., Moody & White, 2003). Individuals are asked to identify those within a defined network (e.g., a classroom or school) with whom they have a particular relationship (e.g., a friendship or academic helping relationship), and from these data, social network analytic methods are used to quantify particular features of a network's structure (e.g., how segregated the peer networks are by a particular demographic feature, such as EL-classification status). In turn, these network-level statistics can be examined in relation to other variables of interest (e.g., Cappella, Kim, Neal, & Jackson, 2013; Gest, Osgood, Feinberg, Bierman, & Moody, 2011), such as whether cross-group integration in the classroom network is associated with academic growth (Molloy Elreda et al., 2019).

To identify the network of academic helping relationships in the classroom, our focus in the present study, we asked students to identify the classmates that they "talk to when trying to get work done in this class."[4] We used these peer nominations to quantify how linguistically segregated each classroom was, or, conversely, how linguistically integrated it was across language learner status, using the Freeman Segregation Index (Freeman, 1978; Gest, Davidson, Rulison, Moody, & Welsh, 2007; Moody, 2001). (See Kibler et al., 2019 for more information on this index and how we employed it in our study.)

For the present study, we focused on classrooms that were most and least segregated at the time of the final survey administration in the spring, which we defined as those that were one standard deviation (SD) or more either above or below the mean of the full sample (N = 46 classrooms) in spring segregation levels. As explained earlier, the eight classrooms we studied qualitatively fit these criteria: four with high segregation and four with low segregation. As we have argued elsewhere (Kibler et al., 2019), although Freeman's (1978) index focuses on segregation, we have made the rhetorical and conceptual choice to discuss this phenomenon in terms of how *integrated* (or *not* segregated) peer social networks are because integration is the network arrangement that is theoretically and empirically supported as being more supportive for EL-classified students. As a result, we refer to classrooms with low segregation as *high integration* (HI) and those with high segregation as *low integration* (LI).

Qualitative Data Collection and Analysis

The field researchers (the first author and graduate students trained in qualitative data collection methods) conducted eight to ten observations of each classroom over the school year (Kibler et al., 2019). An observational protocol (see Kibler et al., 2018) allowed observers to pay particular attention to teacher-student and peer interactions of focal students.

We began our analysis by identifying any instances of participation by the focal students, defining participation broadly as any instance in which a student's verbal or nonverbal behavior was indicated. Using the web-based qualitative analysis software Dedoose, we coded field note excerpts from all eight classrooms for a level of participation for each excerpt. These included off-task or nonparticipatory (Level −1), on-task but not active (Level 0), and active (Level 1).[5] (These levels of participation purposefully included participation that was aligned with assigned tasks as well as conversations that took place in liminal moments that did not have an explicit pedagogical purpose or alignment with the lesson.) To support initial reliability, the lead author and research assistants individually coded and discussed as a group approximately 10 percent of the data, using a consensus process (Hill et al., 2005) to resolve any disagreements and modify the codebook as needed. Following these initial steps, all the remaining data was double-coded by research team members, and any discrepancies were discussed and resolved among group members.

Analysis of the levels of participation (RQ1) led us to notice that the largest difference in participation by integration level was that students in HI classrooms tended to be more likely to actively participate (Level 1) than those in LI classrooms. As a result, we focused our second round of analysis on the 510 Level 1 excerpts (367 in HI classrooms; 143 in LI classrooms) to understand what kinds of active participation were happening in each set of classrooms and how often each kind was occurring (RQ2). Through a rereading of those coded excerpts and a consultation of existing literature, we developed and refined an inductive/deductive (Fereday & Muir-Cochrane, 2006) coding scheme with six key patterns of active participation, representing a variety of interactional contexts, foci, and participants (see Table 3.3).

All Level 1 excerpts were then recoded a final time by at least two members of the research team and a consensus process was used again to (1) ensure agreement and fit with one of these patterns and (2) complete focused coding (Charmaz, 2014) within each pattern. Through this process, we were able to identify key differences in the active participatory practices of EL-classified students in HI and LI classrooms as well as those that occurred in both settings (RQ2).

Table 3.3 Key Patterns of Active Participation

Action/Focus	Interactional Contexts	Participants in Addition to Student
Seeking task-related assistance	dyadic	teacher
Providing or seeking task-related assistance	dyadic	peer
Demonstrating task-related expertise	group or whole class	peers and teacher
Acknowledging a lack of task-related understanding	group or whole class	peers and teacher
Engaging in non-task teacher talk	dyadic or group	teacher (or teacher and peers)
Engaging in non-task peer talk	dyadic or group	peer(s)

Findings

In this section we address each of our research questions in turn. We begin by exploring patterns related to the level of focal students' observed participation in HI and LI classrooms (RQ1) before turning to ways in which types of active participation were similar or different (RQ2) in the two types of classrooms.

Levels of Participation

Table 3.4 shows that while EL-classified students in both HI and LI classrooms were off-task/nonparticipatory at approximately the same rate (11 percent and 13 percent, respectively), students in HI classrooms were more likely to actively participate (38 percent of excerpts) than those in LI classrooms (24 percent of excerpts). In contrast, students in LI classrooms were more likely to simply comply with the demands of the task or conversation than those in HI classrooms (63 percent vs. 51 percent). These trends demonstrate that when students were participating, there was greater voluntary contribution and less "going through the motions" in HI classrooms than in LI ones.

Table 3.4 Level of Focal Student Participation in High- and Low Integration Classrooms

Level of Participation	High Integration Classrooms	Low Integration Classrooms
−1 (off-task/nonparticipatory)	11% (106 excerpts)	13% (76 excerpts)
0 (on-task but not active)	51% (486 excerpts)	63% (382 excerpts)
1 (active)	38% (367 excerpts)	24% (143 excerpts)
Total	100% (959 excerpts)	100% (601 excerpts)

Note: This chart depicts the percentage (and number) of field note excerpts coded for level of participation.

Similarities and Differences in Participation According to Peer Network Linguistic Integration

Similarities

In further analysis of Level 1 (active participation) excerpts, we found two key patterns of participation that were similar in both sets of classrooms: dyadic interaction in which EL-classified students sought assistance from the teacher in the context of teacher-assigned

Table 3.5 Similarities and Differences in Types of Active Participation

	High Integration Classrooms (Excerpts, Classrooms)	All Classrooms (HI Excerpts, LI Excerpts)	Low Integration Classrooms (Excerpts, Classrooms)
Engaging in teacher task-related assistance (dyadic)		Seeking (22, 13)	
		35 (100% of total): 62.9% high; 37.1% low	
Engaging in peer task-related assistance (dyadic)		Seeking (8, 6); providing (10, 6)	
		30 (100% of total): 60% high; 40% low	
Demonstrating expertise related to task (group/whole class)		Providing answer to question (119, 23); providing comment (60, 8); raising hand, but not providing answer (17, 3); other (4,1)	
		235 (100% of total): 85.1% high; 14.9% low	
Acknowledging lack of understanding related to task (group/whole class)		Making generic acknowledgment (8, 2); asking direct question (4,1)	
		15 (100% of total): 80% high; 20% low	
Engaging in teacher non-task talk (dyadic/group)			
Topic	Out-of-school lives (15,4); manners/social expectations (4, 2)	School-related (8, 2)	Unknown (1, 1)
	19 (63.3% of total)	**10 (33% of total): 80% high; 20% low**	**1 (0.3% of total)**
Role	Responding to teacher question or comment directed at student/peer (6, 3)	Asking a question (7,1); commenting (14, 1)	Unknown (1, 1)
	6 (20% of total)	**23 (76.77% of total): 91.3% high; 8.7% low**	**1 (0.3% of total)**
Engaging in peer non-task talk (dyadic/group)			
Topic		Out-of-class lives (14, 5); school-related (11, 4), logistics (14, 12); other (6, 2)	
		68 (100% of total): 66.1% High; 33.8% Low	
Role		Asking a question (11, 1); responding to peer questions or comments (26, 16); other (8, 2)	Refusing (4, 3)
		64 (94.1% of total): 70.3% High; 29.7% Low	**4 (5.9% of total)**

tasks, or dyadic interactions in which students provided or sought assistance from/to peers related to those tasks (see Table 3.5).

The frequency of engaging with dyadic teacher or peer assistance was consistent across integration level, with 60 to 62.9 percent found in HI and 37.1 to 40 percent found in LI classrooms, reflecting the same proportion of overall coded excerpts, given that there were 959 total excerpts in HI and 601 in LI classrooms in our whole dataset (61.5 percent and 38.5 percent, respectively). In other words, EL-classified students were equally likely to seek help from a teacher or seek or provide help to a peer, regardless of the classroom's peer network linguistic integration level. Further, we were not able to discern qualitative differences within the seeking/providing help categories that showed any distinctions by integration level. Because we wish to explore in more depth the types of active participation that differed across classrooms, we do not provide further examples of these trends. Instead, we now turn to the areas in which distinctions between HI and LI classrooms were found.

Differences

The other four types of active participation demonstrated differences in frequency and/or quality of EL-classified students' participation according to peer network linguistic integration. They included demonstrating expertise related to a task in group/whole-class settings, acknowledging a lack of understanding in group/whole-class settings, engaging in teacher non-task talk in dyadic or group contexts, and engaging in peer non-task talk in dyadic or group contexts. We describe these differences with examples from our field notes to highlight the nature of these distinctions by integration level.

Demonstrating academic expertise

One of the primary types of participation that differed by integration level was students' demonstrating academic expertise by providing (or attempting to provide) an answer or an explanation in group and whole-class settings. Although EL-classified focal students in both types of classrooms demonstrated their academic expertise in similar ways, what is notable is the frequency of this participation: even accounting for the relatively greater proportion of total excerpts in HI than LI classrooms (61.5 percent vs. 38.5 percent), in HI classrooms there were far more instances of demonstrating this expertise. Of the 235 total instances of students demonstrating expertise, 85.1 percent of these participatory actions occurred in HI classrooms, compared to 14.9 percent of instances in LI ones. Given that these interactions occurred in public spaces (i.e., in front of groups of peers or even the whole class), this higher frequency of demonstrating expertise in HI classrooms could indicate a greater level of comfort from EL-classified students in this type of classroom and/or more effective teacher facilitation of group and whole-class instruction.

Although the frequency of demonstrating expertise was higher for HI classrooms, the manner in which it occurred was similar across HI and LI classrooms. In both HI and LI classrooms, the most frequent way students demonstrated their academic expertise was by directly answering a teacher's question. When teachers posed questions, students in both types of classrooms volunteered a range of responses. For example, in one interaction in Dr. King-Porter's (HI) math class, when the teacher asked her class, "What's mode?" and a student responded that mode was "the number you see the most," focal student Adrian then said, "It can be two numbers too!" which was a correct response. In another instance, when working through warm-up questions at the beginning of her math class, Ms. Miller (LI) asked the class, "What do I need to do next?" Fawzi raised his hand, was called on by the teacher, and successfully narrated the next steps to the math problem. Focal students also demonstrated academic expertise by expanding on their peers' answers. Interestingly, we found very few instances in either type of classroom in which focal students provided inappropriate or inaccurate answers. Focal students also often raised their hands but were not called on by the teacher. Although it is not clear if they would have provided appropriate responses, the presence of this type of participation likely shows that focal students were willing to engage in sharing what they knew in group and whole-class settings.

In addition to answering teachers' direct questions, EL-classified focal students in both types of classrooms provided unsolicited comments or remarks that were not preceded by raising a hand to signal an intent to participate. In a discussion in Mr. Brown's (HI) ELA class on the book *Holes* (Sachar, 1998), for example, Omar commented, "Stanley still has bad luck," as Mr. Brown discussed the book's plot diagram. Likewise, in Ms. Bayley's (LI) math classroom, Victor shouted out, "It kind of looks like a web!" when the teacher attempted to draw a soup can label on the board to give the class an example of surface area.

Acknowledging lack of understanding

In addition to demonstrating academic expertise, EL-classified focal students in both sets of classrooms also acknowledged to teachers and/or peers when they did not understand something, albeit notably less frequently in LI classrooms (as was the case with demonstrating expertise mentioned earlier). In this type of participation, students acknowledged either not understanding something specific or stated a general lack of understanding in group or whole-class settings. Eighty percent of these instances occurred in HI classrooms and 20 percent occurred in LI classrooms, suggesting that such participation varied by integration level. Generic acknowledgment of a lack of understanding was the most common practice, such as in Ms. Gibson's (HI) classroom when Pedro said loudly, "Nobody knows the answer!" after Ms. Gibson explained subject-verb agreement in one ELA lesson, or in Ms. Bayley's (LI) classroom when Victor shouted to Ms. Bayley "I don't understand!" during one math lesson. Students in both sets of classrooms also asked questions as a way to clarify their lack of understanding. Such interactional moves in front of others—as opposed to signaling confusion privately to a teacher—risked judgment from peers, and the greater frequency of this phenomenon in HI classrooms is notable.

Engaging in teacher non-task talk

EL-classified students in our study also engaged with teachers through non-task talk. Students in both types of classrooms participated in interactions with teachers outside the context of the teachers' planned activities and tasks. Of note, however, was that non-task talk with teachers was much less common in LI classrooms. Indeed, of all of the teacher-student interactions classified as non-task talk, 90 percent occurred in HI classrooms, comprising twenty-seven of the thirty total excerpts in this category. Differences in frequency and content were also evident for both the topic and role taken by the students.

Topics

In addition to the lower frequency of non-task talk interactions with teachers, the topics of conversation in LI classrooms were less personal as well. The few instances of teacher-student interactions in LI classrooms revolved around school-related topics. For example, during one student-teacher interaction, Safwan joked with Ms. Lane (LI) that he designed the online platform that he was using to complete his assignment. In another interaction, Edward asked Ms. Bayley (LI) about some food he left in the classroom previously. While both interactions were initiated by the students, they were brief and restricted to basic classroom needs or topics. In the HI classrooms, there were also numerous teacher-student interactions related to class topics and logistics, but a distinct difference was the added presence of deeper, more meaningful conversations about school-related issues. This was evident in a conversation in Ms. Gibson's (HI) class about the recent English language proficiency test Jiaying took:

Jiaying starts to tell Ms. Gibson that she did her WIDA test yesterday and she feels good. She also says that it has been three years since she moved to the US. Last year she received a 5.8/5.9. Ms. Gibson responds that 6 is a pass, but how she does on that test is not as important because the test is only "one day" and what's more important is "everyday." Ms. Gibson also comments to Jiaying that her understanding is very high. Jiaying responds that she thinks she'll receive highest scores on writing . . . Jiaying then says, this is all because she has the best language arts teacher ever.

While still school-related in nature, Jiaying's initiation of a more personal topic and the extended nature of the conversation suggest a comfort with Ms. Gibson beyond that required for logistical conversations. Jiaying's compliment at the end of the interaction further indicates a positive relationship between Ms. Gibson and her.

There were also types of student-teacher interactions unique to HI classrooms in which teachers and students discussed students' out-of-school lives, activities, and interests. These interactions occurred in all observed HI classrooms and ranged from discussions about pop culture and sleep schedules to more serious issues, such as a discussion about gangs in the community. EL-classified students in HI classrooms also engaged in conversations with teachers about social expectations, such as manners or appropriate behaviors. Collectively, the varied types of interactions students and teachers had outside the context of lessons in HI classrooms and the absence of these conversations in LI classrooms seem to indicate the presence of stronger relationships between EL-classified students and teachers in HI classrooms.

Roles

We found that both sets of classroom interactions pertaining to non-task talk with teachers occurred when students asked the teacher questions or made comments. Unsolicited comments and questions were present in both types of classrooms, but were particularly common in HI ones. Such participation typically occurred in relation to what was happening in the classroom but was not specifically requested. For example, Adrian commented to Dr. King-Porter (HI) on his way out the door that the day's lesson was "fun." Teachers in HI classrooms also frequently opened up space for students to engage without making such non-task talk obligatory. This was evident in the following interaction between Andres and Mr. Hansen (HI):

Brandon and Andrés walk in together. They stare quietly at the screen projection of today's warm-up activity. Mr. Hansen says something about them being so quiet, and Andrés replies that he is just very tired. He adds, with a smiling face, that he is just waiting for Wednesday to come. Mr. Hansen asks him why. Andrés replies that on Wednesday they're going to his "favorite place." Andrés adds that his mom is driving him there.

In the aforementioned interaction, Andres not only accepted Mr. Hansen's invitation to interact but also extended the conversation after the teacher's prompt by offering additional personal information. This again demonstrates a willingness to voluntarily engage in interactions with the teacher, in this case about life outside of school.

Finally, non-task talk with teachers also occurred when the teacher's initiation was directed at another student. For example, during one interaction, Ms. Gibson (HI) asked Pedro's peer why he was so tired, but Pedro jumped in and responded before his peer could, reporting that his peer's lethargy was due to a late bedtime. This interjection indicates a level of confidence in participating in conversations with the teacher even if not explicitly invited to do so.

Engaging in peer non-task talk

In addition to interactions with teachers outside of the context of teacher-provided tasks or activities, the EL-classified focal students in our study also engaged in non-task talk with their peers. In both HI and LI classrooms, these interactions were largely similar: they occurred in proportions that generally reflected the total number of excerpts in each group of classrooms, addressed the same topics, and involved generally similar participatory roles. However, two differences were prominent. In HI classrooms, these peer interactions addressed more substantive topics more often, and they featured more positive, agentive roles for participation. In the following, we discuss not only what topics focal students discussed, since non-task talk could (and did) address a wide range of subjects, but also what roles the focal students played in these interactions.

Topics

Across the three topic areas presented in Table 3.5 (out-of-class lives, school-related topics, and classroom-based logistics), those that were notably more prominent in HI than LI classrooms were discussions of out-of-class or school-related issues, arguably more substantive topics that could provide peers with insights into each other's lives or important information about schooling. Interactions focused on out-of-class topics ranged from conversations about the dating histories of pop stars, which Jiaying discussed in Ms. Gibson's (HI) class with tablemates Aubrey and Diego, to a discussion among peers in Dr. King-

Porter's (HI) class about the work Adrian completed for his out-of-school religious classes, to Omar and his peer's discussion of their favorite foods in Mr. Brown's (HI) class. Topics that were related to school often focused on extracurricular activities, school schedules, and particularly for the eighth graders in this study the high schools they were soon going to attend. Logistically focused interactions, which were more common in LI classrooms, tended to focus on locating and using laptops or other materials (e.g., Ms. Lane, LI). The relative prominence of both school-based and out-of-school interactions in HI classrooms indicates these classroom settings were ones in which peers incorporated issues relevant to their lives, academic or otherwise, outside of the classroom.

Roles

Peer non-task talk featured a range of roles for the EL-classified students whose participation we analyzed. In both sets of classrooms, they asked questions and responded to peers' questions or comments. In total, such practices were more prominent in HI classrooms, comprising more than 70 percent of the total number of peer non-task interactions in our data, a slightly greater proportion than might be expected given the total number of excerpts.

The following example, in which focal student Omar asks several questions of his peers in Mr. Brown's (HI) class, highlights the ways in which such roles often served to keep peer non-task talk moving forward:

> Omar is talking with a small group of students when one starts to tell a story/riddle: "There is a guy who got murdered in a round house. Was it the chauffeur, the maid or the cook? The chauffeur says he was getting gas in the car, the cook was making food and the maid was dusting the corners. Who did it?" Bradley, another student in the group, gives the answer ("the maid"), and a conversation starts about how there are no corners in a round house. Omar asks how it would stand up, and Bradley replies that they could dig a hole and put it in the hole. Omar then asks why someone would dust the corners. Bradley says that usually the corners get dustier, and Cameron says that they get paid to do it.

In this instance, although the conversation was initiated and largely contributed to by other students, Omar's participation played an important role in shaping the interaction and led both Bradley and Cameron to create and extend their explanations in response.

Responding to peers' questions or comments was also a notable component of active participation in peer interactions in both types of classrooms. In many instances, EL-classified students contributed in ways that shared valuable information with peers, such as when Adrian clarified the homeroom schedule for a new student in Dr. King-Porter's (HI) class, or in ways that positioned them as having expertise or viewpoints. An interchange in Ms. Husk's (LI) room demonstrates this latter trend:

> A student sitting next to Zoe tells her that he speaks French, and Zoe says she learned a little bit last year because of an international school she attended. He continues, mentioning that French is spoken in Canada, and that in his opinion, everything is better there. Zoe responds that she likes Canada but doesn't enjoy their food.

In this conversation, Zoe's responses to her peer's comments position her as trilingual (her home language is Korean), an international traveler, and someone with particular opinions about cuisine. Zoe took up her peer's response and expanded upon it, offering new information and a distinct perspective on it based on lived experiences. Questions asked of peers and responses to them in our data set obviously varied in their subject matter and interactional particulars, but the aforementioned examples suggest important ways in which these roles positioned EL-classified students as valued and knowledgeable members of classroom communities, regardless of integration level. That these types of interactions occurred more frequently in HI classrooms, however, suggests it might have been a more common experience for focal students in those classrooms.

A small but notable difference between HI and LI classrooms was one particular role found only in the latter settings: refusing verbal or nonverbal requests from peers. Although these were not found frequently in our data, with only four instances overall, they may imply a lack of cooperation among peers. These instances ranged from refusals to share school supplies to more conflict-laden interactions, such as when Victor refused to return a stuffed animal he had taken from a peer in Ms. Bayley's (LI) class. Given that refusing another student's gesture occurred exclusively in LI classrooms, and appeared in three of four LI classrooms, these patterns might indicate a connection between less linguistically integrated classrooms and negative interactions with peers.

Discussion and Conclusions

Our findings suggest that classroom-level peer network linguistic integration is related to EL-classified students' participation in several ways. Although dyadic interactions related to seeking and/or providing assistance seemed to occur in the same ways and with the same frequency across classrooms, other aspects of participation we investigated differed notably by linguistic integration level. In addition to participating actively more often overall, EL-classified focal students in HI classrooms more frequently shared both expertise and confusion in group and whole-class settings, demonstrating that their "public" personas in the classroom may have been validated to a greater degree in these settings. Additionally, the non-task talk occurring outside of the lesson context in HI classrooms tended to address more substantive topics with peers and simply occurred more often with teachers, suggesting a depth and breadth of peer and teacher connection that was unique to these environments. The academic benefits of supportive individual- and classroom-level networks are well established for both general student populations and immigrant or EL-classified youth (e.g., Bellmore, 2011; Gest et al., 2008; Goza & Ryabov, 2009; Tsai, 2006), but our work is unique in establishing peer network linguistic integration as a classroom-level network feature that is associated with positive classroom participation.

Such patterns also demonstrate important connections between teachers' instructional practices and EL-classified students' uptake of them. Although teachers in HI classrooms appeared to play a more active role in creating opportunities for student-led non-task talk, the instructional tasks in which students engaged were roughly similar across integration level (see Table 3.3), and we did not note systematic differences in the current analysis regarding how teachers facilitated these tasks. [6] However, students appeared to differ across integration levels in their willingness to take up these opportunities for participation and interaction. In this way, social connection that is integrated across language status in the classroom may both facilitate and be facilitated by EL-classified students' willingness to actively participate in classroom settings. Such patterns reinforce Luk's (2004) argument that small talk with teachers can provide venues to both create and further students' sense of belonging and agency in the classroom, and Oriyama (Chapter 4, this volume) finding that a sense of belonging is important for positively viewing participation. Further, given that Carhill-Poza (Chapter 2, this volume) found that many EL-classified adolescents did not have relationships with teachers that supported either academically focused talk or small talk, and our own previous finding that small-talk interactions with teachers were somewhat rare compared to academically focused ones (Kibler et al., 2018), the higher frequency of teacher-student small talk in HI classrooms in the current analysis is particularly notable.

Teaching Implications

Relationships between linguistically integrated peer networks and EL-classified student participation are complex. Because peer networks are created and sustained in ecologically complex settings, it is unlikely that any decontextualized teaching practice will have meaningful or predictable results. Nevertheless, our findings point toward several instructional implications. First, we argue that it is valuable for teachers to have an awareness of the peer networks that exist in their classrooms—particularly for linguistically heterogeneous settings that include EL-classified students—and of how linguistically integrated those networks are. Teachers may not be intuitively attuned to peer dynamics, however (Gest, 2006), and may underestimate the difficulty of establishing and sustaining peer relationships in the classroom (Kurata, Chapter 5, this volume). For these reasons, professional development supporting this awareness is likely necessary to facilitate well-grounded instructional decision-making that supports positive, linguistically integrated peer networks. The current analysis and our previous work (Kibler et al., 2019) suggest that such instructional practices could usefully include forming social connections with students, praising or validating students, facilitating interactive peer learning, providing proactive behavioral support, and addressing discrimination and diversity. Finally, because our findings indicate strong connections between peer network linguistic integration and public or social interactions (rather than dyadic ones), we recommend that teachers attend carefully to building social relationships with EL-classified students and creating classroom communities in which these students are willing to engage in more "public" participation. Teachers' knowledge of student peer networks and their investment in actively cultivating peer relationships that support students' linguistic and academic development are important steps in creating more equitable classroom communities for all students.

Notes

1 In most cases (except where clarity is hindered), we purposefully use the term "EL-classified" student rather than *English learner (EL)* to highlight the fact that our study population was categorized by having a bureaucratic classification—a state-level designation as an EL. There are well-recognized challenges in defining exactly who ELs are (Linquanti & Cook, 2013), and as a result we wish to highlight that the

individuals in our study were sorted by this external mechanism rather than our own sorting and characterizing of students. Employing the term "classified" is also a useful reminder of the ways that socio-institutional mechanisms shape educators' and researchers' labeling of learners (Kibler & Valdés, 2016).

2   While demographics are useful in understanding the context of these classrooms, it should be noted that our previous statistical analysis (Kibler et al., 2019) found that demographic factors were not statistically significantly associated with level or growth/decline of peer network linguistic integration.

3   In our previous study of teacher practices (Kibler et al., 2019), we included classrooms that had both highest/lowest end-of-year levels of linguistic integration and those with the greatest across-year growth/decline in integration. This allowed us to examine teacher practices that may have been associated with both *improving* and/or *maintaining high* linguistic integration (or, conversely, with *worsening* or *lack of improvement in low* integration). In the present analysis, we only focus on classrooms with the highest/lowest integration by the end of the school year, because we anticipated that these classrooms would best and most consistently represent the contrasting conditions and student experiences in high versus low integration classrooms.

4   The use of peer nomination items such as this to identify patterns of relationships within school or classroom peer networks is a well-validated approach, and has been applied extensively across studies of friendships and help-seeking relationships among middle school students (e.g., Moody et al., 2011; Ryan & Shim, 2012) and in studies of cross-race/ethnicity and cross-language peer relationships (e.g., Aboud & Sankar, 2007; Carhill-Poza, 2011; Goza & Ryabov, 2009; Hamm, Brown, & Heck, 2005).

5   Level −1: focal students were neither working on the task assigned by the teacher nor participating in conversation with others in the classroom. Level 0: focal students were compliant; they were on-task (as assigned by the teacher) or participating in conversation but not otherwise contributing verbally or nonverbally beyond what was required or requested. Level 1: focal students were on-task (as assigned by the teacher) or participating in conversations by, for example, seeking out clarification from a teacher or peer, or raising a hand to suggest an answer or idea when not individually called upon or when not all students were expected to respond.

6   In our larger study of teacher practices (Kibler et al., 2019), we found some differences in task facilitation, but these patterns were not systematic enough to present in the current analysis, perhaps because of the smaller data set we investigated here. We also acknowledge that more in-depth, discourse-analytic approaches to examining transcripts of (rather than field notes about) classroom interaction might reveal nuanced differences in these facilitation practices.

References

Aboud, F. E., & Sankar, J. (2007). Friendship and identity in a language-integrated school. *International Journal of Behavioral Development, 31*(5), 445–53. doi:10.1177/0165025407081469

Bellmore, A. (2011). Peer rejection and unpopularity: Associations with GPAs across the transition to middle school. *Journal of Educational Psychology, 103*(2), 282–95. doi:10.1037/a0023312

Bowman-Perrott, L., Davis, H., Vannest, K., Williams, L., Greenwood, C., & Parker, R. (2013). Academic benefits of peer tutoring: A meta-analytic review of single-case research. *School Psychology Review, 42*(1), 39–55.

Braden, S., Wassell, B. A., Scantlebury, K., & Grover, A. (2016). Supporting language learners in science classrooms: Insights from middle-school English language learner students. *Language and Education, 30*(5), 438–58. doi:10.1080/09500782.2015.1134566

Bunch, G. C., Lotan, R., Valdés, G., & Cohen, E. (2005). Keeping content at the heart of content-based instruction: Access and support for transitional English learners. In D. Kaufman & J. Crandall (Eds.), *Content-based instruction in primary and secondary school settings* (pp. 11–25). Alexandria, VA: TESOL.

Cappella, E., Kim, H. Y., Neal, J. W., & Jackson, D. R. (2013). Classroom peer relationships and behavioral engagement in elementary school: The role of social network equity. *American Journal of Community Psychology, 52*(3–4), 367–79. doi:10.1007/s10464-013-9603-5

Carhill-Poza, A. (2011). *English language development in context: The peer social networks and interactions of Spanish-speaking adolescent immigrant students.* Unpublished doctoral dissertation, New York University, New York.

Carhill-Poza, A. (2015). Opportunities and outcomes: The role of peers in developing the oral academic English proficiency of adolescent English learners. *Modern Language Journal, 99*(4), 678–95. doi:10.1111/modl.12271

Carhill-Poza, A. (2017). "If you don't find a friend in here, it's gonna be hard for you": Structuring bilingual peer support for language learning in urban high schools. *Linguistics and Education, 37*, 63–72.

Charmaz, K. (2014). *Constructing grounded theory* (2nd ed.). Thousand Oaks, CA: Sage.

Cohen, E. G., & Lotan, R. A. (1995). Producing equal-status interaction in the heterogeneous classroom. *American Educational Research Journal, 32*(1), 99–120. doi:10.2307/1163215

Cohen, E. G., Lotan, R. A., Abram, P. L., Scarloss, B. A., & Schultz, S. E. (2002). Can groups learn? *Teachers College Record, 104*(6), 1045–68. doi:10.1111/1467-9620.00196

Coleman, J. S. (1988). Social capital in the creation of human capital. *American Journal of Sociology, 94*, S95–S120. doi:10.1086/228943

Creese, A., & Martin, P. (2003). Multilingual classroom ecologies: Inter-relationships, interactions and ideologies. *International Journal of Bilingual Education and Bilingualism, 6*(3–4), 161–7. doi:10.1080/13670050308667778

Daniel, S. M., Martin-Beltran, M., Peercy, M., & Silverman, R. (2016). Moving beyond "yes" or "no:" Shifting from over-scaffolding to contingent scaffolding in literacy instruction with emergent bilingual students. *TESOL Journal, 7*(2), 393–420. doi:10.1002/tesj.213

Duff, P. A. (2002). Pop culture and ESL students: Intertextuality, identity, and participation in classroom discussions. *Journal of Adolescent & Adult Literacy, 45*(6), 482–8.

Fereday, J., & Muir-Cochrane, E. (2006). Demonstrating rigor using thematic analysis: A hybrid approach of inductive and deductive coding and theme development. *International Journal of Qualitative Methods, 5*(1), 80–92. doi:10.1177/160940690600500107

Freeman, L. C. (1978). Segregation in social networks. *Sociological Methods and Research, 6*(4), 411–30. doi:10.1177/004912417800600401

Gest, S. D. (2006). Teacher reports of children's friendships and social groups: Agreement with peer reports and implications for studying peer similarity. *Social Development, 15*(2), 248–59. doi:10.1111/j.1467-9507.2006.00339.x

Gest, S. D., Davidson, A. J., Rulison, K. L., Moody, J., & Welsh, J. A. (2007). Features of groups and status hierarchies in girls' and boys' early adolescent peer networks. *New Directions for Child and Adolescent Development, 2007*(118), 43–60. doi:10.1002/cd.200

Gest, S. D., Osgood, D. W., Feinberg, M. E., Bierman, K. L., & Moody, J. (2011). Strengthening prevention program theories and evaluations: Contributions from social network analysis. *Prevention Science, 12*(4), 349–60. doi:10.1007/s11121-011-0229-2

Gest, S. D., Rulison, K. L., Davidson, A. J., & Welsh, J. A. (2008). Children's academic reputations among peers: Longitudinal associations with academic self-concept, effort and performance. *Developmental Psychology, 44*(3), 625–36.

Goza, F., & Ryabov, I. (2009). Adolescents' educational outcomes: Racial and ethnic variations in peer network importance. *Journal of Youth and Adolescence, 38*(9), 1264–79. doi:10.1007/s10964-009-9418-8

Greenwood, C., Dinwiddie, G., Terry, B., Wade, L., Stanley, S., Thibadeau, S., & Delquadri, J. (1984). Teacher- versus peer-mediated instruction: An ecobehavioral analysis of achievement outcomes. *Journal of Applied Behavior Analysis, 17*(4), 521–38. doi:10.1901/jaba.1984.17-521

Hamm, J. V., Brown, B. B., & Heck, D. J. (2005). Bridging the ethnic divide: Student and school characteristics in African American, Asian-descent, Latino, and White adolescents' cross-ethnic friend nominations. *Journal of Research on Adolescence, 15*(1), 21–46. doi:10.1111/j.1532-7795.2005.00085.x

Harklau, L. (1994). ESL versus mainstream classes: Contrasting L2 learning environments. *TESOL Quarterly, 28*(2), 241–72. doi:10.2307/3587433

Hill, C. E., Knox, S., Thompson, B. J., Williams, E. N., Hess, S. A., & Ladany, N. (2005). Consensual qualitative research: An update. *Journal of Counseling Psychology, 52*(2), 196–205. doi:10.1037/0022-0167.52.2.196

Kibler, A. K., Karam, F. J., Futch Ehrlich, V. A., Bergey, R., Wang, C., & Molloy Elreda, L. (2018). Who are "long-term English learners"? Using classroom interactions to deconstruct a manufactured learner label. *Applied Linguistics, 39*(5), 741–65. doi:10.1093/applin/amw039

Kibler, A. K., Molloy Elreda, L., Hemmler, V., Arbeit, M., Beeson, R., & Johnson, H. (2019). Building linguistically integrated classroom communities: The role of teacher practices. *American Educational Research Journal, 56*(3), 676–715. doi: 10.3102/0002831218803872

Kibler, A. K., & Valdés, G. (2016). Conceptualizing language learners: Socio-institutional mechanisms and their consequences. *Modern Language Journal, 100,* 96–116. doi: 10.1111/modl.12310

Kramsch, C. (2002). In search of the intercultural. *Journal of Sociolinguistics, 6*(2), 275–85. doi:10.1111/1467-9481.00188

Li, L. (2011). Obstacles and opportunities for developing thinking through interaction in language classrooms. *Thinking Skills and Creativity, 6*(3), 146–58. doi:10.1016/j.tsc.2011.05.001

Linquanti, R., & Cook, H. G. (2013). *Toward a "Common Definition of English Learner."* Washington, DC: CCSSO.

Lotan, R. A. (2008). Developing language and mastering content in heterogeneous classrooms. In R. M. Gillies, A. F. Ashman, & J. Terwel (Eds.), *The teacher's role in implementing cooperative learning in the classroom* (pp. 184–200). New York: Springer.

Luk, J. (2004). The dynamics of classroom small talk. *Issues in Applied Linguistics, 14*(2), 115–32.

Martínez, R. A., & Morales, P. Z. (2014). ¿Puras groserías?: Rethinking the role of profanity and graphic humor in Latin@ students' bilingual wordplay. *Anthropology & Education Quarterly 45*(4), 337–54. doi:10.1111/aeq.12074

Molloy Elreda, L., Kibler, A. K., & Gu, Y. (April, 2019). *Peer network dynamics in linguistically diverse middle school classrooms: Associations with students' academic development.* Paper presented at the Society for Research in Child Development, Baltimore, MD.

Molloy Elreda, L., Kibler, A. K., Johnson, H., & Karam, F. (April, 2018). *Academic and language development in linguistically diverse classrooms: Bridging and bonding in the classroom peer network.* Paper presented at the Society for Research on Adolescence, Minneapolis, MN.

Moody, J. (2001). Race, school integration, and friendship segregation in America. *American Journal of Sociology, 107*(3), 679–716. doi:10.1086/338954

Moody, J., Brynildsen, W. D., Osgood, D. W., Feinberg, M. E., & Gest, S. (2011). Popularity trajectories and substance use in early adolescence. *Social Networks, 33*(2), 101–12. doi:10.1016/j.socnet.2010.10.001

Moody, J., & White, D. R. (2003). Structural cohesion and embeddedness: A hierarchical concept of social groups. *American Sociological Review, 68*(1), 103–27. doi:10.2307/3088904

Patton, M. Q. (2015). *Qualitative research and evaluation methods: Integrating theory and practice* (4th ed.). Thousand Oaks, CA: Sage.

Ryan, A. M., & Shim, S. S. (2012). Changes in help seeking from peers during early adolescence: Associations with changes in achievement and perceptions of teachers. *Journal of Educational Psychology, 104*(4), 1122–34. doi:10.1037/ a0027696

Ryan, R. M., & Deci, E. L. (2009). Promoting self-determined school engagement: Motivation, learning, and well-being. In K. R. Wentzel & A. Wigfield (Eds.), *Handbook of motivation at school* (pp. 171–95). New York: Routledge.

Sachar, L. (1998). *Holes*. New York: Farrar, Straus, & Giroux, LLC.

Smith, R. A., & Peterson, B. L. (2007). "Psst . . . what do you think?" The relationship between advice prestige, type of advice, and academic performance. *Communication Education, 56*(3), 278–91. doi:10.1080/03634520701364890

Szpara, M. Y., & Ahmad, I. (2007). Supporting English-language learners in social studies class: Results from a study of high school teachers. *Social Studies, 98*(5), 189–96. doi:10.3200/TSSS.98.5.189-196

Talmy, S. (2010). Becoming "local" in ESL: Racism as resource in a Hawai'i public high school. *Journal of Language, Identity, and Education, 9*(1), 36–57. doi:10.1080/15348450903476840

Tezanos-Pinto, P., Bratt, C., & Brown, R. (2010). What will the others think? In-group norms as a mediator of the effects of intergroup contact. *British Journal of Social Psychology, 49*(3), 507–23. doi:10.1348/014466609X471020

Tsai, J. H. (2006). Xenophobia, ethnic community, and immigrant youths' friendship network formation. *Adolescence, 41*(162), 285–98.

Tseng, V., & Seidman, E. (2007). A systems framework for understanding social settings. *American Journal of Community Psychology, 39*(3–4), 217–28. doi:10.1007/s10464-007-9101-8

van Lier, L. (2000). From input to affordance: Social-interactive learning from an ecological perspective. In J. P. Lantolf (Ed.), *Sociocultural theory and second language learning* (pp. 245–60). Oxford: Oxford University Press.

van Lier, L. (2004). *The ecology and semiotics of language learning: A sociocultural perspective*. Boston, MA: Springer.

van Lier, L. (2008). The ecology of language learning and sociocultural theory. In A. Creese, P. Martin, & N. H. Hornberger (Eds.), *Encyclopedia of language and education, vol. 9: Ecology of language* (pp. 53–65). New York: Springer.

Wasserman, S., & Faust, K. (1994). *Social network analysis: Methods and applications*. Cambridge: Cambridge University Press.

Zuengler, J. (2004). Jackie Chan drinks Mountain Dew: Constructing cultural models of citizenship. *Linguistics and Education, 14*(3–4), 277–303. doi:10.1016/j.linged.2004.02.006

4

Social Networks with Purpose

Heritage Language Networks of Practice among Transnational and Transcultural Japanese Youth in Sydney

Kaya Oriyama

Introduction

While L2 acquisition starts at school or community, heritage language (HL) acquisition begins at home. HL learning, often limited in context, is a long-term process that starts even from birth when one's L1 is or becomes society's minority language. Globalization and advancement of technology have brought about increased connectivity and interdependence between nations, together with ever-growing numbers of unique transnational families that keep kinship ties and a sense of belonging across national borders regardless of settlement or citizenship. Even for these families, both parents and children need to sustain their motivation to develop and maintain the HL over long periods of time for HL acquisition to occur.

Various sociocultural factors (e.g., demography, institutional support, and socialization) and individual factors (e.g., language use, attitude, and motivation) contribute to bilingualism (see Oriyama, 2011, for a summary). In the Australian context, for example, contact with co-ethnolinguistic community (Oriyama, 2012), society's positive attitudes toward HLs and cultures—including positive language, education, and migration policies such as offering HLs as mainstream school subjects—promote HL maintenance (Pauwels, 2005; Rubino, 2019). At the micro-level, family is crucial for HL maintenance. Family language policy—including language ideology, practice, and management (Spolsky, 2004), home HL use and literacy practices (Oriyama, 2012, 2016), extended family networks, visits to the parental homeland where HL is spoken (Pauwels, 2005)—all have a positive effect on intergenerational HL transmission.

Although linguistic minority children are socialized into preference and use of certain language(s) usually at home, school, and community, HL transmission is not a one-way passive process. Children, especially adolescents, can be a driving force in HL maintenance or shift (Spolsky, 2004). This is due to their strong desire to belong to a peer group; they will, for instance, stop using their HL and shift to the peers' language if the peers reject their HL and culture (Cummins, 1984). Such language shift (Fishman, 1991) of linguistic minorities occurs at both the societal and individual levels even from early childhood (Cummins, 1993). Since peer group memberships become the foundation for children's identities (Maguire & Curdt-Christiansen, 2007), studies focused on transnational youth's social networks and identity could provide new insights into the factors contributing to HL development and maintenance. Yet, to my knowledge, no study so far has investigated the interrelationships among (semi-)permanently impermanent (cf. Levitt & de la Dehesa, 2017) transnational youths' HL development and social group memberships.

Such transnational youths are typically from middle-class nuclear families who are *uncertain* about their intention to stay in the country of residence (c.f. Shibuya, 2018) despite physical settlement, and they may engage in circular or multiple migration. Their mental impermanence in the country of residence is more impermanent than Levitt and de la Dehesa's (2017) "(semi-) permanent impermanence," or "long-term residence without settlement or full citizenship" (1521). This makes them different from other transnationals such as business expatriate families, who are certain that they will return to their homelands after several years, or immigrant families who have permanently settled in the host country. They are also different from "early study abroad" sojourners who migrate to English-speaking countries so that their children can acquire English in childhood and eventually return to their homelands (Song, 2010; Orellana et al., 2001). In short, they are neither "transnational settlers" (Hirsch & Lee, 2018) intending to return home someday nor permanently settled immigrants.

Levitt and Schiller (2004: 1013) point out that transnational migrants simultaneously "maintain and shed cultural repertoires and identities" within and beyond the national boundaries. That is, transnationals engage in sociocultural practices (e.g., language and custom) of both homeland and host country, and emotionally belong to both worlds through networks of family and friends. Accordingly, developing and maintaining children's HL and culture is expected to be particularly important for transnational linguistic minority families to maintain such simultaneous existence.

What impacts, then, would such simultaneous sociocultural engagement and psychological inhabitation have on children of (semi-)permanently *uncertain* transnational families, especially on their HL development and identities? Despite the fairly large proportion of these (semi-)permanently impermanent transnational families within the increasing transnational population around the world (Ministry of Foreign Affairs of Japan [MOFA], 2018; Okamura, 2018; Shibuya, 2018), there is little research specifically focused on their children's experiences in relation to their languages and identities. Much less is research on contributing factors in HL development and cultural identities, especially from their perspectives. Even in the studies of HL maintenance and education, it is normally the case that parental intention to stay in the country of residence is unclear. In addition, these transnational children are categorized as one group, such as children of immigrants or second generation, together with transnational sojourners and/or permanent settlers.

In recent years, within Japanese communities living overseas, the numbers of transnational families with school-age children who are uncertain about returning to Japan or staying permanently in the host country have been on the rise (Shibuya, 2018). It is expected that such transnational children are also increasing in Australia where third largest Japanese population overseas (97,223) resides and grows every year, especially in its largest city Sydney, which has the world's second highest concentration of Japanese permanent residents since 2015 (MOFA, 2018). Along with the need to acquire academic language proficiency in the majority language of the host nation, transnational Japanese children are typically expected by their parents to develop and maintain Japanese as an HL. However, contrary to commonly held monolingual assumptions and many parents' expectations, HL, especially its literacy, is difficult to develop and maintain in a minority context, even if both parents speak the HL with their children at home. Some HL learners, however, manage to develop and maintain not only the spoken form but also the written form of the language at higher levels. How and why do they manage? This chapter aims to answer these questions by investigating how the processes and practices of social networks relate to HL maintenance and cultural identity construction among transnational Japanese youths in Sydney whose settlement is (semi-) permanently impermanent.

Socialized into Language, Socialized into Culture

Literacy in HL is crucial, as it provides a solid base for overall HL development and maintenance (Cummins, 2000; Spolsky, 2004). According to a sociocultural theory, literacy is a social practice that is always socioculturally situated (Heath, 1983). As such, it is defined as "not just the multifaceted act of reading, writing, and thinking, but as constructing meaning from printed text within a sociocultural context" (Pérez, 2004: 4). Thus, becoming literate involves more than the mastery of literacy skills; it also requires acquisition of cultural identity consisting of social and cultural beliefs, values, norms, and practices, which are appropriate to members of one's ethnic group (Ferdman, 1991). In other words, children acquire and use literacy as they develop cultural identity that stems from and determines symbolic and practical values of the literacy, or what Bourdieu (1991) calls linguistic capital.

How, then, do children develop cultural identity? As language embodies culture and identity, cultural identity develops through language socialization, the process of one becoming a socially and culturally competent group member by socialization *through* and *into* language (Ochs & Schieffelin, 2017). Language socialization occurs through socially and culturally structured verbal interactions, bidirectionally between people with less or more experience in constructing knowledge, emotion, social action, identities, and power with the language. Since language is a carrier of culture and "a vital part of the development and expression of identity" (Clyne, 2005: 1), we are also socialized into culture through language and literacy, as we develop our cultural identity.

In the case of HL learners who are bilingual, language socialization takes place in two languages and cultures: those of their heritage and the mainstream society's. In terms of cultural identity, experiencing childhood in both languages is essential for bilinguals' sense of belonging to both cultures and groups (Cunningham, 2011). As for literacy, institutional support and sociocultural pressure especially from school are necessary even for L1 learners of majority language (Hatano, 1995). Yet, HL learners usually lack or do not have enough of such support or pressure to acquire HL literacy (Tse, 2001); school, community, and the wider society are dominated by the majority language and culture. Oral language is the foundation of literacy, but they also typically have fewer opportunities for language socialization in HL. Excepting the cases where newly arrived HL speakers are concentrated, they have limited HL contact in their daily environments, especially with other HL speakers through their social networks (c.f. Milroy, 1980).

HL Networks of Practice: From Individual to Sociocultural

Social networks are defined as "the sum of all the interpersonal relations one individual establishes with others over time" (Hamers & Blanc, 2000: 111).

Children's social networks, for example, usually expand from family, school, and community. Social networks supply language models including behaviors and scripts, and convey values, attitudes, and perceptions concerning the language and its users through language (Hamers & Blanc, 2000: 111). Hence, social networks provide opportunities for language socialization. Social networks that make regular contact can support HL maintenance (e.g., Holmes, Roberts, Verivaki, & "Aipolo," 1993), along with supporting factors such as language use and attitudes (e.g., Fishman, 2001). Moreover, depending on the quality of contact, social networks can also influence language use (Milroy, 1980) and attitudes (Gibbons & Ramirez, 2004). For instance, Tse (2001) found that belonging to HL peer groups that value HLs (Spanish, Japanese, Cantonese) during the school year was vital in developing US biliterate youths' HL skills, positive attitudes toward HL learning, and positive HL identity. Such peer networks were formed through participation in school and community, and their influence also confirms Maguire and Curdt-Christiansen's (2007) claim that friendship is the foundation of children's identities, and school is robustly linked with friendship. Accordingly, quality social networks that provide friendships, belonging, and support are likely to shape children and adolescents' language use and learning, attitudes, and cultural identity, and together contribute to language development and maintenance.

Wenger (1998) conceptualized such socially networked groups of quality as communities of practice: groups of individuals who learn from each other through regular high-quality contact, shared interest, knowledge, and resources. Communities of practice "share a concern or a passion for something they do and learn how to do it better as they interact regularly" (Wenger, 2006). The concept developed from a theory of "learning as the production of identity, practice, and meaning" through participation in, and belonging to "social learning systems" (Wenger, 2010: 9).

Three core elements comprise communities of practice: (1) a "domain" of knowledge that defines collective learning needs and creates common ground and identity; (2) a "community" of people who care about this domain and create the social foundation for learning; and (3) shared "practice"—knowledge and resources that community members develop and maintain through interaction (Wenger, McDermott, & Snyder, 2002: 27). Unlike the social networks approach, the communities of practice perspective focuses more on the quality than the quantity of interaction and emphasizes practice (Holmes & Meyerhoff, 1999) resulting in shared learning. Communities of practice differ from networks in that their members are committed to joint ongoing learning, bound by the common cause, identity, and learning need (Wenger, 2010).

However, some communities or networks are more loosely connected or members' goals, identity, or learning needs may differ or change. In such cases, social relations could be in-between social networks and communities of practice. Zappa-Hollman and Duff (2015) developed the concept of individual networks of practice (INoP) to denote all relevant personal relationships within and beyond a social group regardless of their tie strength or distance. An investment in one's own INoP is expected to have two main returns: affective support and academic (cognitive and/or linguistic) support. INoPs are visually presented and they usually include various clusters (the people identifier: e.g., classmates) where nodes (key persons) are grouped. Clusters are connected to the core (focal individual) with ties (the connections) that differ in proximity and strengths.

I modified the INoP and devised an analytical tool "HL network of practice" (HLNoP) as a type of sociocultural network of practice that incorporates the aforementioned sociocultural contexts. HLNoP extends its focus to language practices of social groups situated within linguistic power relations, and how networked members' social group participation, relationships, language ideologies and practices together influence HL development and maintenance, and cultural identity, across time and place. HLNoP represents the focal group members' social relations with HL/majority language groups categorized by domain instead of cluster. Irrelevant nodes are omitted, and the core individuals are connected with relevant social groups labeled by their domain. The core domain that connects all members is shown as circle. The connecting ties and the domain outlines signify their strength/proximity in time, respectively. HLNoP's changes over time/place and language use in the domain are visualized to clarify the process of networking and language socialization. Engagement in HLNoP is likely to result in synergistic benefits for individuals and groups: *affective support, HL peer support, HL practice support, institutional support, cultural support, identity support,* and so on, which together would promote HL development and positive cultural identity.

HLNoP could thus function as a crucial site of HL socialization and cultural identity construction. Therefore, this qualitative study of transnational Japanese youths in Sydney aims to answer the following questions based on biographical, retrospective, and up-to-date data collected from surveys and interviews:

RQ1. What are the major roles of HLNoPs in HL development and maintenance in early childhood and beyond?
RQ2. How do HLNoPs and transnational experience affect cultural identity formation?

Method

Participants

Five transnational Japanese youths (three females and two males including a pair of siblings, aged fifteen to nineteen) and their mothers residing in the North Shore of Sydney, Australia participated in the study. Although the youths (whose parents are both Japanese) are the focus of this study, the mothers were also included to ensure the accuracy of background information. They were recruited by the snowball method (Erlandson, Harris, & Skipper, 1993) through a key person in the Japanese community who knew a mother who has a group of close mother friends with transnational children aged similar to her own. The youths knew each other through this network. They are long-term residents of Australia, born in Australia or migrated originally from Japan at different ages (ranging from one to seven), but their parents are *uncertain* whether to go back to Japan or stay in Australia permanently (key criteria). They are from families of middle to high socioeconomic status, traveling back to Japan at least once every two years. Half of the youth's mothers worked full-time, while the other half stayed at home since their childhoods. As shown in the youths' profiles in Table 4.1, they have various educational and migration backgrounds, but lived in Australia longest. Unlike Japanese HL learners who are Australians or permanent residents who maintained their HL partly through long-term attendance at a Japanese community school (Oriyama, 2016), the transnational Japanese youths in this study either attended a Japanese community school briefly or never attended one. Instead, they attended a small private tutoring school that catered to their various individual needs for different periods, although the school mainly served Japanese expatriate children to develop Japanese/English literacy and prepare them for entrance exams for selective high schools and universities in Japan upon their return. The female and male participants attended the same single-sex/co-ed secondary school, respectively.

Data and Analysis

Data on background including migration history (birth place, age on arrival, length of residence, types and length of schooling, etc.), current and past language/literacy practices (language spoken to/by family members, degree of using HL media and literacy resources, etc.), transnational activities (frequency of visits to Japan, formal schooling in Japan, contacts with relatives in Japan,

Table 4.1 Transnational Japanese Youths' Demographics

Name[a]	Age	Gender	Length of Residence in Australia[b]	Length of Residence in Japan	Length of Japanese Community Schooling[c]	Length of Japanese Study in Australian Schools[d]	Length of Formal Japanese Education in Japan[e]
Takumi	15	M	9	6 (0–2 and 6–10 yrs old)	2 (P1-2) 3 (Y7-9) 2 (Y5-6) T	0*	4 (Y1-4)
Riki	16	M	9	7	8 (Y2-9) T	0*	3.5 (JP1-Y1)
Saori	16	F	16	0	2 (P1-2) 4 (Y1-2 and 7-8) 7 (Y3-9) T	7 (Y1-6 and Y8)*	0
Yuka	17	F	9	8 (0–4 and 8–12 yrs old)	5 (Y1-2 and 7-9) T	1 (Y11)B*	2 (JP1-2) 4 (Y2-6)
Eri	19	F	11.5	1	2.5 (PW1-Y1) HK 2.5 (Y10-12)** T	0*	0

[a] Pseudonyms
[b] Length = length in years.
[c] P = preschool on weekdays (3–5 years old); Y = year (year levels of their weekend community schools follow the standard curriculum in Japan); T = tutoring school; PW = preschool on weekend (4–5 years old); HK = Hong Kong
[d] B = Background Speakers course (equivalent of Year 9, or Year 3 of junior high school graduates in Japan)
[e] Y = year; JP = preschool in Japan (3–5 years old)
* No course other than Background Speakers was available for Japanese background students in secondary school at the time due to eligibility criteria.
** Studied at Year 4 and Year 7 levels.

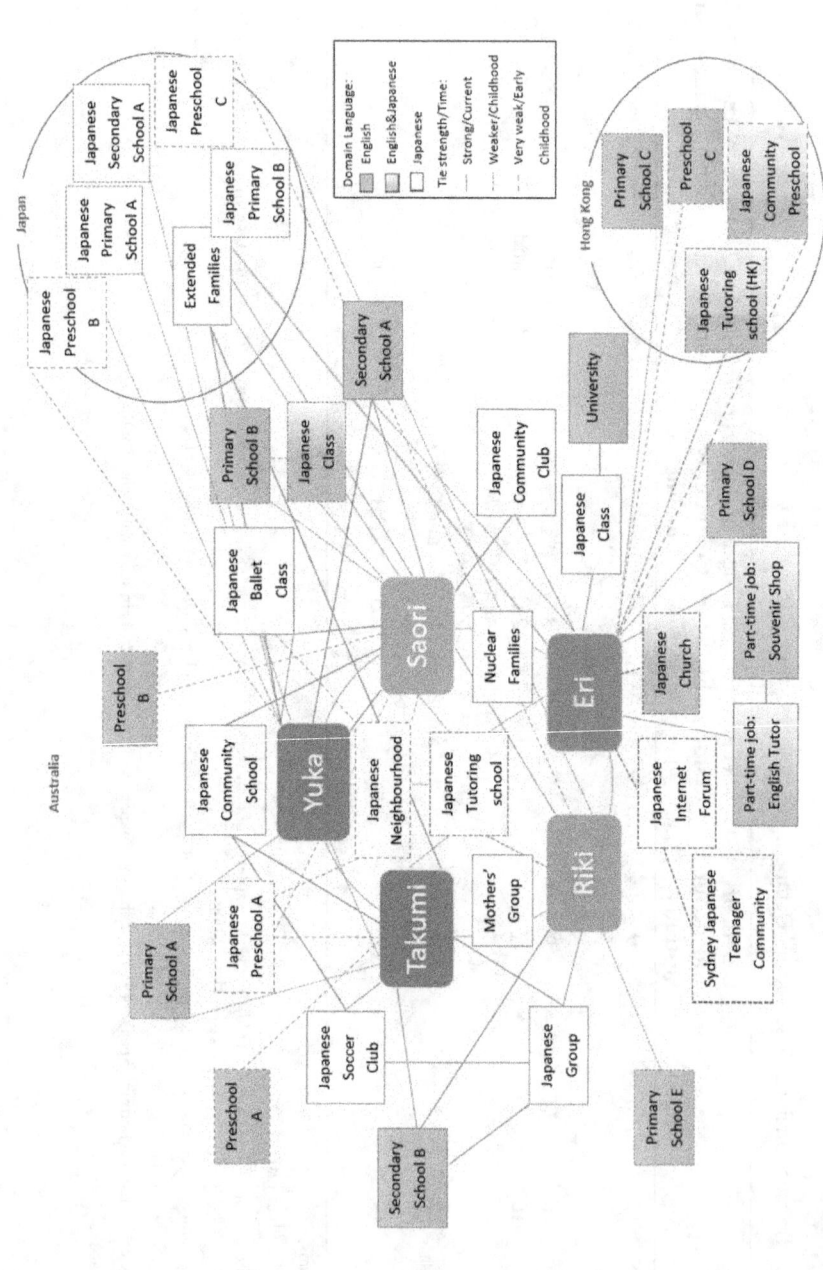

Figure 4.1 Transnational Japanese youths' HLNoPs.

etc.), and language ideology were collected from surveys and interviews with the youths and their mothers (c.f. Oriyama, 2010). In addition, the youths were asked about their experiences and peer relationships at school and the details on their current and past social networks (including through social media), which are important to identify HLNoP (number, frequency, quality of contact with Japanese-speaking friends, etc.). Data on the youths' HL skills and cultural identity (the degree of identification with Japanese/Australian cultures and groups) were also collected from surveys and interviews. The retrospective data collected were used to further understand how HLNoPs developed over time.

Considering the youths' potential differences in HL literacy levels, the surveys were administered in English for youths, but in Japanese for their mothers. The participants filled out the surveys containing twenty-four questions in about fifteen minutes after the interviews. The semi-structured interviews with seventy questions were conducted only in Japanese since the youths were fluent with some individual differences, and they did not require any explanation or translation in English. They were interviewed together as a group as were their mothers. The grouping of the youths provided opportunities for discussions among participants on some topics, and their interview lasted over two hours. The mothers were not present at their children's interviews, and vice versa. The oldest youth, Eri, was unable to attend the group interview with her mother, so she was interviewed individually at a different time. Her interview lasted over an hour and a half. All interviews were conducted once in person and were digitally recorded and transcribed. Since the interview questions were designed to elicit, or elaborate on, the answers in the survey, the interview and survey data were analyzed and grouped together for each category (transnational experiences, language ideologies, practices, and resources) to identify key experiences and factors considered to have contributed to HL development and cultural identity formation at different stages. The role of HLNoP in this process was explored and visualized in Figure 4.1.

Results and Discussion

Transnational youths' language socialization and shared practices through HLNoPs, together with transnational practices, eventually counteracted the youths' home language shift. Moreover, institutional HLNoPs that encouraged HL literacy practices and positive identification with the HL group positively impacted their HL development and maintenance. Their HLNoPs developed mainly through institutional memberships over the years, changing shared domains of practice, as members joined/rejoined and their interest and needs changed (see Figure 4.1). All quotes in English are translated from the Japanese original.

Childhood Peers and Home Language Practices

All mothers stated that they always spoke to their children in Japanese since they were born, despite challenges. However, although all the youths now speak to their parents only or mostly in Japanese, this was not always the case for Takumi, Saori, and Eri, who spent their early childhood in English-medium preschools; they were dominant in Japanese before attending the English preschools, but their English became stronger within twelve months (after three months of English-only preschooling for Takumi aged three, six months for Saori aged four, twelve months for Eri aged five), and they spoke a mixture of Japanese and English at home as Eri's mother explained:

"She mixed English words in a Japanese sentence, so the sentence structure was Japanese. Well, although she would say simple sentences like 'Let's go' and 'Don't touch' in English."

This was despite the fact that Saori and Takumi also attended a Japanese-medium preschool (operated by its headquarters in Japan) twice a week (after the three months of English-only childcare for Takumi) and Eri attended a Japanese community preschool on weekends. Early childhood socialization into the society's dominant language and culture through peers and teachers thus seems to have had a strong impact on the youths' HL acquisition and home language practices. As Clyne (2005) said, this also shows that minority language-speaking children are especially susceptible to language shift to the majority language in the first years of their lives.

Furthermore, although Takumi's older sister Yuka attended an Australian school after first arriving nearly aged five, her home language did not shift as fast as Takumi's. This difference between the siblings indicates that toddler's HL is more vulnerable to language shift. However, since Takumi went back to Japan at age six and returned after four years of Japanese schooling, his Japanese became stronger again. After returning to Australia, he has been always speaking Japanese at home, although he sometimes uses English words.

For Australian-born Saori, it is likely that HLNoP peers, especially through HL schooling, prevented her complete shift to English at home and in other domains, together with the raised "status" of the HL (Rubino, 2019) as a compulsory subject at her primary school, though her Japanese teacher took her Japanese abilities for granted. She had more than ten neighborhood Japanese friends to play with, including those who went to the same Japanese preschool. She attended a Japanese community school until Year 2 and the Japanese tutoring school afterward. She has been taking the same ballet classes by a Japanese instructor with Yuka two to three times a week since childhood (excepting Yuka's four-year return to Japan), and both of them still practiced once a week on a different day. Saori thus had regular opportunities to socialize with other Japanese children outside school. Yet, as Saori's mother said: "Until quite recently, Year 7 or 8, she wasn't interested in Japan and Japanese language. She started studying Japanese after becoming interested in Japanese show business." This coincided with Saori's return to the community school where she shared her interest with friends in Japanese, and her closer friendship with Yuka, who entered the same secondary school. HLNoP thus provided a crucial site for regular language socialization of quality (in terms of language use and models) that helped her maintain the HL despite her disinterest in childhood and motivated her to develop HL literacy in adolescence. Saori can now communicate better with her family and relatives in Japan, for which she feels grateful:

> [I thought studying Japanese was] meaningless, in younger days, but now I think it was good that I've done it. I mean, because the tutoring school and so on, weren't fun then . . . [Japanese literacy] enabled me to express myself better, more fully. There're Japanese expressions that cannot be expressed in English.

As for Eri, who grew up in Hong Kong from infancy until the age of seven, she lost such HLNoP support when she moved to Australia with her mother. In Hong Kong, she attended a British-style English-medium school as well as a Japanese tutoring school and a weekend Japanese community school. She had many Japanese-speaking friends and they communicated with one another in Japanese peppered with English. Within three years of arriving in Australia, Eri became dominant in English, as she lost her HLNoPs and had no contact with other Japanese-speaking children. Her mother worked full-time, and she went to a mostly Anglo-Saxon primary school and daycare where she socialized only in English. She spoke with her mother only in English until lower secondary school years, even though her mother always spoke to her in Japanese. Without her mother's help, she could not even communicate with her father working in Hong Kong or her grandparents in Japan.

Combined with the lack of HLNoP, negative attitudes of her primary/secondary school peers toward her heritage affected her language shift:

> When I became friends with a British girl, her parents asked her if my family went to the war . . . It's a bit painful story but in a geography class, it became a talk about whaling, and my friends glared at me . . . and when we were talking about World War II . . . they thought that all Japanese are the same, somehow, so I got glared at because of that . . . so I think that also influenced more or less my not wanting to learn Japanese. So at least until around lower secondary school, I really hated Japan.

However, participation in an HLNoP along the way aroused her affective and practical needs to acquire HL literacy, awakening her Japanese identity, and reversed her language shift and attitudes toward Japan. Such impacts of HLNoP on HL literacy will be discussed next.

Institutional and Cultural Support for HL Literacy Practices

The youths' HLNoPs that provide institutional and cultural support for literacy were found to promote private HL literacy practices, including book reading, which encourage HL development and maintenance. All youths have come to belong to such literacy-enhancing HLNoPs at some point in childhood, and daily engaged in a variety of literacy practices, such as book/comic book reading, website browsing, internet chat, and emails in adolescence/young adulthood according to the survey. It thus confirms the view that literacy is a key to long-term HL development and maintenance (Spolsky, 2004). While book reading is known to expand vocabulary and improve writing skills, it is especially important for HL learners who lack real-life experiences in HL in quantity and variety. Books provide simulated life experiences; one can experience stories in the books as one's own with imagination and empathy, and acquire words and expressions with emotional connections.

However, kanji (Chinese characters adapted to Japanese, each with two or more ways of reading) are hurdles to clear in order to achieve advanced proficiency and enjoy reading Japanese books for teenagers/young adults. Thus, Riki who loved reading books struggled to learn kanji, even though they became more complex and numerous at higher levels. He studied hard to get good marks on kanji tests as a shared practice at the tutoring school:

> As you expect, you don't remember kanji if you don't use them, so it was extremely hard . . . writing kanji [many times] frantically and stuffing my head

with them before I go to bed every night . . . so that I won't get bad marks on the [kanji] tests, saying to myself, "Let's do my best, Riki!"

The tutoring school functioned as a valuable HLNoP for Riki and other youths; most of their peers were expatriate children trying to keep up with students in Japan, so they influenced them positively in terms of language models and attitudes toward HL learning as Riki said: "It's easier to remember through environment, when you do together with others. If you're just speaking [Japanese] at home, you won't improve."

According to Riki's mother, it was also "the only opportunity" for him to meet and socialize with Japanese peers during his primary school years after his parents withdrew him from a Japanese community school at Year 3 (aged nine). Riki reflected that the community school (with nearly 300 students at the time) was established to provide "a Japanese community" for Japanese children "because they can't speak Japanese at the local school . . . there were few *Asians* and only my sister and I were Japanese at my school, so it was quite fun to have a place for socializing with others like me." The tutoring and community schools thus helped him feel less marginalized, and gave him a sense of belonging in a Japanese community. Moreover, HLNoPs at these schools prevented Riki from losing his Japanese. In fact, his parents enrolled him in both since his Japanese sharply deteriorated only six months after attending just the Australian school since his arrival in the middle of Year 1.

However, Riki quit the tutoring school after Year 9 since the Japanese course offered at upper secondary school for Japanese background students was too difficult for him to earn high scores that count for university entrance, even after years of hard work especially for learning kanji. Riki lamented that his kanji literacy "degenerated" after only a year of not studying and writing kanji. He no longer read every day because "the less I read, the more kanji I forget, and the harder it gets." Riki sometimes likes to read his mother's books on psychology, but he needs to look up numerous kanji words in a dictionary as many as "three times in a minute." Riki's experience confirms Hatano's (1995) claim that acquisition of standard Japanese literacy requires institutional systematic teaching and strong sociocultural pressure. It also shows that it is even more difficult to acquire HL literacy which lacks such support and pressure at the macro-level.

Other institutional HLNoP that encourages cultural interest and private literacy practices was also found to reverse language shift. As discussed previously, Eri lacked HLNoP in her early primary school years. Only after Eri's mother joined a Japanese church to meet other Japanese when Eri was aged nine that she met other Japanese children in Sydney. Eri recalled that she found it extremely unusual to encounter "Asian" people who could not speak English. There she became very good friends with two transnational Japanese sisters who used to live in Hawaii and Canada but engaged in HL literacy practices for leisure (comic books, animations, and Pokémon video games). Eri was greatly influenced by the sisters, quickly becoming a big fan of these entertainments; they shared these items and often played together.

> Around the end of Year 5, I also got my own Game Boy (video game console). I started but every time new sentences appeared on the screen, I ran to my mother, saying "Read it, please!" as I could not understand, but after a while, she became frustrated and said, "Don't play the game if you can't read it by yourself!" ... My mother bought me a Japanese dictionary for children, banged it on a desk, saying "Study with this!" I was like, I'll study so that at least I can play the game by myself!

Coupled with her desire to communicate with her grandparents, Eri started her long journey of HL learning that continued as her university major. In Year 10, she joined the tutoring school where other participants were attending. Studying hard and socializing with more proficient peers and friends in this HLNoP, her Japanese has "markedly improved," according to Eri. Yet, like other participants, she was unable to take the Higher School Certificate (HSC) Japanese course other than "background speakers" that was too difficult, so she forgot many words and kanji in one year after quitting the tutoring school to concentrate on her HSC studies for university entrance.

Language Socialization and Transcultural Identity

The transnational youths' cultural identities were influenced by language socialization through, and experiences with, local and transnational HLNoPs to which they belonged and people in their social networks. Perceptions and understanding of Japanese and Australian cultures and groups also seemed to affect the degree to which they identified with each culture and group. The results show that their identities are situational and *transcultural*, which can be actively constructed by individuals, although influenced by others around them.

Eri, who first lacked HLNoP after moving to Australia, has gone through and reached the last stage of identity formation processes similar to the ones proposed by Tse (2000): (1) ethnic group unawareness, (2) negative attitudes toward one's ethnic group, (3) ethnic identity affirmation, and (4) active participation in one's ethnic group and resolution of identity-related conflicts. Importantly, her engagement in HLNoPs encouraged her home HL use and HL literacy practices, which eventually reversed her language shift. As mentioned earlier, Eri became conscious of her ethnicity with her negative experiences with local school peers. Some of her secondary schoolmates even bullied her in Year 7 (aged thirteen), saying that she was "rootless" due to her transnational background and lack of HL abilities. In her adolescence, such experiences strengthened her desire to learn Japanese so that she could "be Japanese": "After all, I wanted to be proud that I am Japanese by any means possible, and the quickest way within my reach that I could achieve this was to learn the language first and then the culture."

Eri learned Japanese in order to belong to various HLNoPs and construct her Japanese identity. In addition to joining a Japanese teenager community in Sydney through her blog, Eri developed new HLNoPs at her secondary school and tutoring school where she made close friends including Yuka and Saori with whom she still socialized. Although Eri firmly believed that she is Japanese, she recognized possible incongruence in identification by self and others, and the situational nature of identity: "Wherever I cut out or change, I think that I'm Japanese. Well, as expected, I may be different [from Japanese] from the Japanese perspectives, and um, of course I realize that, but as long as I'm in Australia, I'm Japanese no matter what."

Furthermore, her unique transnational upbringing allowed her to be more versatile in her choice of cultural repertoire and identity. She explained the nature of her transcultural identity: "It depends on circumstances. As you expect, I am somewhat like British due to my British-style education, and a little like Hong Kongese because I lived there . . . but after all, what I strongly wish is to be Japanese."

Among other youths, the degree of identification with Japanese and Australians was influenced partly by their peers and transnational experiences and partly by cultural stereotypes. Yuka and Saori, who shared several HLNoPs had no hesitation in identifying who they are: "Japanese." Both of them had many Japanese friends and acquaintances through HLNoPs since childhood. In adolescence, Yuka had seven to eight close Japanese friends and over twenty other friends with whom she socialized mostly in Japanese and emailed only in Japanese, and Saori had about five close friends and around thirty acquaintances who were Japanese but with whom she socialized more often in English. Yuka said that she thinks "more like Japanese," while Saori said that her ways of thinking is "about a half like Japanese." Language of communication with peers thus reflected their cultural identities. Yet, as a circular migrant, Yuka also exhibited transcultural identity like Eri: "She switches—when she's in Japan, she thinks and acts more like Japanese," according to Yuka's mother.

Although Riki's HL socialization was mainly with more proficient expatriate Japanese peers preparing for school/university entrance exams at the tutoring school, he also attended a local school in Japan twice for a week: first time in Year 3, and the second time in Year 6. This transnational practice was fun, and his classmates remembered him, but he found the school in Japan different from Australia: "They cast you into a mold too much. Too many 'you have to' [be/behave in a certain way]." Riki's tutoring schoolmates all went back to Japan, but at secondary school, he had about fifteen Japanese friends (including Takumi) with whom he spoke mostly in Japanese. However, Riki "can get along well with anybody," as he says, and had more multicultural Australian friends, around thirty in total. Perhaps because of his transnational experiences at school in Japan and his peer composition at the time, he felt different from ordinary Japanese: "I'm quite confused . . . In terms of ethnicity, it won't make any difference to the fact that I'm Japanese after all, but I'm different from Japanese living an ordinary life in Japan."

A circular migrant, Takumi had over fifty Japanese friends through his Japanese soccer club with whom he practiced and socialized in Japanese nine times a week (twice a day on some days) at the time of the study. He had more close Japanese friends compared with Australian ones, and even self-organized his enrollment in the community school to socialize more with his friends. Takumi felt "in-between" like Riki who explained his transcultural identity as the following: "Because I act rather freewheelingly, though time to time I'm kind of Japanese-like, but I feel like I understand both Australians and Japanese . . . so I'm in-between."

Such "in-between" identity account was different from those of permanently settled youths of Japanese-heritage in Australia (Oriyama, 2010). Both of them also stated that they did not want to become like "salaried workers (*sarariiman*)" and mentioned negative Japanese stereotypes on education and work ("super serious," "too formal," "too much emphasis on educational background [for employment]," etc.). It was when rather quiet Takumi made most comments, showing that he feels strongly on this topic. As transnationals, they resisted fitting into the negative stereotypes and preferred to choose their future place of belonging despite uncertainty. Their wish to have options and simultaneously belong to two linguistic/cultural communities seemed to have influenced their cultural identity.

The youths therefore exhibited fluid and transcultural identities—though their degree of identification with Japanese and Australians varied. In summary, together with transnational experiences, language socialization through HLNoPs and peer networks played an important role in cultural identity construction, which in turn could influence HL development and maintenance. Cultural understanding deepened through engagement in HLNoPs, and transnational practices allowed the youths to become transcultural and identify with different linguistic/cultural communities depending on circumstances and "based less on prescribed social roles and more on individual choices . . . about what values to embrace and what paths to pursue" (Jensen-Arnett, 2002: 781).

Conclusion and Implications on HL Education

The new construct HLNoP enables the examination of the networked individuals' practices and relationships as a group and the process of network development in relation to the larger sociocultural context including linguistic power relations. Using HLNoP, this study sheds light on the role of HLNoP in the development and maintenance of HL and cultural identity construction among "mentally (semi-) permanently impermanent" transnational youths, a growing but largely neglected population in applied linguistics and transnationalism research. The findings of the study thus provide valuable insights into the practices and experiences of impermanently and simultaneously inhabiting the worlds of multiple languages and cultures from the transnational youths' perspectives. It revealed that all youth have come to belong to educational/religious HL institutions in childhood, through which their HLNoPs expanded over the years. This allowed socialization with more proficient HL users and encouraged HL use in family and private literacy practices, which helped them develop and maintain their HL beyond childhood. The youths who were linguistically marginalized without HLNoP lost/started to lose their HL, until they joined institutional HLNoPs and reversed their language shift.

Although their mothers played a vital role in early to middle childhood in developing the youths' HLNoPs, the youths took an active role from adolescence, as other researchers have found (c.f. Carhill-Poza, Chapter 2, this volume; Kibler et al., Chapter 3, this volume; Durbidge, Chapter 10, this volume). With their HL and cultural knowledge as passport, they developed new/existing HLNoPs to learn from each other and share practices in and through HL for pursuing their common interest (e.g., HL development, Japanese comic books, and video games), though their causes/goals, identities, or learning needs may have differed. Learning is thus social participation and belonging, a process and an experience of transforming our identity and ability to participate in, and belong to a community (Wenger et al., 2002). Consequently, HLNoPs enabled the youths' HL development and maintenance and positive cultural identity even in the face of the majority language dominance in the wider society.

The findings on cultural identity indicate that the transnational youths' cultural identities were situational and transcultural, reflecting their abilities to simultaneously belong to multiple linguistic/cultural communities and their uncertain permanent settlement. That is, their bi/multicultural repertoires enabled them to participate in practices of different communities without borders, but they felt not wholly belonging to one linguistic/cultural community but in the continuum. As shown by Riki and Takumi, cultural identity is also influenced by individual choices, aligned with values and future directions. Overall, language socialization through HLNoPs and transnational schooling, along with attitudes toward HL culture and group, played a crucial role in identity construction. Eri, for instance, stopped home HL use after experiencing negative feelings toward Japan due to lack of HLNoP and the negative reactions of her mainstream school peers. However, friendship and cultural support gained from an HLNoP later ignited Eri's desire to identify with, and be identified as, Japanese in adolescence, which reversed her language shift. Others who had no such negative experience and kept connected with HLNoPs since childhood maintained their HL and Japanese-inclusive identities. As this indicates, language and identity were closely related; they learned and used language to belong to the language community, which is a process of transforming and expressing cultural identity. HL development and maintenance for the transnational youths are thus part of the long-term processes of learning to participate in, and belong to, actual or imagined linguistic/cultural communities within and across national boundaries.

It should be noted that "transnationalism is *costly*" (Mügge, 2016: 120), as it requires social and economic capital such as transnational social networks and money for home-country visits and HL education. Yet, even for our youths who were self-motivated in adolescence and enabled by such socioeconomic capital and institutional HLNoPs to engage in transnational practices that promote HL literacy and positive cultural identity, the development and maintenance of HL, particularly its literacy, were challenging without macro- and micro-level consistent institutional support. The lack of suitable upper secondary HL course and attitudes of people at mainstream school impacted this process.

The study therefore has important implications for transnational children's HL education: HL development and maintenance that foster positive cultural identity and valuable human resources should be supported and recognized by the mainstream society, as it requires more than individual, family, and community efforts or capital. This could include the following: (1) financial aids for HL schools and organizations that create HLNoPs, (2) giving language subject credits at school or university for equivalent HL studies at educational institutions outside school, and (3) offering appropriate HL/bilingual education as part of the mainstream school curriculum to encourage HL studies throughout schooling. At the micro-level, teachers need to support and value diverse students' HLs and cultures to empower them collaboratively (Carhill-Poza, Chapter 2, this volume; Cummins, 2000; Kibler et al., Chapter 3, this volume). Such support and recognition could further promote HL studies and positive cultural identity (c.f. Hill, 2017), raising the value of HLs and multilingualism for the whole societies beyond borders.

Since all youth in this study had an experience of early socialization into the HL and its culture through formal or community schooling, this may have influenced their later HLNoPs, identities, and HL development and maintenance. Future studies on transnational youth could explore this possibility by including those who did not have such opportunities, and those in a different minority context.

References

Bourdieu, P. (1991). *Language and symbolic power*. Cambridge, MA: Harvard University Press.
Clyne, M. (2005). *Australia's language potential*. Sydney: University of New South Wales Press.
Cummins, J. (1984). *Bilingualism and special education: Issues in assessment and pedagogy*. Clevedon: Multilingual Matters.
Cummins, J. (1993). Bilingualism and second language learning. *Annual Review of Applied Linguistics, 13*, 51–70.
Cummins, J. (2000). *Language, power and pedagogy: Bilingual children in crossfire*. Clevedon: Multilingual Matters.
Cunningham, U. (2011). *Growing up with two languages: A practical guide for the bilingual family* (3rd ed.). Abingdon: Routledge.
Erlandson, D., Harris, E., & Skipper, B. (1993). *Doing naturalistic inquiry*. Newberry Park, CA: Sage.
Ferdman, B. M. (1991). Literacy and cultural identity. In M. Minami & B. P. Kennedy (Eds.), *Language issues in literacy and bilingual/multicultural education* (pp. 347–90). Cambridge, MA: Harvard Educational Review.

Fishman, J. A. (1991). *Reversing language shift*. Clevedon: Multilingual Matters.
Fishman, J. A. (2001). *Can threatened languages be saved? Reversing language shift, revisited: A 21st century perspective*. Clevedon: Multilingual Matters.
Gibbons, J., & Ramirez, E. (2004). *Maintaining a minority language: A case study of Hispanic teenagers*. Clevedon: Multilingual Matters.
Hamers, J. F., & Blanc, M. (2000). *Bilinguality and bilingualism* (2nd ed.). Cambridge: Cambridge University Press.
Hatano, G. (1995). The psychology of Japanese literacy: Expanding "the practice account." In L. M. W. Martin, K. Nelson, & E. Tobach (Eds.), *Sociocultural psychology: Theory and practice of doing and knowing* (pp. 250–75). New York: Cambridge University Press.
Heath, S. B. (1983). *Ways with Words*. Cambridge: Cambridge University Press.
Hill, R. (2017). Bilingual Education in Aotearoa/New Zealand. In García, O., Lin, A., & May, S. (Eds.), *Bilingual and Multilingual Education. Encyclopedia of Language and Education* (3rd ed., pp. 329–45). Cham: Springer.
Hirsch, T., & Lee, J. S. (2018). Understanding the complexities of transnational family language policy. *Journal of Multilingual and Multicultural Development*, 39(10), 882–94.
Holmes, J., & Meyerhoff, M. (1999). The community of practice: Theories and methodologies in language and gender research. *Language in Society*, 28, 173–83.
Holmes, J., Roberts, R., Verivaki, M., & "Aipolo," A. (1993). Language maintenance and shift in three New Zealand speech communities. *Applied Linguistics*, 14, 1–24.
Jensen-Arnett, J. (2002). The psychology of globalization. *American Psychologist*, 57(10), 774–83.
Levitt, P., & de la Dehesa, R. (2017). Rethinking "transnational migration and the re-definition of the state" or what to do about (semi-) permanent impermanence. *Ethnic and Racial Studies*, 40(9), 1520–6.
Levitt, P., & Schiller, N. G. (2004). Conceptualizing simultaneity: A transnational social field perspective on society. *International Migration Review*, 38(3), 1002–39.
Maguire, M. H., & Curdt-Christiansen, X. L. (2007). Multiple schools, languages, experiences and affiliations: Ideological becomings and positionings. *Heritage Language Journal*, 5(1). Retrieved from http://www.heritagelanguages.org
Milroy, L. (1980). *Language and social networks*. Oxford: Basil Blackwell.
Ministry of Foreign Affairs of Japan. (2018). Kaigai zairyuu hoojin suu choosa tookei: Heisei 30 nen ban [Annual Report of Statistics on Japanese Nationals Overseas: Heisei 30 version]. Retrieved from https://www.mofa.go.jp/mofaj/toko/page22_000043.html
Mügge, L. (2016). Transnationalism as a research paradigm and its relevance for integration. In B. Garcés-Mascareñas & R. Penninx (Eds.), *Integration Processes and Policies in Europe, IMISCOE Research Series*.
Ochs, E., & Schieffelin, B. B. (2017). Language socialization: An historical overview. In P. A. Duff & S. May (Eds.), *Language socialization, Encyclopedia of language and education* (pp. 1–14).

Okamura, I. (2018). AG5 dayori: Hoshuu jugyookoo no jidoo seito taishoo "Gakushuu jookyoo choosa kekka" hookoku. *Gekkan Kaigai Shijo Kyooiku, 7*. (AG5 letter: Report of the investigation results on the learning state of supplementary school students. *Education of Japanese Children Overseas Monthly, 7*). Available from https://ag-5.jp/archive/tamatebako

Orellana, M. F., Thorne, B., Chee, A., & Lam, W. S. E. (2001). Transnational childhoods: The participation of children in processes of family migration. *Social Problems, 48*(4), 572–91.

Oriyama, K. (2010). Heritage language maintenance and Japanese identity formation: What role can schooling and ethnic community contact play? *Heritage Language Journal, 7*(2), 237–72.

Oriyama, K. (2011). The effects of the sociocultural context on heritage language literacy: Japanese-English bilingual children in Sydney. *International Journal of Bilingual Education and Bilingualism, 14*(6), 653–81.

Oriyama, K. (2012). What role can community contact play in heritage language literacy development? Japanese–English bilingual children in Sydney. *Journal of Multilingual and Multicultural Development, 33*(2), 167–86.

Oriyama, K. (2016). Community of practice and family language policy: Maintaining heritage Japanese in Sydney – Ten years later. *International Multilingual Research Journal, 10*(4), 289–307.

Pauwels, A. (2005). Maintaining the community language in Australia: Challenges and roles for families. *International Journal of Bilingual Education and Bilingualism, 8*(2–3), 124–31.

Pérez, B. (2004). Literacy, diversity, and programmatic responses. In B. Pérez (Ed.), *Sociocultural contexts of language and literacy* (pp. 3–24). Mahwah, NJ: Lawrence Erlbaum Associates.

Rubino, A. (2019). Language competence, choice and attitudes amongst Italo-Australian youth. *Journal of Multilingual and Multicultural Development*.

Shibuya, M. (2018). AG5 dayori: Koochoo choosa ni motozuita hoshuu jugyookoo puroguramu kaihatsu no hookoo sei – guroobaru shakai no jisedai wo sodateru furontia –. *Gekkan Kaigai Shijo Kyooiku, 5*. (AG5 letter: The directivity of developing supplementary school programs based on a principal survey. *Education of Japanese Children Overseas Monthly, 5*). Available from https://ag-5.jp/archive/tamatebako

Song, J. (2010). Language ideology and identity in transnational space: Globalization, migration, and bilingualism among Korean families in the USA. *International Journal of Bilingual Education and Bilingualism, 13*(1), 23–42.

Spolsky, B. (2004). *Language policy*. Cambridge: Cambridge University Press.

Tse, L. (2000). The effects of ethnic identity formation on bilingual maintenance and development: An analysis of Asian American narratives. *International Journal of Bilingual Education and Bilingualism, 3*, 185–200.

Tse, L. (2001). Resisting and reversing language shift: Heritage-language resilience among U.S. native biliterates. *Harvard Educational Review, 71*(4), 676–707.

Wenger, E. (1998). *Communities of practice: Learning, meaning, and identity.* Cambridge: Cambridge University Press.

Wenger, E. (2006). *Communities of practice: A brief introduction.* Retrieved from http://wenger-trayner.com/resources/what-is-a-community-of-practice

Wenger, E. (2010). Communities of practice and social learning systems: The career of a concept. In C. Blackmore (Ed.), *Social learning systems and communities of practice* (pp. 1–16). London: Springer Verlag and the Open University.

Wenger, E., McDermott, R., & Snyder, W. M. (2002). *Cultivating communities of practice: A guide to managing knowledge.* Boston, MA: Harvard Business School Press.

Zappa-Hollman, S., & Duff, P. (2015). Academic English socialization through Individual Networks of Practice. *TESOL Quarterly, 49*(2), 333–68.

Part II

Out-of-Class Social Networks of University Students in Home-Country Settings

5

The Effects of Social Networks on L2 Experiences and Motivation

A Longitudinal Case Study of a University Student of Japanese in Australia

Naomi Kurata

Introduction

Most language learning studies have been conducted in classroom settings or among classroom learners. As Richards (2015) points out, however, there are two aspects of successful learning: what learners do inside class and what they do outside of it. The recent development of online media, communication technologies, and mobility has also significantly expanded what learners can do outside of class (Reinders & Benson, 2017). Language learning and teaching beyond the classroom (LBC) is thus an emerging area of interest in the field of second language acquisition (SLA) that has dominantly focused on classroom settings. As Reinders and Benson (2017) suggest, how learners approach, structure, and feel about their experiences of LBC is particularly important. This is because it is both reflective of and a cause of learners' motivation, attitudes, and sense of identity as language learners or users. These aspects have not been adequately examined to date. One of the most important sources of LBC experiences is the authentic interactions that occur in the learners' personal social networks—"the informal social relationships contracted by an individual" (Milroy, 1987: 178).

Motivation research, on the other hand, has a considerably longer history than research on LBC. Given its educational and theoretical significance in learning processes, motivation has been an important area in the field of educational psychology and SLA for several decades. Previous motivation studies in educational psychology tended to focus attention primarily on achievement-related goals, such as success and failure, and self-efficacy. However, scholars have recently begun to retheorize motivation in terms of value-based and identity-oriented frameworks (Kaplan & Flum, 2009). This trend in part prompted the retheorization of L2 motivation in relation to concepts of self and identity as well (Ushioda, 2011). Therefore, the central concept in recent L2 motivation research is Dörnyei's (2009) L2 motivational Self System, which consists of three major sources of motivation: Ideal Self (future self states that one may aspire to achieve), Ought-to-Self (future self states that one may feel under pressure to achieve), and the L2 learning experience (situated, executive motives related to the immediate learning environment and experience).

A great number of studies have successfully employed Dörnyei's (2009) L2 motivational Self System and offered empirical evidence regarding the motivational function of L2 selves (e.g., Kormos, Kiddle & Csizer, 2011, Nakamura, 2019; Sakeda & Kurata, 2016; Taguchi, Magid & Papi, 2009). Many of these studies rely on quantitative data only and view social contexts as independent background variables that learners have no control over (Ushioda, 2009). However, as Ushioda (2009) maintains, it is important to focus on real persons, rather than on learners as theoretical abstractions as well as on the interaction between the self-reflective intentional agent and the fluid and complex system of social relations, activities, experiences, and so on. Ushioda (2009) then conceptualizes motivation as an organic process that emerges through a complex system of interrelations. Furthermore, an increasing number of L2 motivation studies found the complex and diverse nature of learners' motivation that cannot be fully explained only by the L2 self concept, thereby utilizing multiple motivational concepts, including integrative, instrumental and intrinsic motivation (e.g., Campbell & Storch, 2011; Sakeda & Kurata, 2016). This chapter also draws upon these multiple concepts for comprehensive analysis of L2 motivation.

Employing Ushioda's (2009) aforementioned concept of motivation and taking up Reinders and Benson's (2017) suggestion about the importance of research into the relationships between the construction of LBC experiences and learner identity and motivation, the current study examines how an L2 learner structures her L2 experiences in her social networks and how these experiences are related to her L2 motivation. It particularly focuses on the changes in her social networks, as well as those in her identity as an L2 user and learner for the duration of three and half years of her Japanese learning.

Specifically, this chapter addresses the following questions:

1. What kinds of L2 use/learning experiences occurred in the social networks of an intermediate learner of Japanese at an Australian university?
2. How did these experiences relate to the learner's L2 motivation?
3. How did the learner's social networks change over time and how did these changes affect her L2 experiences and motivation?

Regarding Japanese language education in Australia, see Chapter 7 (Inaba, this volume), which describes it as one of the contexts of her study.

Social Networks, L2 Learning, and L2 Motivation

Most of social network research in language learning settings has been conducted in in-country settings, such as in host countries of immigrants or study abroad contexts (e.g., Bernstein, 2018; Carhill-Poza, 2016; Dewey, Bown, & Eggett, 2012; Hasegawa, 2019; Isabelli-García, 2006; Smith 2002; Wiklund 2002; Zappa-Hollman & Duff, 2015). Compared with this research, there are a limited number of studies in home-country settings (cf. Kurata, 2004, 2011). The major research in these contexts is extensively reviewed in Chapter 1 (Carhill-Poza & Kurata, this volume). Therefore, the section that follows focuses on research into language learners' social networks and their relevance to their learning motivation.

Learners' Social Networks and L2 Motivation

To date, very few studies have directly examined the relationships between L2 learners' social networks and L2 motivation. Isabelli-García's (2006) study is a notable exception. She found that the types of motivation of the four American (Caucasian) university students of Spanish had changed during study abroad in Argentina, depending on the degree to which the students incorporated themselves into social networks. More specifically, the students who incorporated themselves into extended L2 networks showed more gains in linguistic accuracy as well as the better maintenance/formation of integrative motivation than their counterparts who did not develop networks. Isabelli-García then posited that interaction in social networks plays a role as a conduit between motivation and language development in the study abroad context.

With a particular focus on L2 motivational changes and the factors that affect these changes, Campbell and Storch (2011) conducted interviews with eight university students of Chinese at an Australian university. They found that the students' motivation underwent many fluctuations over the course of a university semester. Although this study did not particularly examine the students' social networks and their relevance to their L2 motivation, the analysis revealed that the factors connected to learning environment had the most important impact on changes in the students' motivation. One of these factors was "little practical use of the language" in "people to people contact" that had a negative impact on changes in the students' motivation (Campbell & Storch, 2011: 182). It could be interpreted that one of the principal ways of this practical use of L2 was through authentic interaction in the learners' personal social networks. Therefore, this finding corroborates Isabelli-García's (2006: 255) finding that "the learners' continued motivation was influenced by their success, or lack thereof, in incorporating themselves into social networks."

As discussed in Chapter 1 (Carhill-Poza & Kurata, this volume), this literature provides insights into the relationships between some important features of social networks and certain aspects of L2 learning. Dewey et al. (2012) highlight the necessity to examine a more holistic picture of learners' L2 experience in order to understand the complex relationships between learners' social networks and L2 learning and how motivation and identities mediate these relationships. To date, however, these relationships and mediation have been under-investigated, particularly on beginners' networks in home-country settings. Consequently, the current study attempts to explore the links in these settings by taking up, among others, Zappa-Hollman and Duff's (2015) suggestion for further research on network zones and density, as well as network changes over time. This in turn would allow me to analyze the complex and dynamic nature of network construction and how this affects learning, in particular, L2 motivation.

Theoretical Framework: Sociocultural Approach and Social Network Analysis

As explained in Chapter 1 (Carhill-Poza & Kurata, this volume), this study is grounded broadly on sociocultural perspectives that regard L2 learning as socially constructed in and through interaction in situated activities. I draw upon a number of concepts from sociocultural theory (Lantolf & Thorne, 2006; van Lier, 2004) and poststructural approaches (Norton, 2000; Pavlenko

& Blackledge, 2004; Weedon, 1996). They include "affordance" (van Lier, 2004), "identity" (Norton, 2000), "agency" (Lantolf & Pavlenko, 2001; Norton, 2000), and "social capital" (Bourdieu, 1986).

Regarding social network analysis (SNA), I employ the following criteria proposed by Boissevain (1974) (see Chapter 1 for the definitions of these criteria): interactional criteria—(1) multiplexity, (2) transactional content; structural criteria—(1) size, (2) density, and (3) clusters. In addition, I utilize the concept of network zones (cf. Milroy, 1987). Network zone is the inclusion of members indirectly connected to the focal person; those who are directly linked to the focal person belong to his/her first-order network zone and those who might come in contact with the focal person through those in his/her first-order zone belong to his/her second-order zone.

Methodology

This study is part of a larger research project that examines L2 motivation of intermediate students of Japanese in Australia, with a particular focus on the impact of LBC experiences on their motivation. This chapter focuses on one of the participants, Emily (a pseudonym). I was able to interview her five times over a period of 2.5 years (over the same period of time, other participants were not available for multiple interviews). I used a longitudinal case study approach to gain an in-depth understanding of Emily's experiences of L2 use/learning in her social networks. This approach is still rare in applied linguistics generally and particularly in social network research in this field. However, the approach allows for a detailed description and analysis of how learners' L2 experiences and perspectives are structured in natural settings (cf. Duff, 2008). Moreover, in order to enhance the validity of the study, I triangulated qualitative methodological procedures, namely semi-structured interviews, stimulated-recall interviews, and diary entries. The interview data and diary entries were analyzed in order to identify significant patterns and themes. Further analysis involved coding according to the theoretical categories and constructs that were generated from the data and the aforementioned relevant literature as well as exploring the relations between these categories and constructs.

Emily's Profile and Data Collection

At the beginning of the data collection period, Emily was twenty-two years old and enrolled in a second-year Japanese course as part of her major in Japanese studies at an Australian university. Her nationality is Australian and her home language is English. She had experience in learning multiple languages, including her formal study of French for five years and that of German for four years. She learned a little Japanese in primary school and enrolled in a Japanese introductory course in her second year of university. At the end of the second year, she made a personal trip to Japan for four weeks, which was her only in-country experience. In the following year, she was taking a second-year Japanese course and I interviewed her for the first time. This interview was semi-structured and focused on her linguistic history and L2 experience outside class, including interactions in her bilingual social networks. More specifically, my questions aimed to elicit information about how she constructed L2 experiences and how she felt about them. At the end of this interview, I asked her to record her L2 experience outside class on a table of electronic document for the duration of two weeks.

The second interview that was conducted two weeks after the first one was mainly a stimulated-recall interview based on her diary entries. Emily was asked to recall what she was thinking and how she felt about a particular L2 experience, including events and activities, at the time when she was engaged with them. The third, fourth, and fifth interviews were conducted at six-month or one-year intervals. Each time, I asked her about her L2 experiences between these interviews.

Emily completed her degree at the end of her fourth year of university, and after that she did not study Japanese in class until she went to Japan to participate in the Japan Exchange and Teaching (JET) program in the middle of the following year. This program is for native speakers of English with a bachelor's degree to teach English in primary or secondary schools in Japan for one to three years. Just before she went to Japan, I conducted the final (fifth) interview.

Findings

First Year to the Beginning of Second Year of Learning: Interest in Language and the Impact of L2 Experience during a Trip to Japan on Motivation

Emily originally had intrinsic motivation for learning languages in general. As mentioned earlier, she had experience in learning multiple languages, including her self-study of Russian and Latin, and found it "really fun." She elaborated on her interest in learning foreign languages as "It's like a puzzle that you've kinda got to sit down and work out. I really enjoy doing it." Regarding the selection of Japanese as one of her majors, she wished to learn "something that was sort of completely different from those European languages" that she had studied before. She also expressed her interest in Japanese culture by referring to her childhood memory of watching some Japanese anime and trying some Japanese sweets. She claimed to feel "jealous" of Japanese cultural traditions while describing Australia as "pretty tradition-less." Moreover, she became interested in Japanese history when she studied a history subject in her first year of university. Such interest in the Japanese language, culture, and history seemed to be the basis of her learning motivation. This base was probably constructed by the time she decided to begin her formal Japanese study at the introductory level around the end of first year of university. (See Figure 5.1 for Emily's motivational profile.)

In the middle of her first year of learning (when studying the second half of the first-year Japanese course), Emily had a family issue, which she claimed was the reason "mostly why my study wavered" since she "just lost focus in everything." She also found the content of the second semester of the course "really hard" and felt "really low with my (Japanese) ability." This suggests a downward trajectory of her Japanese learning motivation in her second year of university. It also shows that, to some extent, she felt as an unsuccessful learner,

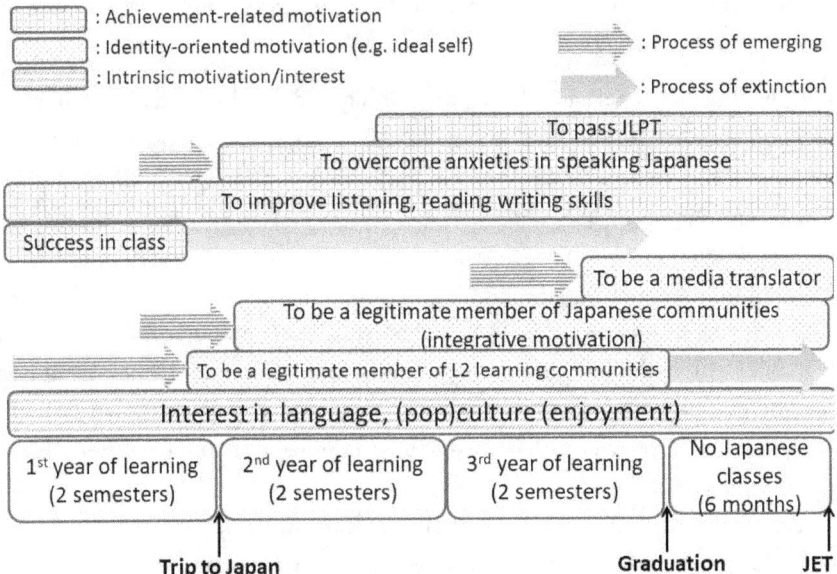

Figure 5.1 Emily's motivational profiles.

which can be viewed as a decline in her achievement-related motivation, or "success in class" (cf. Figure 5.1).

However, at the end of her first year of learning, Emily went on a one-month personal trip to Japan, which seemed to hit a turning point of her Japanese learning history. She described her experience of talking with a taxi driver in Osaka as "the most pleasant memory as a Japanese language learner," and further explained:

Excerpt 1

It was not the best conversation, but I was able to understand what the cab driver was, was saying for the most part and able to respond and, and, it was broken (. . .) but, I was REALLY, really happy and proud of myself that I was able to do that after only a year [of formal Japanese study]. (CAPITAL indicates Emily's emphasis)

Emily also claimed that her interactions with Japanese people during her trip changed her perception of her ability:

Excerpt 2

When I got over there [in Japan], and I actually had to use it [Japanese] and I did that I was like, oh I'm actually kinda good at it? I can, I can keep going? (. . .) I wasn't all that confident at all after coming out of second semester, but definitely going over there sort of motivated me because it made me want to go over there more and achieve that level of fluency that I wanted, so it definitely was a shove in the right direction.

It is clear that her experience during this trip significantly boosted her confidence and motivation. Emily's motivation was thus back on an upward trajectory because of the positive motivational impact of her trip to the host environment.

Another important aspect of Emily's motivation is related to learning Japanese as "enjoyment" or "leisure" (cf. Kubota, 2011; Stebbins, 2007). As mentioned earlier, Emily found language learning itself fun and enjoyable. In addition, her diary entries include her experience of reading manga and seeing "if I could recognize any of the new grammar patterns I learnt this week." She considered reading manga both as a hobby and study because "it's sort of a way that I am studying, but it doesn't feel like studying, I'm doing something that's a little bit more enjoyable and easy."

I also found that Emily utilized a variety of learning resources, such as apps for vocab learning, online dictionaries, as well as following some Japanese language learners' blogging communities (e.g., Lang-8). She explained that members of these communities were those who studied Japanese all over the world and "we sort of help each other" by recommending useful online learning resources and asking and answering questions often with the support of Japanese native speakers. These loosely knitted macro communities in which Emily knew only some of the community members were the only L2-related social networks that she formed in her first year of learning Japanese (see (a) in Figure 5.2). These were low-density, open uniplex networks in which network members usually associate with in a single capacity, in this case fellow learners. I also interpreted this as interest-driven networks as opposed to friendship-driven ones (cf. Chik, 2017).

Emily's diary entries also reported on a short conversation with a Japanese waitress at a Japanese restaurant. However, she described her impression of this experience as "I was horrified when she asked me in Japanese if I spoke it" after she ordered dishes with "a very good (Japanese) accent." She explained that she tended to be very anxious when actually having to speak Japanese with native speakers. This shows her lack of confidence in her oral skills, and she claimed that her perceived challenges in improving her Japanese was speaking and listening. When she looked back over her first year of learning in her interview, she stated that "in my first year I suppose, because it's such a beginner level, I didn't feel the need to sort of reach out and have a conversation partner or try and find ways to engage with the language more," but "I need someone that speaks the language fluently really to be able to help me improve that [speaking and listening] in my own time." I analyzed these data as her increasing awareness of the necessity of her investment in social networks in which she could speak and practice the language in out-of-class settings. This in turn would allow her to obtain expected returns of some types of social and cultural capital, including friendship, L2 use opportunities, L2 development, and affective and linguistic support.

Second Year of Learning: Wider Community Involvement and the Emergence of Identity-oriented Motivation

In recalling her second year of learning Japanese, Emily reported more active engagement in a variety of L2 activities than the previous year. Some examples include watching Japanese TV shows and dramas with Japanese subtitles in order to improve her listening and reading skills, and reading children's books in Japanese. As mentioned earlier, however, she regarded these activities as her "pastime." Therefore, this could be analyzed as achievement-related motivation (i.e., learning with the specific purpose of improving listening and reading skills) as well as intrinsic one (i.e., Japanese learning as leisure and/or enjoyment) (cf. Figure 5.1).

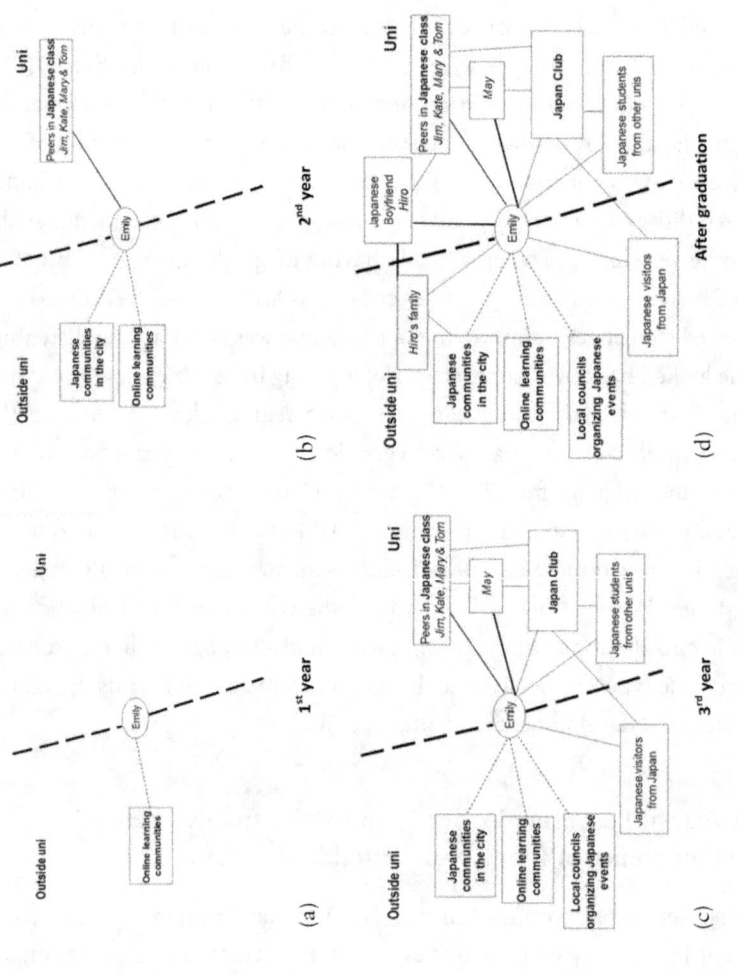

Figure 5.2 Emily's L2-related social networks.

Furthermore, Emily continued to be actively involved in the aforementioned Japanese language learners' blogging communities. She also reported that she was a member of an online language exchange community in which she had her written work corrected by native speakers. In addition, she and another learner whom she met through this community set up an online study group to prepare for Level 3 of the Japanese Language Proficiency Test (JLPT). Emily found such peer support helpful, which in turn seemed to have a positive influence on her motivation for learning Japanese. She further explained that this type of study in online communities was "a lot less intimidating than trying to speak with native speakers" directly.

Regarding her social networks in the university domain, Emily reported having made significantly more friends in her Japanese class than the previous year, and they helped each other not only in class but also outside of it, such as organizing a study session before exams. She explained that having her class friends' support made it easier for her to study Japanese and elaborated on the effect of her peers: "if they are better than you, it makes you want to study more to get back on par with them to engage with them more." Emily thus had expectations to be socially included in the classroom community. It seemed that claiming a legitimate membership in this community was one of Emily's motivations for improving Japanese (cf. Jim, Kate, Mary, and Tom in (b) of Figure 5.2 and identity-oriented motivation in Figure 5.1).

Emily was also keen to become involved with the Japanese community in the city where she lived, which can be interpreted as her integrative motivation. For example, she volunteered for the Japanese Festival with the expectation to meet Japanese people. We can thus see that Emily participated in wider L2-related communities outside and inside her university where she perceived affordances, including more linguistic and affective support than the previous year. This in turn appeared to be conducive to the development of her multifaceted motivational profiles that included identity-oriented motivation, such as her aspiration to be a legitimate member of a variety of Japanese (learning) communities.

In spite of her eagerness to participate in wider L2 communities, however, Emily was not very active in seeking opportunities to improve her oral skills in natural settings. She explained why she was hesitant to have a conversation partner in the aforementioned online language exchange community:

Excerpt 3

I get a lot of requests from people wanting to [do language exchange with me], but I'm still . . . I'm self-conscious, so I sort of don't want to start them and let them see how bad I am but, everyone's got to start somewhere . . . But I know that you just have to get over that hurdle to improve otherwise you never will, but it's hard.

It is clear here that Emily was aware of affective hurdles that she needed to overcome in order to improve her speaking skills. She further commented, "Speaking is definitely the area that needs the improvement more than anything." To achieve this goal, she claimed that it was one of her resolutions in that year to have a language exchange partner and practice speaking Japanese. Emily's awareness of the importance of (meta-) affective strategies (e.g., lowering your anxiety) (Oxford, 2011) was probably developed during her second year of Japanese course. This in turn seemed to help her to form achievement-related motivation, "to overcome anxieties in speaking Japanese" (cf. Figure 5.1).

Third Year of Learning: Multiplex Relations, Expanded Networks, and the Emergence of Ideal Self

Emily's L2-related social networks significantly developed in terms of size, density, and multiplexity when she was studying the third-year Japanese course. The trigger for this development was becoming a committee member of the Japan Club of her university in the middle of the year, since a number of her classmates that she met in the previous year were on the committee. Therefore, the relations between Emily and her classmates (e.g., Jim, Tom, and Mary in Figure 5.2) changed from uniplex (classmates) to multiplex (classmates, club members, and friends) as they met significantly more often than before, not only as peers but also as friends and club members. Moreover, to be on the committee seemed to allow her to have increased opportunities to meet other peer learners and Japanese students in the club, as well as visitors from Japan whom the committee members were asked to show around campus. Emily claimed to have communicated with the visitors in the mixed variety of English and Japanese. She also made friends with many of them afterward and maintained contact by social networking services (SNSs), such as Facebook. Although she reported that she used mainly English with club members, she spoke to another committee member, May (a local student with a Japanese background), mainly in Japanese, and she became her "best friend." Regarding the density of her networks, I found that the club members formed a cluster, that is, a high-density club community since most of the members knew each other.

Another salient feature of Emily's social network development is that she became acquainted with persons who were in the "second-order zone" (Milroy, 1987). For example, she came to know a Japanese student from a different university through May, who met this student at her part-time workplace. The student then introduced Emily to a group of his Japanese friends who studied at his university as international students. In other words, May acted as the conduit between network members in Emily's first-order zone and those in this student's networks. Meeting Japanese students in the club and those in the second-order zone and making friends with them seemed to positively affect her L2 motivation as follows:

Excerpt 4

Having those people [Japanese students she met] that do speak it [Japanese] around you it makes it yeah a lot more urgent to be able to even if they speak English. You want to be able to communicate with them and yeah. So definitely. Definitely pushed me more.

In addition to these expanded networks in the university domain, she reported her involvement in a committee of a local council project to promote sister city relationship in Japan and volunteering for a Japanese cultural festival organized by another local council. These communities are additions to her L2-related social networks in which she was exposed to the language and culture in natural settings (cf. (c) in Figure 5.2).

Another aspect of Emily's motivational profile emerged during her third year of learning. As mentioned earlier, ideal L2 self is one of the three major sources of motivation that constitutes Dörnyei's (2009) L2 motivational Self System. According to him, the gap between the learner's current L2 self and ideal self is a powerful motivator to learn an L2. I found that Emily's career-related ideal self as a translator for an Australian TV station evolved out of her L2 experience outside class (such as watching Japanese movies on TV), and this self-image involved some concrete plans to achieve this ideal self. More specifically, Emily decided to participate in the JET program (an English teaching program in Japan) after graduation, and her main goal during this program was "to be completely immersed in the language," although she would be required to teach English at schools in Japan. She then planned to study a masters in translation, which she hoped would enable her to get a translating job at a TV station. Emily explained the reason for this career interest by comparing with her original future dream to be a teacher of Japanese that involved a vague image with no specific plans, "translation and interpretation is a bit more qualified than teaching and I'd be putting my degree to better use in a way."

As her L2-related social networks significantly expanded, Emily gained more opportunities to be exposed to Japanese "without physically focusing on it," such as her interactions with May. However, she also claimed to continue to make a conscious effort to "have as much Japanese around me as I could." This includes watching reading online news articles, listening to J-pop music in her car, and joining another language exchange community to seek help from native speakers with her writing. Regarding her increasing use of Japanese outside class and the aforementioned goal to participate in the JET program in the following year, she explained their effect as follows:

> Excerpt 5
>
> Just using Japanese outside of the classroom and having that goal with the JET program . . . and knowing that I have to graduate and decide what I wanted to do sort of all of that helped to push me to get my butt into gear and start actually um working hard [hhh] whereas last year was, I had a group of friends that were fun but we never really . . . you know used Japanese outside of class.

Since I conducted this interview toward the completion of her degree, Emily was naturally more conscious about her future career than in the previous year. Together with her emergent future self-image as a media translator, Emily's daily exposure to L2 in her developed social networks with multiplexity and clusters seemed to contribute to more multifaceted intense motivation.

After Graduation: Meaningful Interaction in Further Developed Networks and Formation of a Vivid Ideal Self

In our final (fifth) interview, which was conducted about seven months after the completion of her degree, Emily said that she continued to be on the committee of the Japan Club at her university. This continuous membership helped her to further develop her L2-related networks in terms of size, network zones, and nature of interactions. As mentioned earlier, she entered into the second-order zone through May's friend, who then introduced her to his group of Japanese friends at a different university. Likewise, Jim (a committee member of the club as well as a former classmate and close friend of Emily's) acted as a conduit to introduce her to his friend with a Japanese background (Hiro), who he met at another social club at university. Emily started to go out with Hiro, who was born and raised in Australia; he then introduced her to his family members who formed another second-order zone of Emily's networks (see (d) in Figure 5.2). She explained that these new relationships with him and his family had increased "significantly more chance to meet and to be surrounded by Japanese people and rapid-fire Japanese." Consequently, Emily's involvement in online L2 learning communities decreased. On the contrary, after she completed her degree, she invested more time and effort in her dense and multiplex networks with her close friends than in those that were open, loosely knitted online communities.

Regarding the language selection between Emily and Hiro, she claimed to use mostly English, but she had "been trying to get him" to talk to her in "Japanese only" one day a week and described how she felt about her interaction with him:

Excerpt 6

It's Japanese day where he won't respond to me if I speak to him in English. (. . .) Having that support and that that like I said I'm always scared of making mistakes, it's always anxiety inducing speaking in a foreign language (. . .) having that that support there to be like it's alright to make mistakes. It's okay you don't know what this kanji is, you read that kanji wrong. He'll tell me that but he won't, I know that it's not judging, he's just telling me that I read the kanji wrong. Um so that definitely makes it easier? And and yeah it does motivate me because he's always like here listen to this album or watch this show or watch this YouTube video with me (. . .) like I said they speak it [Japanese] in his household pretty much 100% of the time so Japanese is a big part of his life even though he was raised out here and he's pretty Australian (. . .) the other day he came out and he just bought a book on like business Japanese and he's started to teach himself business Japanese so he's interested in learning Japanese more as well um. So that sort of support helps quite a bit.

This excerpt shows that her close and meaningful relationship with Hiro allowed her to feel that it was "alright to make mistakes" in Japanese as she knew that he would not be "judging" her Japanese but "support" her in learning it. This, in turn, helped her to overcome the aforementioned affective hurdles about speaking Japanese, particularly to native speakers (cf. overcoming anxieties, Edwards & Roger, 2015). Moreover, they shared an interest in learning Japanese, although Hiro would act as an expert to correct her Japanese, including reading kanji. As Palfreyman (2011: 17) notes, interactions with "significant others (other people who are often more significant to them than their teachers are)" play a key role in LBC. I believe that meaningful interactions with Hiro are a source of affordance for Emily's learning, such as linguistic and affective support. This affordance, in turn, would "definitely make it easier" for her to keep learning Japanese and help to improve her L2 motivation.

Emily's L2 experience in her social networks, particularly her relationship with Hiro also seemed to make her aware of the existence of the Japanese community in the city where she lived:

Excerpt 7

Like my boyfriend is Japanese, so I've now realized that they (people from the Japanese community) are everywhere, I've never realized how they're sort of all around (...) Japanese community is growing quite a bit, and I want it to be more accessible and more acknowledged in [the city].

As mentioned earlier, Emily's L2 ideal self as a media translator for an Australian TV station was emerging, but this self-image seemed to become more elaborate and intense than the previous year. For example, she stated that she was keen to bring some "really good quality Japanese movies" to Australia as this TV station never did so. She further claimed that her longer-term goal related to this future job was "to bring Japan more to Australia because Japan is like our closest, one of our closest neighbors." She emphasized that this goal is what she had "really decided on that I want to do" as well as "I want to make Japanese my career." Emily's involvement in wider communities, particularly those in which she participated with Hiro, had a positive impact on the formation of a more vivid and elaborate L2 self-image that also includes an aspect of instrumental motivation.

In addition to the aforementioned increased L2 exposure in her developed social networks, Emily reported that she continued to use and learn Japanese in a variety of ways, even though she did not learn Japanese in class any more. This included watching Japanese TV shows and dramas and learning vocabulary and kanji using apps on her mobile for the purpose of passing N3 of JLPT. She explained, "I'm trying to do a lot more of actually using it (Japanese) rather than just studying practice sentences (...) I'm getting more enjoyment out of what I'm doing (...) I've found myself using Japanese in everyday life." This can be analyzed as a gradual shift of her identity from the one as an L2 learner to that as an L2 user. As Benson (2011a) explains about the term "self-directed naturalistic learning," learners can create an activity for the purpose of language learning or practice, but may shift their focus away from language learning to the content of the activity once they are engaged in it. As shown earlier, Emily made a conscious effort to create opportunities to learn Japanese in out-of-class contexts, such as watching Japanese dramas with Japanese subtitles and participating in wider Japanese communities. She engaged in these activities and shifted her attention from learning form to enjoying content. This is a good example of "self-directed naturalistic learning," and her investment in this type of learning yields a return of enjoyment, meaningful interactions in her social networks, as well as opportunities for L2 learning.

Discussion

The analysis of Emily's L2 learning trajectory in her social networks indicated that the development of her multifaceted motivation and that of her L2-related social networks were closely intertwined. Indeed, as the variety of Emily's out-of-class L2 experiences demonstrates, learners may shape their own learning as agents by, among other things, incorporating themselves into wider communities, which is conducive to increased opportunities of exposure to L2 in natural settings. In Emily's case, such opportunities seemed to be a source of emerging motivation, such as claiming a legitimate membership in L2 communities and maintaining her intrinsic motivation. Conversely, increased L2 motivation appeared to naturally cause her to seek more social interactions in the L2-related communities in which she participated, which in turn facilitated the development of her social networks.

Based on the longitudinal observation of Emily's social networks, the complexity involved in creating and expanding L2-related social networks has become apparent. At an early stage of her learning history, Emily actively engaged herself in learning activities in L2 learners' communities, including online learning communities and those with classmates. These communities can be interpreted as loosely knitted networks, and relationships between members are uniplex as peer learners who usually share an interest in learning an L2. As mentioned earlier, activities among these learners were significantly less intimidating for Emily, who was often hesitant to speak to native speakers of Japanese. Although she was very aware of the necessity to overcome this affective hurdle caused by speaking anxiety, it was not easy for her to do so without affective support and/or useful strategies. In addition, unlike learners in study abroad settings (cf. Isabelli-García, 2006), she did not have many opportunities to meet native speakers, which could make it difficult to establish social networks with these speakers. I argue that such interest-driven communities among L2 learners are good examples of social networks into which they can incorporate themselves and where they receive some linguistic and affective support from each other in their home countries at an early stage of their learning. Furthermore, as Emily's case demonstrates, it is possible for learners to strengthen and/or maintain their intrinsic motivation that such community members usually share. This intrinsic interest could become a basis of their L2 motivational profile on which other types of motivation would be formed at a later stage of their learning journey (cf. Figure 5.1). These communities also tend to share some achievement-related motivation, such as to pass the JLPT, and their overall motivation would be intensified with these two types of motivation.

Friendship-driven L2 social networks, on the other hand, seem to be harder for learners to establish in early stages of learning, in particular in home-country contexts. As shown earlier, in her second and third years of learning, Emily invested more time in her relationships with class peers even outside class and through social club activities, which allowed her to gain social capital, including friendships and extension of her networks with Japanese friends in the second-order zone. According to Boissevain (1974), there would be more intimate ties between two persons with a multiplex relationship than those with a uniplex relation. Moreover, as Isabelli-García (2006) explains, multiplex ties can facilitate participation in more extended conversations. Emily formed multiplex relations with some of her classmates (as class peers, club members, and friends) and some active members of the Japan Club (as friends and club members). Accordingly, they were likely to talk in more various capacities on a wider range of topics in the mixed variety of Japanese and English or mainly in Japanese when she interacted with May. As Emily claimed in Excerpt 5, such interactions, together with her concrete plan to achieve her ideal self, "helped to push me to get my butt into gear and start actually um working hard." This finding is in accord with Isabelli-García's (2006) argument that L2 learners' success in incorporating themselves into social networks with native speakers contributes to the learners' continued motivation. Unlike Isabelli-García's (2006) participants in a study abroad setting, however, Emily's case illustrated the positive impact of peer learners' social networks as well as those with Japanese network members on the learners' continued L2 motivation, and possibly even further development of motivation with multifaceted nature.

Furthermore, drawing on Benson's (2011b: 548) construct of "language learning career" that is subdivided into "phases, processes, incidents and critical incidents," there seemed to be mainly four phases in which Emily conceptualized Japanese: (1) as a subject, (2) as a tool for communication, (3) as a tool for consuming (pop-)culture (enjoyment), and (4) as part of everyday life. Benson (2011b: 548) refers to "critical incidents" as those "that were recounted in order to account for a change of direction or a transition between phases in the learning career." It can be analyzed that the transition between aforementioned phases (1) and (2) was marked by Emily's experience in her L2 host environment, including her interaction with the taxi driver during her first trip to Japan. As explained earlier, this critical incident seemed to make her aware of certain level of usefulness of her Japanese skills for communication, which represented a turning point in her overall language learning career in the sense that Emily's motivation was back on an upward trajectory after suffering from her family issue. Before this incident (in her first year of learning), she seemed to consider Japanese just as a subject and her sense of success or failure as a learner in class seemed to dominate her motivational intensity, although she already had intrinsic motivation to some extent (cf. Figure 5.1). After the incident, in contrast, she seemed keen to become involved in L2 (learning) communities in which she could communicate with L2 speakers, which resulted in the development of her L2-related social networks as well as that of her identity-oriented motivation (e.g., desire to be a legitimate member of these communities).

The third phase of Emily's language learning career (Japanese as a tool to consume culture) seemed to evolve from her increasing exposure to Japanese (pop-) culture, such as manga, possibly soon after the aforementioned critical incident. The second and third phases were thus coexisting and the latter also seemed to be closely related to her intrinsic motivation (e.g., interest in consuming pop culture for enjoyment and as learning activities) as well as one of her important learning strategies that she seemed to employ. This is a strategy that Emily described as "striking a balance between learning grammar, kanji and finding enjoyment out of it (watching Japanese dramas etc.)." She emphasized the importance of this strategy: "if I was just going to be drilling kanji over and over again, I'd get sick of it and I wouldn't study anymore." As Palfreyman (2011) shows, learners utilize strategies to pursue their goals within particular contexts, which partly structure their learning experiences. Emily seemed to actively shape her learning experiences by using, among other things, this strategy, which helped her to attain multiple goals related to both of her achievement-related and intrinsic motivation, and also identity-oriented motivation in the long run.

The critical incident that contributed to the emergence of the fourth phase of Emily's language learning career (Japanese as part of everyday life) was probably her completion of her Japanese course (graduation) and meaningful interaction with her boyfriend (Hiro). As Emily's learning trajectory shows, she gradually accumulated learning experiences, including those in her social networks, and continued to learn naturalistically even after the completion of her degree. Emily found herself "using Japanese in everyday life rather than just studying practice sentences" and "getting more enjoyment" out of what she was doing by using Japanese during this phase. Moreover, she seemed to invest in her relationship with Hiro, which yielded social capital, such as close relationship with him and an expansion of her social networks through him (in the second-order zone). This in turn allowed her to maintain or develop many facets of her motivation, in particular identity-related motivation. For example, she was probably eager to be recognized as a legitimate speaker/user of Japanese by Hiro and his family members. This formed significant part of Emily's L2 motivational profile. Therefore, Emily's language learning career demonstrates that L2 learning is not simply a matter of acquiring grammar and vocabulary of the language or how to communicate in it. It is also a process that is closely connected with the development of identities, including future self-images (cf. Reinders & Benson, 2017). Block (2007) also claims that classroom experiences are in themselves unlikely to have a strong influence on L2 identity, which is far more likely to emerge from critical experiences of using the language outside the classroom in situations that destabilize identity. Emily seemed to actively structure out-of-class L2 experiences mainly in her social networks where she perceived and utilized linguistic and affective affordance, which in turn allowed her to develop her L2 identity from a learner with little confidence in speaking into a user in everyday life.

Pedagogical Implications and Future Research

Emily's case indicates that some L2 beginners in their home country can actively create and develop social networks in which L2 is used in the first few years of their language learning career, which seems to positively affect the development of their multifaceted L2 motivation. However, her case also highlights the necessity for educators to be aware of the complex processes of the development of their learners' L2-related social networks. As mentioned earlier, given the affective hurdle of speaking anxiety that many adult learners experience as well as few opportunities to communicate with native speakers in home-country settings, it is difficult for learners to establish social networks with native speakers of their L2 at an early stage of their learning career. Moreover, the current study stresses the importance of long-term investment by learners in social networks as Emily's 3.5-year L2 motivational trajectory demonstrates. Therefore, it is not effective for educators to advise beginner students to simply go out and meet native speakers to improve their L2 proficiency. Instead, it is essential to give students some guidelines for constructing learning environments in which

L2 opportunities may arise in out-of-class contexts. Specifically, beginner learners should be encouraged to incorporate themselves into some interest-driven peer social networks, including online learning communities and L2-related social clubs. As Emily's case demonstrates, if students invest in these communities, they may have linguistic and affective affordances, which in turn are conducive to the development of their motivation. In addition, learners may gradually develop multiplex and close relations with some community members who might introduce them to some other peers and native speakers in the second-order zone. This could facilitate the formation of friendship-driven social networks in which learners might engage in meaningful L2 social interactions.

Furthermore, it is important for teachers to be aware of a variety of L2 activities in which their students can engage outside class. As Emily's case shows, students could significantly invest in these activities and receive some social capital (e.g., friendships and expanded networks) and cultural capital, such as some learning strategies as returns (Bourdieu, 1986). We should not fail to capitalize on L2 (-related) knowledge and skills that students learn outside class and bring to class. They include affective strategies, such as striking a balance between hard work on grammar, vocab, and so on and finding enjoyment from being exposed to L2 outside class in order to sustain their motivation. Utilizing students' out-of-class learning experiences, as Reinders and Benson (2017) argue, teachers and students can collaboratively create a better environment in which all students can shape their own learning experiences as agents, both inside and outside class, so that they could develop their language learning career.

It must be acknowledged that given the case study of one learner, the results of the current chapter cannot be generalized to all learners of Japanese in home-country contexts. It is thus important to further examine a larger number of learners' social networks and their effect on motivation, ideally learners with a wider variety of linguistic and cultural backgrounds and learning histories. This should include two groups: those who do not continue their formal study of Japanese but engage in L2 activities outside class and those who only self-study an L2 outside of class settings. In addition, it would be worthwhile to conduct surveys and interviews with language teachers to examine their beliefs about their students' L2 use and learning outside class as well as the impact of social networks on their learning. This examination would help us to consider how we can effectively connect out-of-class learning with classroom learning in order to improve individual learner's L2 environment.

References

Benson, P. (2011a). *Teaching and researching autonomy*. London: Pearson.

Benson, P. (2011b). Language learning careers as an object of narrative research in TESOL. *TESOL Quarterly*, *45*(3), 545–53.

Bernstein, K. A. (2018). The perks of being peripheral: English learning and participation in a preschool classroom network of practice. *TESOL Quarterly*, *52*(4), 798–844.

Block, D. (2007). *Second language identities*. New York: Continuum.

Boissevain, J. (1974). *Friends of friends*. Oxford: Basil Blackwell.

Bourdieu, P. (1986). The forms of capital. In J. G. Richardson (Ed.), *Handbook of theory and research for the sociology of education* (pp. 241–58). New York: Greenwood.

Campbell, E., & Storch, N. (2011). The changing face of motivation: A study of second language learners' motivation over time. *Australian Review of Applied Linguistics*, *34*(2), 166–92.

Carhill-Poza, A. (2016). "If you don't find a friend in here, it's gonna be hard for you": Structuring bilingual peer support in urban high schools. *Linguistics & Education*, *37*, 63–72.

Chik, A. (2017). Learning a language for free: Space and autonomy in adult foreign language learning. In G. Murray & T. Lamb (Eds.), *Space, place and autonomy in language learning* (pp. 44–60). London: Routledge.

Dewey, D. P., Bown, J., & Eggett, D. (2012). Japanese language proficiency, social networking, and language use during study abroad: Learners' perspectives. *The Canadian Modern Language Review*, *68*(2), 111–37.

Dörnyei, Z. (2009). The L2 motivational self system. In Z. Dörnyei & E. Ushioda (Eds.), *Motivation, language identity and the L2 self* (pp. 9–24). Bristol: Multilingual Matters.

Duff, P. A. (2008). *Case study research in applied linguistics*. New York: Lawrence Erlbaum Associates.

Edwards, E., & Roger, P. S. (2015). Seeking out challenges to develop L2 self-confidence: A language learner's journey to proficiency. *The Electronic Journal for English as a Second Language*, *18*(4), 1–24.

Hasegawa, A. (2019). *The social lives of study abroad: Understanding second language learners' experiences through social network analysis and conversation analysis*. New York: Routledge.

Isabelli-García, C. (2006). Study abroad social networks, motivation and attitudes: Implications for second language acquisition. In E. Churchill & M. DuFon (Eds.), *Language learners in study abroad contexts* (pp. 231–58). Clevedon: Multilingual Matters.

Kaplan, A., & Flum, H. (2009). Motivation and identity: The relations of action and development in educational contexts – An introduction to the special issue. *Educational Psychologist*, *44*, 73–7.

Kormos, J., Kiddle, T., & Csizér, K. (2011). Systems of goals, attitudes, and self-related beliefs in second-language-learning motivation. *Applied Linguistics, 32*, 495–516.

Kubota, R. (2011). Learning a foreign language as leisure and consumption: Enjoyment, desire, and the business of eikaiwa. *International Journal of Bilingual Education and Bilingualism, 14*(4), 473–88.

Kurata, N. (2004). Communication networks of Japanese language learners in their home country. *Journal of Asian Pacific Communication, 14*(1), 153–78.

Kurata, N. (2011). *Foreign language use and learning: Interaction in informal social networks.* London: Continuum.

Lantolf, J. P., & Pavlenko, A. (2001). (S)econd (l)anguage (a)ctivity theory: Understanding second language learners as people. In M. P. Breen (Ed.), *Learner contributions to language learning: New directions in research* (pp. 141–9). London: Longman.

Lantolf, J. P., & Thorne, S. L. (2006). *Sociocultural theory and the genesis of second language development.* Oxford: Oxford University Press.

Milroy, L. (1987). *Language and social networks.* Oxford: Basil Blackwell.

Nakamura, T. (2019). *Language acquisition and the multilingual ideal: Exploring Japanese language learning motivation.* London: Bloomsbury.

Norton, B. (2000). *Identity and language learning: Gender, ethnicity and educational change.* London: Longman.

Oxford, R. L. (2011). *Teaching and researching language learning strategies.* Harlow: Pearson Longman.

Palfreyman, D. (2011). Family, friends, and learning beyond the classroom: Social networks and social capital in language learning. In P. Benson & H. Reinders (Eds.), *Beyond the language classroom* (17–34). Basingstoke: Palgrave Macmillan.

Pavlenko, A., & Blackledge, A. (2004). *Negotiation of identities in multilingual contexts.* Clevedon: Multilingual Matters.

Reinders, H., & Benson, P. (2017). Research agenda: Language learning beyond the classroom. *Language Teaching, 50*(4), 561–78.

Richards, J. (2015). The changing face of language learning: Learning beyond the classroom. *RELC Journal, 46*(1), 5–22.

Sakeda, M., & Kurata, N. (2016). Motivation and L2 selves: A study of learners of Japanese at an Australian university. *Electronic Journal of Foreign Language Teaching, 13*(1), 49–67.

Smith, L. R. (2002). The social architecture of communicative competence: A methodology for social-network research in sociolinguistics. *International Journal of the Sociology of Language, 153*, 133–60.

Stebbins, R. A. (2007). *Serious leisure: A perspective of our time.* New Brunswick: Transaction Publishers.

Taguchi, T., Magid, M., & Papi, M. (2009). The L2 motivational self system among Japanese, Chinese and Iranian learners of English: A comparative study. In Z. Dörnyei & E. Ushioda (Eds.), *Motivation, language identity and the L2 self* (pp. 66–97). Bristol: Multilingual Matters.

Ushioda, E. (2009). A person-in context relational view of emergent motivation, self and identity. In Z. Dörnyei & E. Ushioda (Eds.), *Motivation, language identities and the L2 self* (pp. 215–28). Bristol: Multilingual Matters.

Ushioda, E. (2011). Why autonomy? Insights from motivation theory and research. *Innovation in Language Learning and Teaching, 5*(2), 221–32.

van Lier, L. (2004). *The ecology and semiotics of language learning: A sociocultural perspective*. Boston: Kluwer Academic.

Weedon, C. (1996). *Feminist practice and poststructuralist theory* (2nd ed.). Cambridge: Blackwell.

Wiklund, I. (2002). Social networks from a sociolinguistic perspective: The relationship between characteristics of the social networks of bilingual adolescents and their language proficiency. *International Journal of the Sociology of Language, 153*, 53–92.

Zappa-Hollman, S., & Duff, P. A. (2015). Academic English socialization through individual networks of practice. *TESOL Quarterly, 49*(2), 333–68.

6

Changing Informal Language Learning Networks in a Gulf Arab Community

David M. Palfreyman

Introduction

Contacts with speakers of a second language (L2) or through the medium of an L2 are generally thought to be helpful for learning a language, hence the long-time popularity of pen friends, language clubs, and years abroad, in addition to more formal contacts such as language courses. In this chapter, I am concerned with social networks as systems of social relationships, constituted in social practice, which offer resources of various kinds for language learning; with how students in a second language institutional setting draw informally on their networks beyond the institution to understand and use a second language; and with generational change and continuity in these phenomena. I will build on previous studies (e.g. Palfreyman, 2006, 2011) that consider the nature and availability of resources for language learning in learners' social networks. I will focus on a community of female Emirati university students, and compare recent self-reported survey data about students' informal learning networks with data collected from a previous cohort in the same university fifteen years earlier (Palfreyman, 2006).

Research Context

The central context of this research is the Dubai female campus of a federal government university (referred to henceforth as GU) in the United Arab Emirates (UAE). As recently as the 1960s, the arid territory of the modern UAE had no large cities, no universities, and very few schools. In the traditional local culture, women's participation in life outside the home, including education, was limited. Following the establishment of the UAE state in 1971 and the growth of oil revenue, the country—and Dubai emirate in particular—showed a dramatic pace of modernization and globalization, involving enthusiastic investment in technology and foreign expertise/labor. Since the 1970s, the population of the modern UAE has comprised an overwhelming majority of immigrant workers, with residence status which, although temporary, often lasts many years or decades. These workers come mainly from the Indian subcontinent, the Arab/Islamic world and the Philippines, but also from 'Western' countries such as the United Kingdom, France, and the United States. Indigenous Emirati citizens are a numerical minority—approximately 8.8 percent of the population in 2010, according to UAE government (2019)—but form a cohesive community and are highly influential and supported in many ways by the government including the provision of free higher education.

Arabic remains the language of the country's national affairs and of its identity as part of the Arab/Muslim world, as well as the main medium of instruction in government schools, which cater to the Emirati population. However, for the country's population as a whole—particularly in Dubai, where the proportion of foreigners is highest—English is the main lingua franca; it is also the main medium of instruction in higher education (Findlow, 2006).

GU was established in the late 1990's as a progressive but gender-segregated environment for female students, to encourage traditional Emirati families to allow their daughters to enter higher education. In GU's early years, the majority of students were the first in their family to study at university. The majority of current students at GU have studied in Arabic-medium state schools, then taken an English test to join the university, where almost all courses are taught in English, usually by non-Arabs. Their time at university involves a rapid, content-based development of their academic and general English skills. Beyond the university, the students are exposed to films and other media in English, as well as using English as a lingua franca in service encounters.

Gender roles in the Emirati population have changed more slowly than other aspects of life, but women are now found much more in leadership positions—indeed, this has become part of the country's "nation branding" (Allagui & Al-Najjar, 2018). Concurrently, many more females are continuing in higher education than males, who often prefer/need to become breadwinners as early as possible. Indeed, Ridge (2009) quotes an estimate from the National Admissions and Placements Office (NAPO) that 27 percent of young Emirati males were in higher education, compared with over 70 percent of Emirati females. The majority of these female students are in federal government institutions, which are still gender segregated and cater almost exclusively to Emiratis.

Social Network Analysis and Language Learning

Interaction is an important component in L2 learning, in at least two respects. On the one hand, interacting with others (at least partly) through the medium of an L2 provides practice in integrating various aspects of language performance (Lightbown, 2019) and helps build the learner's developing language system (Ortega, Tyler, Park, & Uno, 2016). Another way in which interaction affects learning generally is through the co-regulation of behavior, thought, and emotions, that is, through a "transitional process [...] within which learners and others share a common problem-solving plane, and [self-regulation] is gradually appropriated by the individual learner through interactions" (Hadwin & Oshige, 2011: 247). Co-regulation involves the learner and some other (typically more competent) actor collaboratively supporting and building the learner's understanding within his/her Zone of Proximal Development (Vygotsky, 1978). It includes a range of collaborative processes in and about language, including negotiation of meaning and form (Lyster & Ranta, 1997), scaffolding (Donato, 1994), and languaging (Swain, 2006).

A learner's interactions in and around the L2 do not typically happen with random strangers, but within the context of some established and/or socially sanctioned relationship; that is, in practicing or developing knowledge of the L2, the learner taps into her social networks. These include not only formal, learning-specific contacts with teachers and classmates in classroom activities but also, depending on the social context, informal interactions with close networks of peers or other familiar individuals, or with a looser network of contacts with people encountered in roles such as 'shop assistant' (in retail interactions) or even 'helpful local' (e.g., to ask the way). I will refer to the set of contacts outside the classroom in interaction with whom a learner has opportunities to develop their L2 as their informal language learning network (ILLN).

The affordances (opportunities for engagement) offered by social networks underlie "funds of knowledge" (nonmaterial resources for everyday living) in a particular community, which may be validated by power dynamics in the wider social context to become social capital (Rios-Aguilar & Marquez Kiyama, 2018). In contrast to formal contacts in a classroom setting, ILLNs are built on existing networks originating in and sustained by other aspects of social life:

family networks into which a person is socialized; friendship networks based on affinities and trust; and transactional networks based on social roles rather than individual relationships. A network with rich affordances for language learning is likely to offer perceived sources of (linguistic and affective) competence, trust, common goals, and accessibility (Kurata, 2010; Palfreyman, 2011). From their various networks, language learners may gain not only practice opportunities and assistance but also affective resources like encouragement.

Networks exist in the context of particular communities, which offer and structure opportunities and reasons for interaction. In previous research, I have investigated the ILLNs of female Emirati undergraduates in the UAE, surveying a large sample (Palfreyman, 2006) and interviewing individuals (Palfreyman, 2011). For these learners, the family provided a constant and close social network, within the gendered social parameters of a Gulf Arab community, although the learners also learned in other networks of friends (within or beyond the same community) and affinity groups, such as online communities.

Networks are not abstract, but involve doing things together: participating in social practices (i.e., socially recognized kinds of activity such as studying for an exam, going to the cinema, or chatting) through which social ties are (re)constituted over various timescales. Zappa-Hollman and Duff (2015) study the social networks through which international students in Canada gain information and support while taking part in practices such as studying together or socializing. They show how each student sees herself/himself as contributing to her/his individual network of practice as well as benefiting from it—affectively, informationally, or otherwise. These networks and practices are also linked to particular locations, or rather social spaces, such as a shop where a learner practices the L2, a café where students meet or a 'Language Café' purposely designed to foster the development of ILLNs (Murray & Fujishima, 2013). As well as communities, practices, and spaces, networks involve nonhuman actors such as institutions and, notably, technologies (Latour, 1996) with which people interact. In this chapter, I will consider primarily the human elements of ILLNs; but these are intimately linked with material elements such as books, as well as discursive elements such as gender or family roles (Palfreyman, 2014).

The affordances of ILLNs emerge from and are shaped by all these elements; and within this context each learner exercises some kind of agency. This begins with gaining access to an ILLN—an issue of particular interest for those working with migrants and international students, in terms of who learners communicate with, in what situations and in which language (Mitchell, Tracy-Ventura, & McManus, 2015; Norton, 2000). Ohara (2017) studies how members of a class interact with each other in and around a language course and how these networks enable learners to "take charge of their learning." Kurata (2010) points out how interlocutors' understanding of their relationship and the purpose of their conversation affect the learner's ability to create opportunities to use Japanese. In the UAE context, Palfreyman (2011, 2014) highlights community discourses which shape how learners can build and benefit from an ILLN.

Social networks may be seen as evolving complex dynamic systems (Mercer, 2014), so the aforementioned parameters involve a balance between persistence and constant (incremental or sudden) change. In this study, I am concerned with generational change and continuity in an Emirati female undergraduate community, that is, changing ILLNs in the community over some years (rather than change in the ILLN of individuals). Gal (1978) notes that females are often found to be leaders in linguistic change, in response to changing macro-social patterns; and her research found that the social class composition of an informant's contacts was a better predictor of language choice than the informant's own class membership. Studies of minority language networks in families of migrant (e.g., Li Wei, 1993) and indigenous origin (e.g., Gruffudd & Morris, 2012) have identified network patterns in language use in different generations. More broadly, Ross (2002), for example, shows how generational changes can affect how people understand their environment and its affordances. On a global scale, Edmunds and Turner (2005) argue that with globalization of media and of other aspects of life, generational groups such as "Baby Boomers" (or, recently, "Generation Z") show coherence across different societies in the world, albeit with different consciousness in different contexts.

For the Emirati community, 2003 (when the data in Palfreyman (2006) was gathered) was a time of global change, with the recent advent of the internet and the globalization of capitalism, as well as cultural polarization in the wake of the 9/11 attacks—all in the context of a conservative tribal society already in the process of accelerated economic, demographic, and technological change, as described earlier. Since then, these trends have all progressed and interacted in different ways, with the rise of social media and leveling-off of growth in the UAE economy. Traditionally (before the oil boom), young Emirati females would have had little social contact outside their immediate family, especially with males; but, recent changes in education, economy, and technology have opened up these contacts somewhat (Palfreyman, 2011). Within this overall historical and macro-social context, Daleure, Albon, Hinkston, Ajaif, & McKeown (2018) surveyed Emirati college students and their guardians regarding overall academic achievement and family support. They suggest that there are considerable disjunctions in educational level, experience, and outlook between the present generation of college students, their parents' generation, and their grandparents' generation. Parents' overall support for their children's further education is coupled with often mismatching advice and a lack of monitoring (as well as high expectations of employment as a family resource)—although the latter resources are often supplemented by support from educated older siblings, as found previously in Palfreyman (2006).

Methodology

Following is the overarching research question of this study: *Compared with the situation in the "same" context described by Palfreyman (2006), what are the affordances of current students' informal language learning networks (ILLNs), and how do they draw on and contribute to these networks?*

The present study aims to compare the characteristics of the social networks of contemporary students with those from the 2003 cohort, so the methodology was kept as similar as possible to that described in Palfreyman (2006). The data involved is mainly quantitative and based on multiple-choice questions in an online survey to gain a reasonably sized sample from each cohort; this is supplemented by some analysis of short open question responses in the survey. The community of female undergraduate students at GU is of interest precisely because GU has been at the forefront of development in higher education in the country. This study attempts to gain some insight into the changing contacts and practices of students in this particular community, and how these may shape students' learning of English outside the university.

The online survey elicits responses on the following topics:

- Demographic/relational information about the respondent
- Family members in the respondent's household and their education, experience, and proficiency in English (six questions)—related to language/learning competence in students' family networks
- Contact with family and friends (five questions)—related to strength of ties in students' networks
- Respondent's use of English inside and outside the home (two questions)—related to English practices in students' broader networks
- Respondent's attitude to various language learning resources (one question)—related to material resources in students' ILLNs

- How respondent draws on personal contacts for help with English (five questions)—related to co-regulation of learning in students' ILLNs
- How respondent helps others with English (one question)—related to students' role in the ILLNs of others in their social network.

The survey was sent by email to two related samples of informants in 2018 for comparison with the first sample from 2003. As shown in Table 6.1, the 2018 survey used a limited "snowball sampling" strategy, with a core group of students (sample 2) forwarding the survey to their own contacts (sample 3). The advantage of snowball sampling in the present study is that it "relies on and partakes in the dynamics of natural and organic social networks" (Noy, 2008: 329) and, if used reflexively, can give insight into social knowledge and relations (Noy, 2008: 329). My request to the core respondents was simply to pass the survey link on to "their contacts" outside the class, and they interpreted this in various ways. For example, one student passed it on to classmates in another course using the institutional learning management system, and another gave it to her family's driver and housemaid; so the third sample included relatives, friends, and other kinds of contact.

Table 6.1 Sampling Strategies and Respondent Demographics for the Two Years

	2003 (N = 129)	2018 (N = 102)
Sampling strategy	Sample 1: All students on GU's Dubai campus invited by email	Sample 2: invitation sent to a class of fifteen third-year students on the same campus as in 2003 (fourteen responses) Sample 3: respondents from sample 2 forwarded the invitation to contacts of their choice within/outside the university (eighty-eight further responses).
Gender	Female: 100%	Female: 95%; male: 3%; prefer not to say: 2%
Nationality	Emirati: 100%	Emirati: 91%; other Arab: 7%; other nationality (not Arab): 2%
Occupation	GU students: 100%	GU students: 42%; students at another university/college: 35%; GU graduates: 7%; graduates of another university/college: 6%; high school students: 2%; other working persons: 5%; other: 3%
Residence	Dubai: 54%; Sharjah: 26%; Ajman: 15%; Umm Al-Quwain: 5%	Dubai: 44%; Ajman: 18%; Sharjah: 17%; Abu Dhabi: 12%; Ras Al-Khaimah: 4%; Fujairah: 3%; Umm Al-Quwain: 2%

Statistical analysis that follows is largely based on comparison of the 2003 sample of GU students with the demographically comparable 2018 respondents (i.e., Emirati, female, and studying at GU, n=41). Students in both samples were self-selecting, and so presumably also comparable in their willingness to respond to a survey in English. Responses were analyzed statistically for differences between (sub)samples (Mann-Whitney U-test).

Findings

As contextualizing information for what follows, I will first briefly consider descriptive demographic statistics about the personal networks of the core 2018 respondents (sample 2) as indicated by the contacts they recruited (sample 3). In the other subsections, I will consider changes in how GU students use English and seek/receive help with the language, by comparing the 2003 responses (sample 1) with responses from the most comparable subgroup of the 2018 respondents: the forty-one female GU students (i.e., all of sample 2 plus their contacts in sample 3 who fulfill these criteria). First, I will compare opportunities for practicing English, then the competence and accessibility of students' family contacts, and then students' practices in drawing on family and other contacts as an ILLN and in giving help to others' ILLNs.

GU Students' Individual Networks (2018)

Eleven of the fourteen respondents in sample 2 recruited further respondents, and the survey for sample 3 began with two additional questions to offer some insight into the individual networks of the core respondents. More than half the contacts responding were recruited by two core participants, MY (28.4 percent of sample 3) and KA (23 percent)—also two of the most engaged and high-achieving students in the class—while two core respondents recruited just one respondent each. Table 6.2 shows that the majority of the core respondents recruited mainly from friends; only HA and HB drew in mainly family members, while KA, one of the two highest recruiting, recruited an even spread of family members, friends, and "other" contacts. As noted earlier, the core respondents were all female students at GU (all Emirati except one "other Arab"). The recruited respondents were almost all also female; and 91 percent of them were Emirati (most of the

Table 6.2 Core Respondents (Sample 2) and their Recruited Contacts (Sample 3)

Core Respondent (Residence)	Relation to Recruited Contacts (% of Sample 3, Descending Order)	Residence of Recruited Contacts (% of Sample 3, Descending Order)	Occupation of Recruited Contacts (% of Sample 3, Descending Order)
AA (Sharjah)	Friend (6.8)	Sharjah (6.8)	HE student elsewhere (6.8)
Other	Friend (1.4); other (1.1)	Dubai (1.4); Sharjah (1.4)	GU student (2.7)
FH (Sharjah)	Friend (1.4)	Sharjah (1.4)	GU student (1.4)
FI (Dubai)	Friend (4.1); family (1.4)	Dubai urban (4.1); UAQ (1.4)	GU student (5.4)
HC (Dubai)	Friend (8.1)	Dubai urban (5.4); Dubai extra-urban (1.4); Abu Dhabi urban (1.4)	GU graduate (4.1); other HE graduate (2.7); other working person (1.4)
HA (Dubai)	Family (5.4); friend (1.4)	Dubai urban (2.7); Abu Dhabi urban (2.7); Dubai extra-urban (1.4)	GU student (4.1); HE student elsewhere (2.7)
HB (Sharjah)	Family (1.4)	Abu Dhabi urban (1.4)	GU graduate (1.4)
KA (Ajman)	Friend (8.1); other (8.1); family (6.8)	Ajman (12.2); Sharjah (4.1); Fujairah (4.1); RAK (1.4)	HE student elsewhere (16.2); GU student (4.1); other HE graduate (1.4); other working person (1.4)
MY (Dubai)	Friend (20.3); family (5.4); other (2.7)	Dubai urban (20.3); Sharjah (2.7); Ajman (2.7); Dubai extra-urban (1.4); Abu Dhabi urban (1.4); UAQ (1.4)	HE student elsewhere (14.9); GU student (9.5); high school student (1.4); other working person (1.4); other (1.4)
MA (Ajman)	Friend (8.1); family (1.4)	Ajman (4.1); Dubai urban (2.7); Abu Dhabi extra-urban (1.4); RAK (1.4)	GU student (5.4); HE student elsewhere (1.4); other HE graduate (1.4); high school (1.4)
MM (Dubai)	Friend (5.4); other (1.4)	Dubai urban (4.1); Sharjah (1.4); Ajman (1.4)	GU student (5.4); HE student elsewhere (1.4)

remainder being "other Arab": 7 percent). That is, although living in a society full of people of both genders and many nationalities, the students largely recruited people similar to themselves. Table 6.2 also shows that these students tended to recruit most often from their hometown and that contacts were similar to the core respondents in occupation: primarily students in higher education, either at GU (37.8 percent) or another university/college (40.5 percent). Overall, then, for the purpose of this survey, the core students tended to mobilize networks of friends of a similar age and social position to their own, and based in their hometown, but not necessarily from their current institution.

Social Networks and English, 2003–2018

I now examine differences and similarities between the 2003 and 2018 data regarding the ILLNs of female GU students—a demographic which comprises all of the 2003 sample (n=112) and a subset of the 2018 sample (n=41). The focus here is on the students' English learning-related practices at home and in public contexts.

English Practice Opportunities in Looser Networks

In 2003, the English skill reported as most frequently used outside the home or university context was speaking (Table 6.3), followed by listening, with reading and writing less frequent but still used every day by a considerable proportion of students. In 2018, all four skills showed increased reported frequency; for example, 56 percent of students (compared with 49 percent in 2003) reported

Table 6.3 Frequency of English Use (Scale: 1 (Rarely)—2 (Once a Week)—3 (A Few Times a Week)—4 (Every Day); Mann-Whitney U-Test)

	Outside Home/University		At Home	
	2003	2018	2003	2018
Speaking	3.36	3.44	2.97	2.46*
Listening	3.04	3.56***	2.98	2.76
Reading	2.83	3.12	3.19	2.78
Writing	2.46	2.85	3.13	2.90

*p<0.05, **p<0.01, ***p<0.00

speaking English outside the home every day. For listening, this increase is clearly statistically significant (Mann-Whitney U-test, p<0.001), from an average of "once or twice a week" in 2003 to nearer "every day"; indeed, listening overtakes speaking as the most cited skill outside the home. For the other three skills, the increase does not reach significance. As in 2003, the examples given in 2018 generally relate to shopping/eating out (e.g., "I use it to communicate when I go restaurants or grocery stores") and secondarily medical contexts (e.g., "I use it in the doctors office if he/she only speak English") as well as "studying at university" (even though the question explicitly excluded the university context). Listening is mentioned mainly in interactional contexts (e.g., "listen to English speaker people when explaining about something or asking me"; "If I want to buy something you just speak and listen to their reply"), sometimes for listening to lectures at the university, or occasionally in relation to listening to songs or the radio.

Learning from Home: English Use and Funds of Knowledge

I turn now to the data about students' use of English at home and the affordances of their family environment for co-regulation of language learning. The responses for both years indicate that English is (unsurprisingly) used less for speaking and listening at home than outside (Table 6.3); reading and writing in English, on the other hand, are *more* frequent at home, reflecting students' academic work. In 2018, students' self-reported frequency of using English at home was somewhat lower than in 2003 in all four skills. Only speaking, however, showed a statistically significant change (Mann-Whitney U-test, p<0.05)—from "once or twice a week" to nearer "rarely." In 2003, speaking English at home was reported for particular purposes, especially communication with foreign domestic workers (and sometimes for privacy from family elders); similar examples appeared in the 2018 data: "I talk to the maids in English [and] I communicate with my sisters in English to help them improve their English." Note that the first part of this comment concerns use of English as a lingua franca; whereas the second part raises the topic of deliberate co-regulation of language learning at home, to which I will now turn.

In the rest of this section I present findings about the family 'landscape' of education/experience, competence and contact within which students' English learning may be co-regulated. At home, all students reported at least one parent living with them (Table 6.4), except for a minority who reported living with their husband and sometimes one child. The average household size seems to be smaller in the 2018 data than in 2003, although this can be only estimated

Table 6.4 Family Members Living with the Respondent (% of Respondents; Mann-Whitney U-Test)

	2003 (%)	2018 (%)
Mother	86.0	85.4
Father	82.9	70.7
Older sister(s)	60.5	34.1**
Older brother(s)	68.2	43.9**
Younger sister(s)	68.2	51.2
Younger brother(s)	66.7	58.5
Husband	3.1	12.2

*p<0.05, **p<0.01, ***p<0.00

from the survey responses because the survey asks about sibling categories such as "older sister(s)," without specifying how many in each category. However, in 2003, 38.8 percent of students reported having a sibling in all four of these categories; in 2018, this proportion was down to 12.2 percent. Every category of family member (except husband) was less frequent overall in 2018 than in 2003, but this difference is statistically significant (p<0.01) only for older sisters and older brothers—perhaps because older siblings now move out of the home more often than in the past, and/or are less numerous in families.

There have been striking changes in family members' educational background. Parents and older brothers, who in 2003 were less likely than other family members to be educated, have made significant gains, due to the fast growth of education in the UAE. Students' parents in particular are much more likely to have received schooling and university education (Table 6.5). Older brothers still lag behind older sisters in university education but have made a statistically significant gain from 2003. In terms of exposure to life abroad and employment, the family profile remains generally similar to that in 2003; but in employment, as in education, mothers show a significant increase (Table 6.5). Regarding potential English models within the family, older siblings still most often hold this position. Differences between the 2003 and 2018 samples for all family member categories are in line with those for education and employment, but the only statistically significant difference is an increase for fathers.

Amount of time spent with each category of family member has not changed significantly (Table 6.6): it remains generally the case that students have the most contact with their mother (a fair amount of time every day), then younger siblings and older sisters, and then their father, and least frequent contact with older brothers (somewhere between "once or twice a week" and "a little time every day"). In contrast, average contact with friends outside university remains lower (Table 6.7): meeting friends is between "rarely" and "once a week," while talking to

Table 6.5 Family Members' English-Related Experience (% of Respondents as Applicable; Mann-Whitney U-test)

	Studied K-12		Studied HE		Lived Abroad		Working		English Better Than Mine	
	2003	2018	2003	2018	2003	2018	2003	2018	2013	2018
Mother	31.3	82.9***	4.5	31.4***	8.0	17.1	5.4	22.9*	5.4	11.4
Father	35.0	72.4***	8.4	34.5**	7.5	10.3	81.5	86.2	16.7	34.5*
Older sister(s)	68.5	92.9	72.4	92.9	11.5	0.0	59.3	57.1	59.8	50.0
Older brother(s)	66.0	83.3	53.8	83.3*	17.8	11.1	88.8	77.8	66.3	44.4
Younger sister(s)	81.8	90.5	24.2	38.1	2.2	0.0	5.7	0.0	11.2	19.0
Younger brother(s)	79.1	83.3	11.5	25.0	1.1	4.2	18.2	20.8	11.2	16.7

*p<0.05, **p<0.01, ***p<0.00

Table 6.6 Time Spent with Family Members Weekly (as Applicable; Scale: 1 (Once or Twice a Week)—2 (a Little Time Every Day)—3 (a Lot of Time Every Day); Mann-Whitney U-Test)

	2003	2018
Mother	2.50	2.44
Father	1.97	2.06
Older sister(s)	2.26	2.13
Older brother(s)	1.69	1.96
Younger sister(s)	2.48	2.27
Younger brother	2.28	2.19

$^*p<0.05, ^{**}p<0.01, ^{***}p<0.00$

Table 6.7 Frequency of Contact (Scale: 1 (Rarely)—2 (Once a Week)—3 (a Few Times a Week)—4 (Every Day); Mann-Whitney U-Test)

	2003	2018
Phone friends	2.76	2.54
Meet friends	1.58	1.44
Messaging	2.82	3.63***

$^*p<0.05, ^{**}p<0.01, ^{***}p<0.00$

them on the phone is between "once a week" and "a few times a week." However, as one might expect, there has been a significant increase in online messaging, from a median response of "a few times a week" in 2003 to "every day" in 2018.

Overall, then, the social networks of these students outside the university remain home-centered and female-centered, with frequent contact especially with their mother. However, since 2003 there have been significant increases in the education of some family members; whereas in 2003 a typical student's mother was a housewife with minimal education, she is now much more likely than before to be educated and in employment. This makes mothers seem a more likely resource for co-regulation of students' studies—but perhaps not for language learning, because (compared to 2003) mothers are not significantly more often seen as competent in English. Older brothers are also more likely than before to be university educated, but seem still to have less contact with respondents than other family members do.

Co-regulation of Learning: Seeking and Receiving Help with English

A series of questions in the survey asks in different ways about help networks for English. Responses to "How often do other people help you with English at

Table 6.8 Mean Frequency of Help with English at Home (Scale: 1 (Never)—2 (Rarely)—3 (Sometimes)—4 (Often); Mann-Whitney U-Test)

	2003	2018
How often others help at home (1–4)	3.13	2.37***
How often help others at home (1–4)	3.25	3.24
Net help (±3)	0.11	0.88***

*p<0.05, **p<0.01, ***p<0.00

home?" indicate the overall frequency of help from others, with a significant decrease from 2003 to 2018 (Table 6.8). This may reflect a decrease in help available and/or in help needed. In both years, a student living with her birth family who had difficulty with English while at home would typically think of asking a friend (rather than a family member) about it (Table 6.9). A later question "Who helps you most?" again showed the importance of friends over family members, albeit again with a decrease falling short of significance (Table 6.10). Respondents' answers to the open questions sometimes specified *kinds* of friend, giving some insight into their networks, for example "close friends," "friends who are in my class," or "virtual friends."

The second most cited recourse for help in both years was "sister" (Table 6.9). Respondents often did not specify "older" or "younger," although it seems likely that older sisters, being more educated and in employment, would be more called upon. For the question "Who helps you most?" the one significant change since 2003 was an increase for sisters (Table 6.10), positioning sisters slightly above friends for the 2018 sample in this question.

Respondents also suggested sources of help other than immediate kin. In fact, "husband" was the most preferred single social resource in the 2003 survey (Table 6.9), but this was applicable only for the small proportion of students who were married (3.1 percent). Interestingly, and in contrast, 12.2 percent of the 2018 sample were married and yet none of these students mentioned asking their husband about English—possibly due to the educational imbalance between male and female Emiratis mentioned earlier. Of the unmarried majority of students in both samples, some mentioned other relatives (usually female) such as aunt, sister-in-law, and niece; others mentioned nonfamily household members such as "nanny" or "housemaid," who would be foreign workers.

Interestingly, there are certain differences between home English-related practices of students from different cities, mainly in 2003. At that time, students from the smaller, more distant emirates of Ajman and Umm Al-Quwain were significantly more likely to ask their father for help with English than students from Dubai and its medium-sized, less wealthy, and more conservative

Table 6.9 Cited First Source of Help with English (as Applicable; Scoring: 0 (Not Mentioned)—1 (Second Resort)—2 (First Resort); Ranked for 2018; Mann-Whitney U-Test)

	2003	2018
Friend	0.94	0.80
Sister	0.85	0.68
Web	0.04	0.63***
Older sister	0.13	0.33
Father	0.14	0.17
Teacher	0.18	0.17
Brother	0.62	0.16*
Younger sister	0.00	0.14
Mother	0.05	0.11
Nobody	0.12	0.07
Cousin	0.04	0.07
Older brother	0.23	0.05
Younger brother	0.03	0.00
Laptop	0.04	0.00
Husband	1.00	0.00
Dictionary	0.12	0.00
Myself	0.06	0.00

*p<0.05, **p<0.01, ***p<0.00

Table 6.10 Cited main Source of Help with English at Home (% of Applicable Respondents, Ranked for 2018; Mann-Whitney U-Test)

	2003 (%)	2018 (%)
Sister (all mentions)	2.3%	28.6%**
Friend	48.1	27.5
Older sister	0.0	14.3
Mother	1.1	11.8
Web	1.0	10.5
Father	0.0	10.3
Teacher	44.2	7.5***
Nobody	1.9	7.5
Myself	1.0	7.5
Younger sister	0.0	4.8
Brother	0.0	3.2
Cousin	0.0	2.5
Husband	25.0	0.0
Computer/laptop	1.0	0.0
Older brother	0.0	0.0
Younger brother	0.0	0.0
Dictionary	0.0	0.0

*p<0.05, **p<0.01, ***p<0.00

neighbor city Sharjah. This could be because in the smaller emirates only the most cosmopolitan families with supportive fathers would have sent daughters to university in Dubai. Students from Ajman and especially Umm Al-Quwain were then also the most likely to report speaking English at home, while Sharjah was the lowest in this regard. Furthermore, students from Ajman were the most willing to ask a brother for help, while this was rare among students from Sharjah. This all suggests that Sharjah students were living more in line with conservative gender roles, while those from Ajman were a more cosmopolitan (and smaller) group. In 2018, on the other hand, these variables no longer differed significantly between students from different cities.

With the exception of decreases in recourse to brothers and an increase for sisters, the differences described earlier between the two years do not reach statistical significance. However, if we consider not only personal contacts but also other sources of help, there is another, clearly significant change: an increased preference for online resources (Table 6.9)—despite the question being phrased as "*Who* do you ask?" (emphasis added). In 2003, students referred to "the internet" or "websites"; in 2018, it was more often mentioned as branded services such as "Google" or "YouTube." In 2003, such resources were ranked low, on a par with "mother" or "younger brother"; in 2018, they were ranked a close third, below "friend" and "sister," and replacing "brother." Also in 2018, the later question "Who helps you most?" despite again using the word "Who" and being preceded by a question about "other people," elicited mentions of online resources such as Google. In a similar vein, students in 2018 were significantly more likely to say that internet chat and websites are useful for learning English (Table 6.11). They were also significantly less likely than before to say that an Arabic-English dictionary is useful.

Table 6.11 Usefulness of Resources for English Learning (Scale: 1 (Not Useful)—2 (a Bit Useful)—3 (Useful)—4 (Very Useful); Ranked for 2018; Mann-Whitney U-Test)

	2003	2018
Talking to other people	3.61	3.73
Watching films	3.63	3.71
Using websites	3.20	3.63**
Reading stories	3.48	3.61
Chatting on the internet	2.73	3.44***
Reading magazines and newspapers	3.24	3.41
English-English dictionary	3.14	3.24
Arabic-English dictionary	3.58	3.17**
Grammar book	3.01	3.07

*p<0.05, **p<0.01, ***p<0.00

Finally, the question "Who helps you most?" prompted students to mention their teacher (Table 6.10), whom they had rarely mentioned in response to the earlier question, "Who would you ask?" In 2003, 44.2 percent of students mentioned their teacher helping them most, although both questions are pre-contextualized in relation to help "at home"; this high response put the teacher second only to friends. In 2018, on the other hand, "teacher" was mentioned by significantly fewer respondents (Table 6.10), positioning the teacher as less important than internet resources, which had increased as described earlier. It seems that students in both years tend to look outside the family for help with English. In 2003, the teacher was seen as a primary source of expertise—one student in 2003 outlined a narrative which suggests a feeling of isolation from this expertise at home: "First? I cry in my bed then I ask my teacher the next day" (note that family is not mentioned). Online services, although available in 2003, seem to have become more accessible to the majority of students and bridged this gap.

Overall, then, a shift has taken place in the way students value family members as a source of help with English. In 2003, older brothers were seen as well qualified to help (in terms of education and English knowledge) and were likely to be called upon despite students' relatively infrequent contact with them. Parents were perceived as less educated and less competent in English than other family members—especially mothers, who were the most in contact with students but seen as least competent to help with English. Since 2003, the new older generation (especially females) has benefited from growing educational opportunities; now older sisters are seen as better qualified than before, as well as continuing to be more accessible than brothers. As a result, students are less likely to resort to asking their brothers, despite those brothers being on average more educated than they were in 2003. Husbands, too, for the minority of married students, were previously preferred as a source of help but seem less likely to have this role nowadays.

However, family members in general are not the most preferred source of help with English, despite being often qualified and in constant contact with students. Help tends to be sought primarily from friends, and (nowadays) online resources. Networks of social and technological resources blend together, comprising friends contacted via messaging services, friends who are considered "virtual," and online services such as Google. In 2003, teachers were the second most favored resource according to one question, but the use of online services has now taken this position.

Table 6.12 Cited Main Recipient of Help with English at Home (% of Applicable Respondents, Ranked for 2018; Mann-Whitney U-Test)

	2003 (%)	2018 (%)
Younger sister	31.2	31.8
Sister (all mentions)	58.1	31.0
Younger brother	9.9	20.0
Friend	29.0	19.5
Brother	28.1	15.6
Older sister	1.6	12.5
Mother	3.2	11.4
Father	2.3	6.7
Older brother	0.0	5.3
Cousin	2.8	2.4
Nobody	0.9	0.0
Husband	0.0	0.0

Help to Family and Friends

Turning now to how respondents co-regulate others' language learning, the mean response to the question "How often do you help other people (family or friends) with English?" (from 1 "Never" to 4 "Often") was almost the same in both years (Table 6.8). This contrasts with the significant decrease mentioned earlier for the question, "How often do other people help you?" The difference between each student's responses to these two questions gives an indication of how she perceives her net contribution to her home-based network. Unsurprisingly, considering the trends already mentioned, on average this net balance has shifted significantly, from a small positive to a larger positive Table 6.8.

In terms of the recipients of this help, students in both samples were most likely to mention a sister, although this response is somewhat less frequent in the more recent data (Table 6.12). Where specified, this is much more likely to be a younger sister than an older sister. Younger brothers are the next most frequently mentioned, followed by mother. Fathers are mentioned at a similar rate to older sisters.

Discussion

ILLNs, like brain synapse networks (Abbott & Nelson, 2000), depend on an infrastructure of connections, but these connections vary in their potential to be used and using a connection affects its level of potential for future activation. In 2018, students' most mobilized networks for the academic, English-based task of doing the survey were not native speakers of English, but friends/acquaintances of the same gender and ethnic group as themselves (female Emiratis) and at a similar age and stage of education to themselves, often from networks based in their hometown. Secondarily, they involved family members, and the most-recruiting core respondents also drew on networks of other contacts. The students clearly had ready networks of contacts in which they could exert some kind of influence for this task.

Students' *use* of English in speaking and listening continues to be a feature of their looser networks outside the home (with foreign workers in various contexts, including at university), while Arabic is the oral language of the home. However, for reading and writing the opposite pattern holds: literacy in English (and probably in Arabic, too) is more common in the home—not as part of the domestic frame but typically in university assignments which extend into time at home.

Comparing the picture in 2018 with 2003, it may be that students are now on the whole using English outside the home more often than before, but less within the home, suggesting a polarization of language use—although this change is statistically significant only for listening outside and speaking at home. At first sight, it seems odd that students in 2003, who on the whole were rather less proficient in English than the current generation, should have spoken (or at least perceived themselves as speaking) English at home more than students today. This is a matter for further investigation; it may reflect a change in language practice at home, but it may also reflect a change in perception of English over the last fifteen years: a decrease in the salience of English in the home and a social normalization of the language vis-à-vis its previous "exotic" status (Palfreyman & Al-Bataineh, 2018).

Regarding learning networks, there has been a significant reduction in perceived frequency of receiving help with English at home; this may well be due to students' higher proficiency in English nowadays, and but also due to relational factors. Friends are still the primary source of help with English. However, the family as an arena for learning (about) English has changed in important ways: family members are in general more educated than fifteen years ago, more likely to be in employment, and more likely to be proficient in English.

The difference in education and experience between the 2003 cohort and their parents was a result of recent, sudden changes in the local context, and that gap has now reduced to an extent. However, the social barriers between female students and their male relatives remain, and their contact with friends outside the university seems to be mainly via telecommunications rather than in person (cf. Inaba, Chapter 7, this volume). Students' face-to-face contact networks outside the university remain centered around the home and female relatives (as well as looser contacts in public spaces); but now that these relatives are more educated, it is less common for students to look to male relatives with whom they have less regular contact. It seems that asking older brothers was a strategy which is no longer necessary, and so the general patterns of gender interaction in the society reassert themselves. Note, however, that weaker ties between genders are not unique to this society (e.g., Thelwall, 2008). Interestingly, when I told the core group of 2018 students the preliminary results of this study, they applauded when I mentioned female relatives being more educated than in the past, and more valued as a source of help—an attitude of approval commonly expressed by students in this community, in line with the national narrative of Emirati female empowerment referred to earlier.

Another significant change is the rapid development and uptake of technologies which both support and replace social networks. Technologies such as smartphones and messaging support students' building and making use of friendship networks, and this was explicitly mentioned by some students (cf. Durbidge, Chapter 10, this volume). More noticeable is the students' readiness to use online sources of information, as opposed to personal contacts, in order to deal with language learning challenges. The significant decrease in seeking help from more knowledgeable others with whom the student is not in constant contact (teachers and older brothers) is associated with a significant increase in resort to online services such as Google and YouTube. These online sources seem to be seen as both knowledgeable and easy to access and understand, meaning that students have presumably developed strategies for learning from them despite the lack of personal interaction around them. This again is not unique to the UAE but has had a strong impact on where/how students seek support regarding their L2 learning.

Finally, students' readiness to help others with English has remained moderately high. This help is directed primarily to family members considered less competent (mother and younger siblings), especially females.

Implications for Teaching and Research

Palfreyman (2006) suggested trying to link institutional learning with students' own learning practices and community "funds of knowledge" (Moll et al., 1992). Now it seems that the teacher and other sources of help are being replaced to some extent by readily available online services. Weller (2011) suggests that learning and education are being transformed by the increasingly free availability and accessibility of content online, which has made knowledge and expertise a much less scarce resource than in the past. Although online services such as Google and YouTube have developed to help users find their way within this abundance, learners still need to make decisions and evaluate options for their own learning needs and exercise autonomy within their own overall ecology (Palfreyman, 2014). Weller suggests that pragmatic and social approaches such as problem-based learning and communities of practice could support a "pedagogy of abundance" to enable learners to deal with this wealth of resources. This could involve using discussion and comparison, possibly drawing on actual learner vignettes to help learners "own their knowledge of and dynamic capacities in the L2 on their own terms" (Levine, 2015: 105).

One focus of such pedagogy could be on using on/offline social resources, which are ubiquitous from traditional educational contexts to more recent social blended learning environments (e.g., Eisenchlas & Trevaskes, 2007; Wang, Fang, Han, & Chen, 2016). Another could be a metacognitive focus on recognizing one's own teachable/learnable moments, especially outside class, using social and (mobile) online resources "anytime/anywhere," recognizing when the learner needs help or clarification, where to get it, and how to benefit from it. Within the classroom, Levine (2015) suggests discussing challenging situations learners have found themselves in or suggesting ones they might encounter (examples for the UAE might be writing an assignment or mediating language for family members on a visit to the doctor) and discussing how to deal with them. The aim would be to prepare students to deal with the language not only in the abstract or as produced by native speakers but also in life/study situations.

Pedagogical tasks could also require learners to look for, select, and make use of a range of resources. Learners can interact with human resources (visitors brought into the classroom, sought in other parts of the institution or in the learners' home or neighborhood, or contacted by phone or Skype) and discuss how they searched and what they found, what worked, what didn't, and why.

Further research in this field would benefit from ethnographic studies of how learners orient to social resources and how their learning identity is shaped by them (e.g., Hajar, 2018). Such studies can investigate what kind of help learners seek, and how—for example, by asking specific questions or by looking for a model to copy—and why. On the other hand, more quantitative study could relate such social learning to differences in gender or academic ability in different contexts.

References

Abbott, L. F., & Nelson, S. B. (2000). Synaptic plasticity: Taming the beast. *Nature Neuroscience, 3*(11), 1178–83. https://doi.org/10.1038/81453

Allagui, I., & Al-Najjar, A. (2018). From women empowerment to nation branding: A case study from the United Arab Emirates. *International Journal of Communication, 12*, 65–85.

Daleure, G. M., Albon, R., Hinkston, K., Ajaif, T., & McKeown, J. (2018). Family involvement in Emirati College Student Education and linkages to high and low achievement in the context of the United Arab Emirates. *FIRE: Forum for International Research in Education, 1*(3), 8–31. https://doi.org/10.18275/fire201401031024

Donato, R. (1994). Collective scaffolding in second language learning. In J. P. Lantolf & G. Appel (Eds.), *Vygotskian approaches to second language research* (pp. 33–56). New Jersey: Ablex.

Edmunds, J., & Turner, B. S. (2005). Global generations: Social change in the twentieth century. *British Journal of Sociology, 56*(4), 559–77. https://doi.org/10.1111/j.1468-4446.2005.00083.x

Eisenchlas, S., & Trevaskes, S. (2007). Intercultural competence: Examples of internationalizing the curriculum through students' interactions. In D. Palfreyman & D. L. McBride (Eds.), *Learning and teaching across cultures in higher education* (pp. 177–92). London: Palgrave Macmillan.

Findlow, S. (2006). Higher education and linguistic dualism in the Arab Gulf. *British Journal of Sociology of Education, 27*(1), 19–36.

Gal, S. (1978). Peasant men can't get wives: Language change and sex roles in a bilingual community. *Language in Society, 7*(1), 1–16. https://doi.org/10.1017/S0047404500005303

Gruffudd, H., & Morris, S. (2012). *Canolfannau Cymraeg and social networks of adult learners of Welsh: Efforts to reverse language shift in comparatively non-Welsh-speaking communities.* Swansea: Academi Hywel Teifi.

Hadwin, A., & Oshige, M. (2011). Self-regulation, coregulation and socially shared regulation: Exploring perspectives of social in self-regulated learning theory. *Teachers College Record, 113*(2), 240–64.

Hajar, A. (2018). *International students challenges, strategies and future vision: A sociodynamic perspective.* Bristol: Multilingual Matters.

Kurata, N. (2010). Opportunities for foreign language learning and use within a learner's informal social networks. *Mind, Culture, and Activity, 17*(4), 382–96. https://doi.org/10.1080/10749030903402032

Latour, B. (1996). On actor-network theory: A few clarifications. *Soziale Welt, 47*(1996), 369–81.

Levine, G. S. (2015). A nexus analysis of code choice during study abroad and implications for language pedagogy. In J. Cenoz & D. Gorter (Eds.), *Multilingual* education: Between language learning and translanguaging (pp. 84–113). Cambridge: Cambridge University Press

Lightbown, P. M. (2019). Perfecting practice. *The Modern Language Journal, 103*(3), 703–12. https://doi.org/10.1111/modl.12588

Lyster, R., & Ranta, L. (1997). Corrective feedback and learner uptake: Negotiation of form in communicative classrooms. *Studies in Second Language Acquisition, 19*(1), 37–66.

Mercer, S. (2014). Social network analysis and complex dynamic systems. In Z. Dörnyei, A. Henry & P. D. MacIntyre (Eds.), *Motivational dynamics in language learning* (pp. 73–82). Bristol: Multilingual Matters.

Mitchell, R., Tracy-Ventura, N., & McManus, K. (2015). *Social interaction, identity and language learning during residence abroad.* European Second Language Association (EUROSLA). https://doi.org/10.1097/00001888-194309000-00011

Moll, L. C., Amanti, C., Neff, D., & Gonzalez, N. (1992). Funds of knowledge for teaching: Using a qualitative approach to connect homes and classrooms. *Theory into Practice, 31*(2), 132–41.

Murray, G., & Fujishima, N. (2013). Social language learning spaces: Affordances in a community of learners. *Chinese Journal of Applied Linguistics (Quarterly), 36*(1), 140–57. https://doi.org/10.1515/cjal-2013-0009

Norton, B. (2000). *Identity and language learning: Gender, ethnicity and educational change.* London: Longman.

Noy, C. (2008). Sampling knowledge: The hermeneutics of snowball sampling in qualitative research. *International Journal of Social Research Methodology, 11*(4), 327–44. https://doi.org/10.1080/13645570701401305

Ohara, T. (2017). *Articulating the social dimensions of learner autonomy in the Japanese language classroom.* University of New South Wales. https://www.unsworks.unsw.edu.au/primo-explore/fulldisplay/unsworks_46499/UNSWORKS

Ortega, L., Tyler, A. E., Park, H. I., & Uno, M. (Eds.). (2016). *The usage-based study of language learning and multilingualism.* Washington: Georgetown University Press.

Palfreyman, D. (2006). Social context and resources for language learning. *System, 34*(3), 352–70. https://doi.org/10.1016/j.system.2006.05.001

Palfreyman, D. M. (2011). Family, friends, and learning beyond the classroom: Social networks and social capital in language learning. In P. Benson & H. Reinders (Eds.) *Beyond the language classroom* (pp. 17–34). London: Palgrave Macmillan.

Palfreyman, D. M. (2014). The ecology of learner autonomy. In G. Murray (Ed.), *Social dimensions of autonomy in language learning* (pp. 175–91). London: Palgrave Macmillan.

Palfreyman, D. M., & Al-Bataineh, A. (2018). "This is my life style: Arabic and English": Students' attitudes to (trans)languaging in a bilingual university context. *Language Awareness, 27*(1–2), 79–95.

Ridge, N. (2009). *The hidden gender gap in education in the UAE.* Policy brief. Dubai School of Government. https://www.mbrsg.ae/getattachment/2dee9885-631c-40a2-9e5f-d5c292a80e01/The-Hidden-Gender-Gap-in-Education-in-the-UAE

Rios-Aguilar, C., & Marquez Kiyama, J. (2018). A complementary framework: Funds of knowledge and the forms of capital. In J. Marquez Kiyama & C. Rios-Aguilar (Eds.), *Funds of knowledge in higher education* (pp. 7–24). London: Routledge.

Ross, N. (2002). Cognitive aspects of intergenerational change: Mental models, cultural change and environmental behavior among the Lacandon Maya of Southern Mexico. *Human Organization, 61*(2), 125–38.

Swain M. (2006). Languaging, agency and collaboration in advanced second language proficiency. In H. Byrnes (Ed.), *Advanced language learning: The contribution of Halliday and Vygotsky* (pp. 95–108). London and New York: Continuum.

Thelwall, M. (2008). Social networks, gender, and friending: An analysis of MySpace member profiles. *Journal of the American Society for Information Science and Technology, 59*(8), 1321–30. https://doi.org/10.1002/asi

UAE Government. (2019). *Population and demographic mix.* https://www.government.ae/en/information-and-services/social-affairs/preserving-the-emirati-national-identity/population-and-demographic-mix

Vygotsky, L. S. (1978). *Mind in society: The development of higher psychological processes.* Cambridge, MA: Harvard University Press.

Wang, Y., Fang, W. C., Han, J., & Chen, N. S. (2016). Exploring the affordances of WeChat for facilitating teaching, social and cognitive presence in semi-synchronous language exchange. *Australasian Journal of Educational Technology, 32*(4), 18–37. https://doi.org/10.14742/ajet.2640

Weller, M. (2011). A pedagogy of abundance. *Revista Espanola de Pedagogia, 69*(249), 223–36.

Wei, L. (1993). Mother tongue maintenance in a Chinese community school in Newcastle Upon Tyne: Developing a social network perspective. *Language and Education, 7*(3), 199–215. https://doi.org/10.1080/09500789309541359

Zappa-Hollman, S., & Duff, P. (2015). Academic English socialization through individual networks of practice. *TESOL Quarterly, 49*(2), 333–68.

7

How Do Social Networks Facilitate Out-of-Class L2 Learning Activities?

Case Studies of Australian and Swedish University Students of Japanese

Miho Inaba

Introduction

Out-of-class language learning and authentic language-use activities are considered as crucial factors in mastering a target language (Benson, 2011). Recently, the development of information and communication technology (ICT), furthermore, has significantly transformed the language learning environment by enabling language learners to access a variety of resources, tools, and communities to support their learning even when learners study their target language in their home countries. In the field of second language acquisition (SLA), therefore, research on out-of-class language learning has recently attracted attention (Sockett, 2014; Sundqvist & Sylvén, 2016). However, it is also true that the extent to which learners take advantage of such opportunities differs widely because, as I have discussed elsewhere (Inaba, 2018), out-of-class language learning is triggered and facilitated by various individual, contextual, and societal factors. Among these factors, learners' social networks (e.g., friends, classmates, and family members) in both their first language and the target language play a crucial role, particularly in promoting opportunities to use their target language outside of the classroom.

This chapter discusses how learners' social networks facilitate out-of-class language learning, including "significant others" in their social network, that is, those "who have an important influence or play a formative role in shaping the behavior of another" (Scott, 2014: 683). It does so by exploring Japanese language learners from the viewpoints of Activity Theory, which is one of the strands of Vygotskyan sociocultural theory (Lantolf & Thorne, 2006). The Activity Theory perspective enables us to explore how learners' social networks and the influential individuals in those networks facilitate the activities of learning and using a target language outside of the classroom. As an example of learning a foreign language other than English, learners of Japanese provide us with insightful examples, because the popularity of Japanese pop culture overseas in combination with ICT development has enabled learners of Japanese to access authentic resources and connect with Japanese-speaking peers. Both of these factors significantly influence learners' exposure to the target language outside of the classroom (e.g., Imura, 2018; Williams, 2006). Although my original study conducted in Australia and Sweden involves multiple case studies of eighteen students of Japanese at the tertiary level, this chapter focuses on two students for in-depth analysis and utilizes data from the other participants to support the arguments. In this chapter, I use "language learning activities" as an umbrella term to indicate any language-related activities, including language use in authentic contexts, such as watching Japanese cartoons and communicating in Japanese. The main reason for this is that language learning and language-use activities are frequently inseparable, as seen in the examples in the previous studies on out-of-class language learning (Chik, 014; Palfreyman, 2011).

Social Network Perspective and L2 Learning beyond the Classroom

A social network is a notion originally introduced in the field of social science which signifies "a finite set or sets of actors and the relation or relations defined on them" (Wasserman & Faust, 1994: 20). The concept of actor indicates social beings: for example, students and their classmates in language learning contexts. The social network perspective explores the structure of the relationships between connected individuals and how such relationships influence individuals or groups in a network through, for example, the flow of information and materials (Carolan, 2014). In sociology, furthermore, the concept of significant others explained earlier has become a commonplace one to indicate those who play a particularly influential role in social networks (Haller & Woelfel, 1972).

This perspective of the social network has been utilized in a number of academic fields, including sociolinguistics, with the aim of examining the influence of social relations on linguistic behaviors within a community (e.g., Miloy, 1987). In the field of SLA, although it is still in its infancy, an increasing number of studies have begun to explore how learners' social networks affect SLA, in particular the impact of social relations with native speakers on learners' oral proficiency development (e.g., Dewey, Brown, & Egget, 2012; Isabelli-García, 2006; Kurata, 2004; Smith, 2002). Although these studies have examined different contexts of learning (e.g., either study abroad or study in one's home country), their findings clearly indicate that meaningful connections with native speakers of a learner's target language had a positive impact on proficiency in L2, including linguistic awareness through frequent communication with native speakers (Kurata, 2004), as well as motivation and positive attitudes toward the target culture (Isabelli-García, 2006). However, the scope of these studies is relatively limited because they focused on the impact of learners' relations with native speakers on L2 oral proficiency development.

Rather than focusing on a network of native speakers, Zappa-Hollman and Duff (2015) examined the academic socialization of three Mexican students in a study abroad context and their social networks, including relations with peers from their home university as well as other international students. The most remarkable finding of their study is that the students' out-of-class interaction with their L2 English-speaking peers (i.e., students from their home university) played a key role in their successful engagement in the course assignments, providing not only academic resources but also emotional support.

Indeed, multiple studies have been conducted on out-of-class language learning to examine how social and contextual factors affected language learning beyond the classroom, including the influence of fellow L2 speakers. For example, Lam's (2000) case study of a Chinese-background immigrant adolescent, Almon, illustrated how he improved his English language skills and gained confidence as a student of English as a Second Language (ESL) by actively utilizing English to engage in his hobby, Japanese pop culture. Specifically, he used English to create a homepage about his favorite Japanese pop singer and to communicate with other fans of Japanese pop music. Similarly, Chik (2014) explored the possibility of language learning through online digital gaming communities and found that learning and teaching activities occurred informally among peers while chatting about games on gamers' blogs and forums.

Palfreyman (2011), furthermore, explored authentic language-use activities engaged in by five United Arab Emirates (UAE) female university students with regard to English and other foreign languages. By analyzing interview data with the students and their families, Palfreyman found that family members, not just friends and local communities, played significant roles as a language community, for instance, by providing students with opportunities to teach English to or talk in English with siblings and parents, in addition to providing encouragement and motivation. Meanwhile, Gao (2010) highlighted the influence of other important individuals on the strategic language learning behaviors by mainland Chinese undergraduate students at a university in Hong Kong, which utilized English as the medium of instruction. Drawing on sociocultural perspectives, Gao found that students' social resources (e.g., parents, English teachers, and peers at university-based societies), in addition to societal discourses (e.g., the value of English in a Chinese context) and cultural artifacts (e.g., English examinations and availability of English TV programs), shaped learners' motivation, beliefs, and capacity for L2 learning and affected their choice of language learning strategies while at university. This finding also demonstrates the usefulness of the sociocultural perspective in exploring the influence of social resources on language learning processes.

These studies clearly indicate that language learning and authentic language use outside of the classroom is shaped through interactions with other individuals. However, most research on out-of-class language learning has focused more on individual social agents than social networks, thus ignoring the features of social networks in terms of language learning outside of the classroom. In addition, the majority of the participants in these studies are ESL learners, whereas the cases of learners of other languages remain underexplored despite the fact that ICT now enables those learners to access various resources and authentic language-use opportunities (Benson, 2013). Accordingly, this study focuses on Japanese language learners and how their social networks facilitate their out-of-class language learning activities.

Activity Theory

To explore the influence of learners' social networks on out-of-class language learning activities, following Gao's (2010) study, I have employed sociocultural perspectives, in particular, Activity Theory. This theory has its origins in the work of Vygotsky (1978) and his colleagues on human mental development and was constructed by Vygotsky's collaborator, Leont'ev (1978). Activity Theory incorporates the notion of "mediation," which is Vygotsky's fundamental claim that individual human action to achieve their objects in the social-material world is mediated by artifacts, such as physical and symbolic tools and cultural concepts (Lantolf, 2000; Lantolf & Thorne, 2006). For instance, a learner of Japanese (subject) utilizes a website about Japanese grammar (artifact) to understand a Japanese text (object). Leont'ev (1978) developed Vygotsky's notion of mediated action and employed the concept of activity as the fundamental unit of analysis for unifying and understanding individual mediated actions and social contexts (Engeström, 1999). In Leont'ev's framework, activities signify any interactions mediated by artifacts between a subject (human) and an object and are inextricably connected to the concept of motive, which is the biological or social need or desire to lead human activity toward a specific object. In the case of students of Japanese, they undertake various language learning activities, for example learning Japanese words in a textbook (a specific object) with a desire to achieve native-level fluency in Japanese (motive). However, this traditional conceptualization of activity does not fully depict the societal and collaborative dimensions of each action (Engeström, 1999). To overcome this dilemma, Engeström (1987, 1999, 2001) further developed Activity Theory and proposed an activity system model by adding three additional elements to the traditional tripartite conceptualization (subject, mediating artifact(s), and object) of mediated activity: the community or communities in which the subject is embedded; the rules and norms that regulate the activity; and the division of labor among members of the community. In this activity system model, all these factors are potentially interrelated. Examining learners' out-of-class language learning as an example, peers in a language class (members of a community) might become language practice partners, provide useful information to support language learning (mediating artifacts), and eventually shape a learner's beliefs (subjective factor) and influence their motivation for language learning (motive). This example shares common ground with Carolan's (2014) claim regarding the importance of the social network perspective in exploring how learning occurs: "networks play a key role in shaping opinions, beliefs, and understandings and ultimately in shaping behaviors" (15). In other words, Activity Theory supports the exploration of learners' social network and language learning by providing a concrete analytical lens to explore the factors that are influenced by learners' social networks in facilitating out-of-class language learning activities.

As Zappa-Hollman and Duff (2015) pointed out, however, the concept of community in sociocultural perspectives, including Activity Theory, presupposes a group that shares the same purpose, and excludes looser connections between individuals who do not share any particular purposes (Kuttii, 1996; Zappa-Hollman & Duff, 2015). Moreover, as I have discussed elsewhere (Inaba, 2018), out-of-class language learning activities may be embedded in a number of activity contexts with different purposes, such as social activities with friends and personal leisure activities. In addition, a person's social relations with others are not necessarily rooted in a community as understood from a sociocultural perspective; for example, such relations may consist simply of friends whom learners occasionally meet at events. The concept of a social network covers this type of social relations, which are outside the concept of community from a sociocultural perspective. Therefore, this study employs both Activity Theory and the concept of social networks to comprehensively examine how learners' social networks mediate their language learning activities outside of the classroom. In doing so, it aims to answer the following research questions:

1. What are the features of Japanese language learners' social networks, specifically in terms of out-of-class language learning activities?
2. Which individuals are significant in these networks, and how do these significant others facilitate the language learning activities outside of the classroom?

As explained previously, the concept of significant others in the second research question has been commonly utilized in sociology and indicates someone who has an important influence on an individual's self-image or identity (Scott, 2014). In this study, I apply this term specifically to designate members of a learner's social networks who play a key role in facilitating the learner's L2 learning activities outside of the classroom.

Methodology

Contexts of the Study

The participants of the current study are tertiary-level Japanese language learners in two different countries, Australia and Sweden. The educational systems available for learning Japanese differ considerably in the two countries, and such differences, in addition to other contextual and individual factors, are reflected in the students' learning histories.

In Australia, Japanese is supported by government-level promotion of languages other than English and other related programs, such as the National Asian Languages and Studies in Schools Program (Japan Foundation, 2017a). Because of this nationwide promotion, the majority of learners are school-age adolescents. However, Japanese is also the most widely taught language in Australia at university as well (de Kretser & Spence-Brown, 2010). In Sweden, although the number of secondary schools that offer Japanese as a third language has been increasing, universities are the main providers of Japanese language education (Japan Foundation, 2017a).

Here, I touch once again upon the popularity of Japanese pop culture overseas and its influence on the learning environments of learners of Japanese. Japanese pop culture, manifested in such productions as Japanese comic books (*manga*) and Japanese cartoons (*anime*), is a significant phenomenon and a major motivation for nonnative Japanese language learning overseas, including in Australia (Armour, 2015; Northwood, 2018). In Sweden, too, for example, it has been reported that institutions other than schools (e.g., lifelong learning centers) have increasingly begun to offer Japanese courses for school children because those children have become interested in Japanese through pop culture (Japan Foundation, 2017b). Indeed, as discussed in the following sections, the data clearly demonstrate the notable influence of Japanese pop culture on their out-of-class language learning activities and their social networks.

Focal Participants

As mentioned earlier, my original study involves multiple case studies of eighteen students of Japanese. Among them, fifteen participants were from an Australian university and three were from a Swedish university. Whereas the students in Australia were recruited in August 2008 and March 2009 through announcements in all classes and advertisements university-wide, the students in Sweden were recruited in February 2014 through emails targeted to the students of the Japanese program at the university. Although there is approximately a five-year gap between the data collection in Australia and that in Sweden, the influence of ICT and Japanese pop culture was evident in both studies.

To conduct an in-depth analysis into the effect of learners' social networks on their out-of-class language learning, one participant from each context will be discussed in this chapter—Melissa (an Australian university student; pseudonym) and Fredrik (a Swedish university student; pseudonym). These students were chosen because they provided detailed data on their out-of-class language learning experiences and their social networks, which included examples similar to those found among the other participants.

Table 7.1 provides basic information on the focal students. Both Melissa and Fredrik were enrolled in a Japanese course at their respective universities. In both cases, the initial motive to start learning Japanese was Japanese pop culture. However, there were several key differences in their backgrounds. On the one hand, Melissa is an Australian and a native speaker of English. At the university,

Table 7.1 Background of the Participants

Name (Pseudonym)	Melissa	Fredrik
Nationality	Australian	Swedish
Learning experience with Japanese before university	None	Self-study
Level of course taken during the data collection	Intermediate	Beginner
Length of Japanese study at university before the data collection	Approx. two years	Approx. eleven months
Experience in Japan (before the data collection period)	Approx. ten-week in-country summer program	Short trip (a couple of weeks) in Japan
Major	Language arts (Italian and Japanese)	Engineering
Home language(s)	English	Swedish and Cantonese

Melissa was studying Japanese in addition to Italian. She also volunteered at a *Manga* library owned by the university and run by student volunteers. It is also worth mentioning that Melissa had participated in an in-country summer program before the data collection period. Fredrik, on the other hand, is Swedish with an Asian background. However, because Fredrik was born in Sweden, he speaks Swedish as his first language and speaks Cantonese only with his parents. Fredrik majored in engineering at university and first took an evening course of Japanese at university. After completing the evening course, he took a full-time Japanese course at the same university while studying engineering. Fredrik had no experience of a long-term stay in Japan prior to the data collection. However, after taking the full-time course for a year, he participated in an in-country summer course in Japan before leaving the Japanese course to focus entirely on the engineering study. It is also worth mentioning that Fredrik's Asian background was part of his motive to study Japanese. Regarding his current motivation to study Japanese, he mentioned becoming friends with, for example, Japanese exchange students, because he did not feel "I'm at home" (March 21, 2014) in Sweden, whereas he thought "Oh I return back to where I originally came from" when he traveled to China and Japan (March 21, 2014).

Data Collection

To explore how one's social networks facilitate out-of-class language learning activities, this study employs a qualitative research method. Thus, data were collected through semi-structured interviews and language learning diaries for one to two weeks. Diary entries were obtained in addition to conducting interviews to gather richer data with concrete examples of out-of-class language learning and other influential factors in the participants' learning environments in a nonintrusive manner and from an "insider" perspective (Dörnyei, 2007: 157). Diary entries were also utilized as triggers to elicit participants' reflections in the subsequent interview, similar to the use of video/audio recordings in stimulated-recall interviews. The learning diaries were written in English, and the interviews were conducted in English, even with Swedish students, because English was a language common to both the participants and the researcher.

The basic data collection procedure was as follows: (1) a semi-structured interview (sixty to ninety minutes) was conducted to gather information on the participants' backgrounds; (2) the first language learning diary entry was obtained in a digital format via email, and a subsequent interview was conducted; (3) the second diary entry was obtained in the same manner as the first diary entry, followed by an interview. Although this procedure was employed in both Australia and Sweden, the duration of time for the data collection and the available data differed for Melissa and Fredrik. On the one hand, Melissa participated in the study in 2009 for one semester and completed two diary entries in addition to two interviews. As her participation was only one semester, the second diary study was conducted approximately one month after the first. Fredrik, on the other hand, participated in this study from the spring semester of 2014 until January 2015; this time span included several months after he had completed the Japanese course. In addition, Fredrik did not submit his learning diary for the second round of the data collection, which was conducted nine months after the first diary study. However, the interview with him included valuable examples of authentic language use and transformation in his social network after leaving the language course. All the interview data were transcribed for analysis.

The transcribed interview data and the diary entries of each case were coded to determine what types of social networks were involved in and the significant themes in relation to the social networks, based on the factors outlined in Engeström's (1987, 1999, 2001) activity system model (e.g., to provide information about resources and to motivate them to use the language). Subsequently, the coded data were thematically analyzed to examine what aspects of their out-of-class language learning activities their social networks influenced/facilitated.

Findings

The analysis shows that the social networks of Melissa and Fredrik were roughly divided into three types: (1) networks that had already existed before university, including friends at school and siblings; (2) networks in an academic context at university or related to language learning, such as classmates, friends at university, and an online study group; and (3) networks with native speakers of Japanese. Furthermore, in these social networks, there were individuals who particularly influenced the participants' out-of-class language learning activities, that is, their significant others (see Figures 7.1 and 7.2). The following sections will discuss how social networks and significant others facilitated out-of-class language learning for Melissa and Fredrik.

Friends at School and Siblings—Triggered Interests in Japanese Pop Culture and Learning Japanese

Japanese pop culture was one of the significant motivators to learn Japanese among the participants of the current study, and both Melissa and Fredrik explained that their friends at school had been integral to their developing an interest in this media. Melissa's social network, in relation to her initial interest in Japanese pop culture, consisted of friends at school who studied Japanese as a school subject and both an older and a younger sister at home. The members

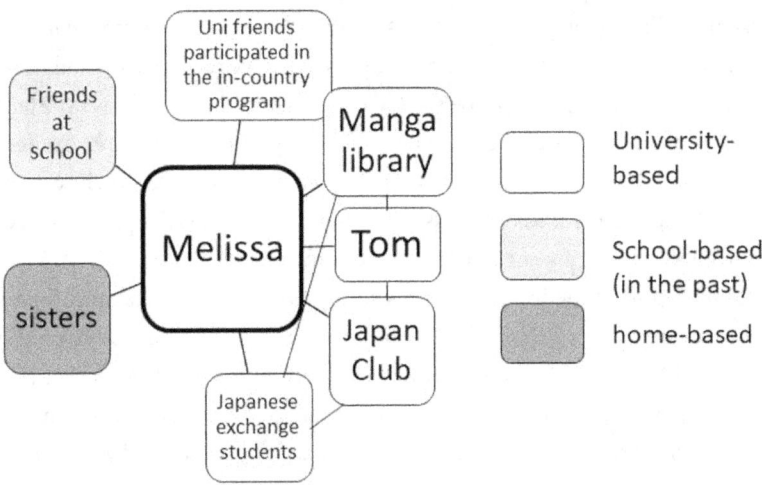

Figure 7.1 Melissa's social network for out-of-class language learning.

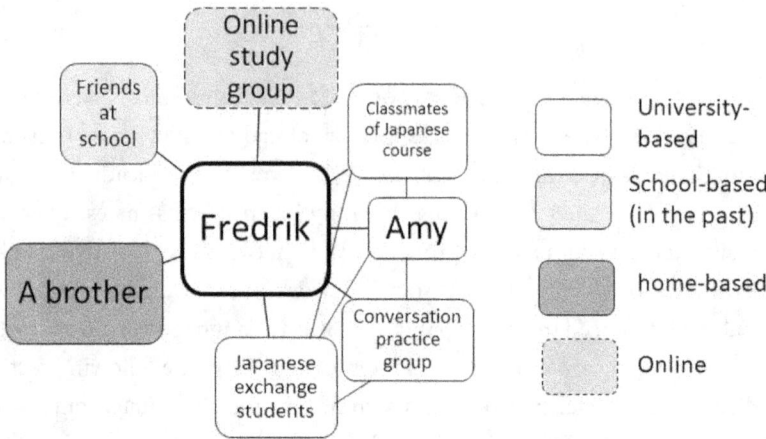

Figure 7.2 Fredrik's social network for out-of-class language learning.

of Fredrik's social network included friends at school and a younger brother at home.

For example, Melissa noted how her friends at school had fostered her interests in Japanese *anime*, although she did not study Japanese: "because they were doing Japanese, they sort of knew about *anime* and said, 'okay, try watching this and try watching this'" (April 30, 2009). Fredrik, meanwhile, explained that his interest in Japanese pop culture had been fostered from childhood through *anime* and video games.

A number of participants in this study also noted their siblings' influence on their interest in Japanese pop culture, or vice versa. During the interview, for instance, Fredrik explained how his hobby (drawing *anime* and *manga*) had affected his younger brother: "at junior high, I started drawing a lot, and then my brother became influenced. So, he started drawing too. Sometimes we started like a project, yeah" (March 21, 2014). Melissa also reported that she recommended *anime* to her siblings and shared resources (DVDs of *anime*), which were often obtained from their friends and classmates. In other words, the participants also influenced their existing social network at home.

Fredrik reported the influence of his young brother on his learning Japanese. Since Fredrik and his brother had become interested in Japanese pop culture, they started learning Japanese on their own. Although Fredrik explained that his younger brother "motivated me to not really learn Japanese, but more like drawing *anime, manga*" (April 4, 2014), his younger brother had recommended a Japanese self-study app to him when he was in high school. Fredrik used this app continuously, even during the data collection period, showing that his brother's recommendation had a long-term impact on Fredrik's Japanese study. These examples illustrate how the participants' social networks and the factors in their activity systems were interlinked and influenced each other, as Engeström (1987) claims. The school friends provided resources of Japanese pop culture and triggered the participants' interests in this media, which not only eventually fostered their motives to learn Japanese but made their network at home became a Japanese pop culture fan group. Furthermore, as Fredrik's example shows, the Japanese pop culture fan group introduced a tool of learning Japanese. In other words, his activity system related to Japanese pop culture gained another aspect, that is, learning Japanese.

Peers and Classmates at University—Further Developing Learners' Interests in Japanese Pop Culture

Friends at university also played a significant role in terms of Japanese pop culture, but in a slightly different way from their school friends and siblings, as discussed earlier. The social network of Melissa at university included her friends who volunteered together at the *Manga* library and those who studied together in the in-country summer program (see Figure 7.1), and the peers at the *Manga* library played an influential role in triggering the snowball effects for her interests in Japanese pop culture, as discussed in the following section. The members of Fredrik's social network at university only included his classmates on the Japanese course (see Figure 7.2). However, similar to Melissa, one of his classmates, Amy (pseudonym), had a significant impact on his out-of-class language learning activities.

Fredrik explained that Amy triggered "this huge change" (April 4, 2014) in his viewing activities, shifting his preference from *anime* to Japanese drama. Indeed, in his diary entries, he reported that he searched for dramas on the website that the classmate told him about and watched the drama for a couple of hours on the weekends. Furthermore, Fredrik explained that he preferred dramas to *anime* "because I like . . . it teaches more somehow like, it's more real life" (April 4, 2014). He also explained his current motivation for learning Japanese, which was triggered by watching: "lately I've been developing like 'Oh I want to see how it is living in Japan,' how do you say, *seikatsu* ['life' in Japanese]" (April 4, 2014). These comments imply that watching Japanese TV dramas ignited his interest in a different area of Japanese culture (i.e., life in Japan) and added a new layer onto his motive to learn Japanese. As pointed out in the previous section, the factors in Fredrik's activity system were interrelated to each other: the peer as an information provider introduced Fredrik to the artifacts (information and resources in the new genres of Japanese pop culture) and triggered the motives (learners' interests in the new genres and learn Japanese).

Similarly, Melissa's interest in Japanese pop culture shifted from *anime* to Japanese TV drama when she started studying Japanese at university. Behind this change lay the influence of friends at the *Manga* library where both Melissa and her friends worked as volunteers. In the interview, Melissa explained that she began watching Japanese TV dramas at university because her friends at the *Manga* library would "talk about drama, and I want[ed] to watch it too" (June 23, 2009). Melissa's interest in Japanese TV dramas led her to develop an interest in Japanese pop songs, again through the support from her friends:

> I saw the drama of *Gokusen* [a Japanese TV drama series about school life], and I think that it had Matsumoto Jun [a member of a J-pop boy band] in it. And my friends said he is in a band and gave me some of the band's music. I think that's how I started it, and I like the music, and music is easy for me to listen to because I drive. And so, I really got into it that way. (April 30, 2009)

Melissa also mentioned that listening activities were the most common activities during the data collection period. It is reasonable to conclude that this suggestion from her friends had a significant impact on her out-of-class language learning activities. Furthermore, it is also worth mentioning that Melissa recognized the positive influence of these listening activities on her Japanese study in a formal context, citing a concrete example:

> for instance, on today's test, there is *yaburu*, "to tear." I didn't know what it was, I wouldn't know if I just looked at it at the test. But I learnt *yaburu* by listening to a song, because I understood all of the sentences except for *yaburu*, so I looked it in a *jisho* [dictionary] and it said *yaburu*. (April 30, 2009)

Melissa also reported that she sometimes found the words she learned in class while listening to songs. From an Activity Theory perspective, her Japanese study in formal context and out-of-class language learning activities can be understood as different with different motives (e.g., gaining a degree for Japanese study at university contrasted with enjoying pop culture for out-of-class language learning activities). However, they influenced each other regarding the linguistics tools to support Melissa's activities of learning and using Japanese. In other words, her peers' suggestions had an impact on not only her out-of-class language learning activities but also her Japanese study at university and facilitated her language learning processes.

Communications with Japanese Speakers (1)—
Practicing Japanese and Source of Motivation

As stated previously, the opportunity for communication with native speakers of a target language and its influence on learners' speaking competence is one of the main themes in previous studies on social networks in SLA. Both Melissa and Fredrik had Japanese acquaintances and friends in the university context. Melissa was acquainted with Japanese exchange students at the *Manga* library as well as the Japan Club at the university, in which both students of Japanese and international or exchange students from Japan participated (see Figure 7.1). Fredrik had also become acquainted with Japanese exchange students at the university (see Figure 7.2).

Fredrik reported that he often participated in a conversation practice group and social gatherings at the university, and communicated with Japanese exchange students in Japanese, Swedish, and English. These communication opportunities increased his motivation for learning Japanese in two different ways. First, communication with the exchange students enabled Fredrik to recognize the gap between his current Japanese competence (i.e., tool) and the proficiency level that he aimed to achieve (i.e., object of activity), which in Activity Theory means that a contradiction exists and triggers a motive to overcome it (Engeström, 1987). Indeed, this gap motivated Fredrik to study Japanese more:

> Every time I meet exchange students, I'm not really able to, really able to speak Japanese. I have like this motivation, I want to be better at Japanese, so next time maybe I could communicate properly. (April 4, 2014)

Second, communication with the exchange students also became an opportunity to fuel Fredrik's motivation, influenced by his Asian background (see "Focal Students" section). When Fredrik participated in the language exchange group with Japanese exchange students, he was highly impressed with how much they had improved their Swedish proficiency and commented as follows:

> I always like, have this in my mind that Japanese people are always hard working and really enthusiastic and ambitious people. And I want to become like one of them. (April 4, 2014)

Relatedly, Fredrik also explained "well, it also origins from start when I like, decided studying Japanese" (April 4, 2014). In Activity Theory, Fredrik's motivation can be understood as his social need to be part of a Japanese community. Leont'ev (1978), for instance, argued that a subject's need becomes a motive of activity when his/her need meets an object (i.e., the need is objectified). From this viewpoint, it can be said that the communication with the exchange students enabled Fredrik's social need to meet its concrete object (i.e., to become a hard worker, which he viewed as a Japanese attribute), or at least clarified his need, and consequently enhanced his motive to learn Japanese. Indeed, although Fredrik remarked that he could not really speak Japanese, I observed his consistent efforts to use Japanese on Facebook and in emails as well as in face-to-face communication with the author. However, Fredrik's experience was the exception. As discussed in the following section, Melissa utilized English with her Japanese network.

Communication with Japanese Speakers (2)—Practicing Japanese, Or Not?

Melissa had Japanese native speaker acquaintances, for example, Japanese exchange students, and occasionally communicated with them via Facebook's online chat function. However, they most often communicated in English: "I think it's mostly just English because they're learning English" (May 12, 2009). Ten of the eleven Australian students who used Facebook with Japanese friends also reported that they mainly communicated in English on this platform, though the participants provided different reasons for this dominant use of English (see Inaba, 2018).

In contrast, Melissa reported that she often communicated in Japanese on Facebook with her Australian friend, Tom (pseudonym—see Figure 7.1), who studied Japanese at a university in Japan as an exchange student around the time of the data collection period. Tom and Melissa became friends through the volunteer work at the *Manga* library and participating in the Japan Club activities. As to the reason for this utilization of Japanese, Melissa explained:

> when he is over there, he finds a bit embarrassing to practice Japanese because he, he thinks all his friends are really good at it [Japanese], and he is not, and so, if I'm there, he gets excited "Oh, let's practice" because he is not so embarrassed with me, because I make mistakes too. (June 23, 2009)

From an Activity Theory perspective, these contrasting examples can be understood by the differences in their motives and other factors related to their activity system for learning English and Japanese. With her Japanese native speaker friends, on the one hand, Melissa prioritized her friends' motives for practicing English, contradicting her own motive to practice Japanese. It is also worth noting that the status of English as a lingua franca could have affected the motives of Japanese native speakers while communicating with Melissa, who is a native English speaker. On the other hand, Melissa and her Japanese language-learner peers shared the motive of wanting to practice Japanese. Furthermore, as the previous excerpt indicates, due to their similar proficiency levels, both felt comfortable communicating in Japanese. In other words, this shared aspect (proficiency level) affected her friends' motive (eagerness to communicate in Japanese) and promoted practicing Japanese with Melissa. Thus, a number of factors could have affected their choice of language, and having native speaker peers does not always lead to communication in the target language.

Online Study Group—Language Learning Support after Course Completion

Fredrik's experience after leaving the Japanese course illustrates the possibility of online communities supporting self-study learners. Fredrik stopped taking the Japanese course after participating in an intensive in-country summer course in order to complete his engineering degree. Consequently, Fredrik was rarely able to participate in the conversation practice group and the social gatherings with Japanese exchange students due to the intensive schedule of his engineering course. Furthermore, during the final interview, Fredrik noted that "to get myself motivated enough" (January 18, 2015) was the greatest challenge to improving his Japanese language skills, particularly because there were no longer any tests or teachers to evaluate his progress.

Around the time of this final interview, however, Fredrik joined an online community of Japanese language learners who aimed to pass the second highest level (N2) of the Japanese Language Proficiency Test (JLPT; the proficiency test organized by the Japan Foundation and Japan Educational Exchange Services, 2012). Through the online study group, Fredrik exchanged his contact details on Twitter with approximately thirty learners of Japanese around the world, including those from Australia, Japan, and the United Kingdom. Fredrik reported that "we usually discuss sort of Japan-related things including the language ... [and] we chat a lot together, and we help each other a lot [in English and Japanese on Twitter]" (January 18, 2015).

This peer group, connected through Twitter, played a role similar to that of his Japanese classes and related peer groups (e.g., the conversation practice group). For instance, the Twitter group provided Fredrik with opportunities to use the language, which might enable him to assess his Japanese language skills as he had done in his face-to-face communication with the Japanese exchange students. Furthermore, although the communication on Twitter did not provide the same immediate diagnostic opportunities as the Japanese classes had done, discussing the language could be compared with a teacher's explanation of grammar and idioms. It is also noteworthy that this online group shared the same motive (i.e., passing the N2 of the JLPT). This motive is at least one of the key factors connecting language-learner peers and building a supportive network for learning Japanese.

Concluding Remarks and Implications for Language Teaching

Drawing on the perspective of Activity Theory, this study examined the role of social networks in facilitating out-of-class language learning activities by Japanese language learners. In answering the first research question, I found that the learners' social networks are inextricably connected with Japanese pop culture. Prior to university, Japanese pop culture was introduced through the learners' existing networks with friends at school as well as siblings and became a significant motivator to start learning Japanese. At university, their underlying interest in different genres of Japanese pop culture was triggered through communication with classmates and school friends, further influencing their exposure to the language outside of the classroom. Though they often engaged in these activities individually, their shared interest in Japanese pop culture was a key factor in uniting the members of their network. Furthermore, Melissa's example of watching her peers' favorite Japanese drama implies that both their social relations and their interest in Japanese pop culture were potentially reinforced through their communication about the media, because they were able to share more information as well as experiences. It is also important to note that the pop culture and the language are inseparable. As the pop culture resources involve the use of Japanese, their interest in Japanese pop culture becomes a trigger of learning Japanese.

In answering the second research question, the analysis revealed that the participants' social networks included a number of significant others, such as Melissa's friends at university and Fredrik's classmate, as well as Japanese exchange students. These significant others in the participants' social network mediated out-of-class language learning activities in a variety of ways. The Japanese exchange students in Fredrik's case, for example, not only provided communication opportunities in the target language but also motivated Fredrik to learn Japanese by enabling him to recognize and asses his current language skills and clarify his social need in relation to the target language. Moreover, the examples of both Melissa and Fredrik illustrate that their friends and classmates functioned as informational and material providers of Japanese pop culture and thus triggered the learners' interest in different genres of this media. Consequently, learners started utilizing new types of materials (resources) or engaging in new types of activities involving the target language. Here, I would remind readers that these significant others were members of social networks that were bound by a shared interest in Japanese pop culture and following their friends' recommendations is an essential aspect of participating in the network which motivate Melissa and Fredrik to explore new genres of the pop culture. In this way, out-of-class language learning, enjoying various aspects of Japanese pop culture, and their social relations are linked to each other, and as Carolan (2014) claims, their social network played a key role "ultimately in shaping behaviors" (p. 15).

Findings, furthermore, parallel previous studies about learners of English in that the shared interests of members of their existing social networks are key factors in facilitating language learning (Gao, 2010; Palyfreman, 2011). However, the current study illustrates that shared interests also differ from previous studies: whereas the value of English as a lingua franca plays a critical role in the studies by Gao and Palyfreman, a shared interest in Japanese pop culture is one of the most significant factors among the learners of Japanese in this study.

It is also worth noting that communication with native speakers might not necessarily involve utilizing the target language because native speakers are also social agents with their own reasons for communicating with Japanese language learners. In particular, as observed in Melissa's case, the importance of English as a lingua franca might be a disadvantage for native speakers of English seeking to learn a foreign language. Rather than connecting with native speakers, as Fredrik's online study community and Melissa's interactions with her Japanese language-learner friend illustrate, sharing motives or interests that involve target languages might be an essential condition to producing and maintaining language learning opportunities (cf. Kurata, Chapter 5, this volume; Lam, 2000, an example of an ESL student).

These findings also have clear pedagogical implications. Firstly, given that the peer recommendations for Japanese pop culture resources supported out-of-class language learning activities, arranging opportunities for students to exchange information about topics in which they are equally interested could enable learners to seek out classmates who share the same interests. In this way, teachers can also familiarize themselves with their students' interests and choose materials and topics that might deepen those students' interest in learning the language, and thus further facilitate autonomous language learning outside of the classroom.

Secondly, although communication with native speakers is beneficial for students, not only in terms of practicing their target language but also in order to enhance their motivation, the results suggest that connecting with native speakers of a target language is insufficient to create and maintain opportunities for using a target language. In other words, it might not be sufficient to arrange communication opportunities with native speakers; intervention by a teacher in social networks is also necessary. For instance, arranging study groups or pairs for language exchange activities based on common interests might be profitable to promote communication between language learners and native speakers of the target language. Moreover, teachers need to be aware of how difficult it is to stay connected with one's peers based solely on a language course after completing that course. Establishing a peer community, especially an online community, would be one solution to support the transition from classroom-based learning to autonomous learning after course completion.

This study has several limitations. The case studies offered here are only two students, and therefore the findings are not generalizable to a larger population. It is also important to note that this study only analyzed university students who were studying Japanese as a foreign language. Thus, it would be helpful to explore cases of learning different languages within different contexts, particularly self-study learners, because one might reasonably assume that the role of one's social network differs considerably from those who learn a language in a classroom context. Finally, this study spans a limited time, from one semester to approximately ten months; in other words, it was not sufficient to fully examine the developmental aspect of a social network and out-of-class language learning. Longitudinal data (e.g., throughout a degree program at a university) would be required to more fully explore how social networks and out-of-class language learning influence each other and evolve. Despite these limitations, however, the current study does demonstrate the role of one's social network in developing and expanding out-of-class language learning and language-use activities in foreign language contexts.

References

Armour, W. S. (2015). The geopolitics of Japanese soft power and the Japanese language and studies classroom: Soft power pedagogy, globalization and the new technologies. In I. Nakane, E. Otsuji, & W. S. Armour (Eds.), *Languages and identities in a transitional Japan: From internationalization to globalization* (pp. 37–56). New York: Routledge.

Benson, P. (2011). Language learning and teaching beyond the classroom: An introduction to the field. In P. Benson & H. Reinders (Eds.), *Beyond the language classroom* (pp. 7–16). Basingstoke: Palgrave Macmillan.

Benson, P. (2013). Learner autonomy. *TESOL Quarterly, 47*(4), 839–43.

Carolan, B. V. (2014). *Social network analysis and education: Theory, methods & application.* Thousand Oaks, CA: Sage Publications.

Chik, A. (2014). Digital gaming and language learning: Autonomy and community. *Language Learning and Technology 18*(2), 85–100.

de Kretser, A., & Spence-Brown, R. (2010). *The current state of Japanese language education in Australian schools.* Carlton South: Education Services Australia.

Dewey, D. P., Brown, J., & Eggett, D. (2012). Japanese language proficiency, social networking, and language use during study abroad: Learners' perspectives. *The Canadian Modern Language Review, 28*(2), 111–37.

Dörnyei, Z. (2007). *Research methods in applied linguistics.* Oxford: Oxford University Press.

Engeström, Y. (1987). *Learning by expanding: An activity-theoretical approach to developmental research.* Retrieved from http://lchc.ucsd.edu/mca/Paper/Engestrom/expanding/toc.htm

Engeström, Y. (1999). Activity theory and individual and social transformation. In Y. Engeström, R. Miettinen, & R. L. Punamaki (Eds.), *Perspectives on activity theory* (pp. 19–38). New York: Cambridge University Press.

Engeström, Y. (2001). Expansive learning at work: Toward an activity theoretical reconceptualization. *Journal of Education and Work, 14*(1), 133–56.

Gao, X. A. (2010). *Strategic language learning: The roles of agency and context.* Bristol: Multilingual Matters.

Haller, A. O., & Woelfel, J. (1972). Significant others and their expectations: Concepts and instruments to measure interpersonal influence on status aspirations. *Rural Sociology, 37*(4), 591–622.

Imura, T. (2018). A portrait of Japanese popular culture fans who study Japanese at an Australian university: Motivation and activities beyond the classroom. *East Asian Journal of Popular Culture, 4*(2), 171–88.

Inaba, M. (2018). *Second language literacy practices and language learning outside of the classroom.* Bristol: Multilingual Matters.

Isabelli-García, C. (2006). Study abroad social networks, motivation and attitudes: Implications for second language acquisition. In E. Churchill and M. Dufon (Eds.), *Language learners in study abroad contexts* (pp. 231–58). Clevedon: Multilingual Matters.

Japan Foundation. (2017a). *Survey report on Japanese-language education abroad 2015.* Tokyo: Japan Foundation. Retrieved from https://www.jpf.go.jp/j/project/japanese/survey/result/dl/survey_2015/Report_all_e.pdf

Japan Foundation. (2017b). *Nihongo kyōiku kuni·chīki betsu jyōhō 2016: Ōstoraria (Country and regional information about Japanese language education 2016: Australia)*. Tokyo: Japan Foundation. Retrieved from https://www.jpf.go.jp/j/project/japanese/survey/area/country/2016/australia.html

Japan Foundation and Japan Educational Exchanges and Services. (2012). Japanese-Language Proficiency Test. Retrieved from https://www.jlpt.jp/e/index.html

Kurata, N. (2004). Communication networks of Japanese language learners in their home country. *Journal of Asian Pacific Communication, 14*(1), 153–78.

Kuttii, K. (1996). Activity theory as a potential framework for human-computer interaction research. In B. Nardi (Ed.), *Context and consciousness: Activity theory and human-computer interaction* (pp. 17–44). Cambridge, MA: MIT Press.

Lam, W. S. E. (2000). L2 literacy and the design of the self: A case study of a teenager writing on the Internet. *TESOL Quarterly, 34*(3), 457–82.

Lantolf, J. P. (2000). Introducing sociocultural theory. In J. P. Lantolf (Ed.), *Sociocultural theory and second language learning* (pp. 1–26). Oxford: Oxford University Press.

Lantolf, J. P., & Thorne, S. L. (2006). *Sociocultural theory and the genesis of second language development*. Oxford and New York: Oxford University Press.

Leont'ev, A. N. (1978). *Activity, consciousness and personality*. Englewood Cliffs, NJ: Prentice Hall.

Miloy, L. (1987). *Language and social networks*. Oxford: Blackwell.

Northwood, B. M. (2018). The influence of Japanese popular culture on learning Japanese. *East Asian Journal of Popular Culture, 4*(2), 189–204.

Palfreyman, D. M. (2011). Family, friends, and learning beyond the classroom: Social networks and social capital in language learning. In P. Benson and H. Reinders (Eds.), *Beyond the language classroom* (pp. 17–34). Basingstoke: Palgrave Macmillan.

Scott, J. (2014). *Dictionary of sociology* (4th ed.). Oxford: Oxford University Press.

Smith, L. R. (2002). The social architecture of communicative competence: A methodology for social-network research in sociolinguistics. *International Journal of Sociology of Language, 153*, 133–60.

Sockett, G. (2014). *The online informal learning of English*. Basingstoke: Palgrave Macmillan.

Sundqvist, P., & Sylvén, L. K. (2016). *Extramural English in teaching and learning: From theory and research to practice*. London: Palgrave Macmillan.

Vygotsky, L. S. (1978). *Mind in society: The development of higher psychological processes*. M. Cole, V. John-Steiner, S. Scribner, and E. Souberman (Eds.). Cambridge, MA: Harvard University Press.

Wasserman, S., & Faust, K. (1994). *Social network analysis: Methods and applications*. Cambridge and New York: Cambridge University Press.

Williams, K. (2006). *The impact of popular culture fandom on perceptions of Japanese language and culture learning: The case of student anime fans*. Unpublished PhD dissertation, University of Texas, Austin, US.

Zappa-Hollman, S., & Duff, P. A. (2015). Academic English socialization through individual networks of practice. *TESOL Quarterly, 49*(2), 333–68.

Part III

Social Networks in Study Abroad Contexts

8

Implementing Mental Contrasting to Improve English Language Learner Social Networks

Hannah Trimble-Brown, Dan P. Dewey, Vashti Lee,
and Dennis L. Eggett

Interaction is of particular interest to learners who participate in a study abroad program. Although beneficial, communication with native speakers comes with many challenges, regardless of how involved or helpful the study abroad program is. Mental contrasting with implementation intentions (MCII) is a self-regulation strategy that has helped individuals successfully alter their behavior in a variety of areas, including healthier eating, better relationships, and improved time management skills (Oettingen, 2012; Kirk, Oettingen, & Gollwitzer, 2013). MCII involves visualizing a future goal and its associated outcomes, as well as imagining potential obstacles and making a plan to overcome them. Recently, this self-regulation strategy has been applied to building social relationships (i.e., social networks) by learners studying abroad in the United States (Lee, Dewey, Brown, & Belnap, 2018). The Lee et al. (2018) study investigates the specific impact of MCII on social networks during study abroad and suggests that utilizing MCII can increase both students' second language (L2) interactions and the variety of social circles to which they belong. In an effort to further determine the impact of this form of self-regulation on L2 engagement with other individuals abroad, this chapter explores the effects of MCII on social networks among 107 English language learners studying abroad in an intensive English program in the United States over a period of fourteen weeks. It compares control and treatment groups, and students who are in their first semester (new) versus those returning to the program. Surveys and freewrite responses provide us with both quantitative and qualitative data for a better understanding of a relatively new area of research.

Review of Literature

Based on the research that interaction in the L2 increases L2 proficiency (Johnson, K., & Johnson, H., 1999; Allwright, 1984; Savignon, 1997; Fraser 2002), study abroad programs often advertise themselves as "a short cut to linguistic fluency" (Wilkinson, 1998). Study abroad programs, defined here as international experiences involving in- and out-of-class language learning (Freed, 1995), often assume participants will naturally use the L2 since they are immersed in the target language. Although these programs capitalize on the benefits of interaction in the L2 while abroad, the social and linguistic intricacies of the second language cause a range of problems for many participants, including developing friendships and making contact with native speakers during their experience (Mendelson, 2004). Many students begin a study abroad program with high hopes of linguistic benefits, yet encounter difficult and sometimes unexpected challenges associated with building social relationships and using the L2 with locals (DeKeyser, 2010; Pérez-Vidal & Juan-Garau, 2011; Tullock, 2018; Wilkinson, 1998).

These informal social connections, also known as social networks (Milroy, 1980), comprise several challenges for students while studying abroad. Factors that inhibit social network development may include high program academic demands and low program support for interaction with locals (Dewey, Ring, Gardner, & Belnap, 2013), gender bias and cross-cultural differences in gender behavior (Trentman, 2012), lack of access to universities, shopping, and night life, and individual factors such as personality types, difficulty fitting in, challenges making friends, desire to remain within one's L1 social group, negotiation of identity, and so forth (Ring, Gardner, & Dewey, 2013). The sheer amount and variety of challenges that students must confront can be daunting and demotivating. We do also acknowledge that not all study abroad programs have an ideal atmosphere for social interaction and not all offer well-established opportunities that facilitate students' social network growth. Additionally, social network development depends on individual students' agency (Tullock, 2018; Ryan & Mercer, 2011) and their ability to mitigate some of the challenges associated with social network formation during study abroad.

In order to facilitate social interaction between students and native speakers throughout the duration of the study abroad, programs have created opportunities to help students engage with the locals, such as offering a peer mentoring or tutoring program, organized social activities, direct enrollment for classes with native speakers, introductions to clubs, teams, and other social circles, and implementation of an L2 language pledge (cf. Hasegawa, Chapter 9, this volume), or through encouraging interaction with the community through volunteer work or community clubs (Ring et al., 2013; Dewey, Bown, & Eggett, 2012).

Despite the well-organized program interventions that enhance the overall study abroad experience, the students themselves must use their agency to choose to be actively engaged in creating a positive experience and communicating in the L2 with those around them. Bown, Dewey, and Belnap (2015) point out the important responsibilities that each student has, stating that "the learners themselves must regulate their own learning and the learning environment, in as much as the sociohistorical context allows them to" (216). Lantolf and Pavlenko (2001) also target learner responsibility, writing that students are agents who "actively engage in constructing the terms and conditions of their own learning" (145). Therefore, it is not enough to create a well-designed program; students must take charge of their own learning, especially when it comes to overcoming obstacles to social network development.

In order to take learning into their own hands and excel, language learners need to learn to self-regulate. Self-regulation refers to the processes that individuals utilize to manage their emotions, thoughts, and behaviors effectively. In regard to academic achievement, such self-regulation presents itself by making plans, setting goals, self-evaluating personal progress, and implementing different strategies. Self-regulation helps language learners experience greater academic success (Zimmerman, 1990), learn the target language faster, more effectively and enjoyably, and face the anxiety and complex challenges that are involved in the process (Oxford, 2011; Wen-Ta Tseng, Dörnyei, & Schmitt, 2006; Ortega, 2013). Macaro (2001) states that these types of proactive learners seem to learn more from their language experiences.

Within the context of language learning and study abroad, self-regulation strategies have been used by students to enhance their social network development. An example of this is seen in research done by Bown, Dewey, and Belnap (2015), who analyzed how learners studying Arabic abroad in Jordan used self-regulation to monitor their actions and engage in strategies that lead to positive social networking experiences. They found that learners made L2 communication goals, engaged interlocutors by showing interest in them and asking quality questions, refused to switch to the L1 even if the native Arabic speaker did, and utilized pre-speaking techniques such as studying vocabulary along with topics of interest. These self-regulation techniques empowered the learners and aided them in creating successful social contacts while on their study abroad.

One specific tool for self-regulation that has the potential to help learners develop social networks is MCII. It might be thought of as following both a motivational and a cognitive model of self-regulation. In other words, this technique focuses on motivation to achieve a specific goal, as well as instruction that can condition and help individuals practice a new behavior. It promotes clear visualization of one's goals and a combination of two primary ideas addressed in the self-regulation research: (1) mental contrasting and (2) implementation intentions. The first idea, mental contrasting, promoted by Gabriele Oettingen (2000), involves envisioning a successful future and then contrasting it with the reality of the present. The second strategy, implementation intentions, takes the form of if-then statements ("if X occurs, then I will put plan Y into action") and helps individuals react positively to real challenges they anticipate prior to their actual occurrence (Gollwitzer & Sheeran, 2006). This combined strategy, MCII, is also sometimes referred to by the acronym WOOP, which stands for wish, outcome, obstacle, and plan.

The positive findings from utilizing MCII in areas such as coping with social insecurity and improving relationships (Houssais, Oettingen, & Mayer, 2013) suggest that this strategy would also be beneficial in social network development during study abroad. MCII has only been applied in one piece of study abroad–related research to date. In Lee et al. (2018), eighty-four English language learners (ELLs) in an intensive English program in the United States were involved in a study which evaluated the impact of MCII on students' English-speaking social networks. Results report that students who utilized this self-regulation technique significantly outperformed non-MCII users in areas of durability (frequency of English use) and dispersion (the number of social groups one belongs to), but no other significant differences were found. This is the only known study of MCII and L2 social networks to date.

The present study seeks to increase our understanding of how MCII can promote social networks among L2 learners on study abroad in an intensive English program. Our research questions are as follows:

1. Are there significant differences in the social network development (measured by size, intensity, durability, dispersion, and density) of students who are taught MCII techniques and those not taught?
2. How do those who are in their first semester of the program (new students) compare in their social network development with those who have been in the program two or more semesters (returning students)? Does MCII impact new and returning students differently?

3. Do the students perceive MCII as a positive, neutral, or negative tool in regard to helping them to develop their social networks throughout the semester?

Method

Participants

One-hundred and seven English language learners (fifty-five males, fifty-two females) participated fully in this study. All participants were English language learners at the same intensive English program in the United States, which is located near two universities (Brigham Young University and Utah Valley University). Most students at this institution are from middle-class or wealthy families and seek to earn degrees in the United States before moving back to their home countries. On average, they study for two to three semesters at this intensive English program before enrolling in an American university or returning home. Nearly three-quarters of our sample (seventy-four participants) were returning students. The thirty-three students in their first semester of the program are referred to as new students throughout the chapter, and the rest as returning (Table 8.1).

The intensive English program provided limited structured opportunities to meet locals, only offering an optional peer mentoring program to students. Access to other English speakers in the community was available; students could find these opportunities through public transportation, many community events, a variety of university activities, church programs, and roommates. It is important to note that since this intensive English program is affiliated with

Table 8.1 Participant Demographics

First Language Background	Age	English Ability
Spanish (59%)	Range: 18–56	Range: Intermediate to Advanced*
Portuguese (15%)	Median: 24	
Chinese (14%)		
Korean (3%)		
Japanese (2%)		
Other (Burmese, Malagasy, Russian, Turkman, Mongolian, and Berber Languages, comprising 1% each)		

*According to the American Council on the Teaching of Foreign Languages (2012) proficiency guidelines.

Brigham Young University, a private church university, most of the students who come to study English are religious and choose to attend nearby religious services and activities in English. Our participants were no exception and participated in a religious community with English speakers in a variety of ways.

Materials

Data on the participants' English-speaking social networks were collected through the Study Abroad Social Interaction Questionnaire (SASIQ), and students' perceptions of MCII were measured using a brief survey. Qualitative insights about attitudes toward this self-regulation strategy were obtained from students' responses to weekly writing prompts. Each of these instruments is described in further detail in the following section.[1]

SASIQ

This questionnaire was originally created by Dewey and colleagues (Dewey et al., 2012; Dewey, Belnap, et al., 2013; Dewey, Ring, Gardner, & Belnap, 2013) and has been used in a number of studies to measure social networks; it is based on the Montreal Index of Linguistic Integration (Segalowitz & Ryder, 2006). This questionnaire has been used to determine the size, durability, intensity, density, and dispersion of learners' social networks (Dewey et al., 2014; Baker-Smemoe, Dewey, Bown, & Martinsen, 2014). Size refers to the number of friends a learner interacts with and was measured by asking learners to list the names of their English-speaking friends (up to 15). Durability measures the frequency of interaction with an individual, by asking participants to indicate how often they spoke English with each of the individuals they had listed. Five options were available: *never, rarely, sometimes, often,* and *very often*. Intensity, or the closeness of the relationship, was determined through use of a Likert scale that ranged from *acquaintance* to *very-close friend*, which was numerically represented from 1 to 8. Density refers to the number of connections within a social group. Lastly, dispersion measures the number of social groups that an individual belongs to, such as school, church, roommates, work, and so on. The original survey questions were adapted to the English level of the participants, mainly through simplification of the instructions. For example, "Do your friends know each other? If your friends know each other, click and drag their names into the same box." Although these simpler questions were not piloted in advance of the study, they were carefully crafted to target an English level that could be understood by the lowest proficiency groups being surveyed.

MCII Survey

The MCII survey contained six questions designed to assess the students' perceptions toward MCII and the degree to which they implemented the technique. Students responded to each question using a six-point Likert scale, ranging from *strongly disagree* to *strongly agree*. The questions were as follows: (1) "WOOP [MCII] helped me to meet more English-speakers (native and nonnative)," (2) "WOOP helped me to develop close English-speaking friends," (3) "WOOP helped me to overcome my obstacles to speaking English with people," (4) "WOOP helped me to speak more English," (5) "I will continue using WOOP to make social goals," and (6) "I used WOOP every week."

MCII Writing Prompts

In addition to quantitative measures, qualitative data were gathered from the participants via responses to weekly writing prompts. The prompts targeted different aspects of social network development and MCII, such as goal setting, describing outcomes, foreseeing obstacles, and making a plan. The following questions were included, all of which were repeated at least twice over the course of the fourteen-week semester: "What WOOP social interaction goal do you have this week?"; "What is an outcome you expect from speaking English with other people?"; "What is an obstacle that stops you from interacting with others in English? Remember, the obstacle needs to be in your control"; "What is your plan to overcome this obstacle?"; and "How did using WOOP help your social interaction last week?"

Design

Out of the six existing proficiency levels already established at the intensive English program, the highest four levels were selected for the study; we did not include the two lowest levels due to insufficient English proficiency. There were enough classes at each level to form a control and treatment class. In other words, there were a total of eight classes; four made up the control group and four the treatment. Care was taken to ensure that both of the classes within each level were taught by the same instructor to mitigate possible teacher variables, and all classes were focused on the same skill area, writing. Overall, there were a total of forty-seven students in the control group (an average class size of eleven students), and sixty in the treatment (an average class size of fifteen students). Within the treatment group, there were eighteen new students and forty-two returning. The control group had fifteen new students and thirty-two returning.

Procedures and Analyses

The SASIQ was administered to all participants during the second week of the semester and was administered again during the last week of classes. Administrators were on site to answer questions or clarify any portion of the survey if the students needed assistance. Due to the large variance in the number of friends that the participants listed, only the three highest-rated friends (in terms of intensity) were averaged to calculate intensity. Durability was coded numerically from 0 (never) to 4 (very often). After data were collected from the pre- and post-SASIQs, all participants' changes in social network measures were calculated. We then conducted a two-way analysis of covariance (ANCOVA) on these overall changes, controlling for the pre-SASIQ scores. In addition, post hoc Tukey tests were run in order for us to see the interaction effect of new versus returning students.

All students in the treatment group took the MCII survey immediately following the post-SASIQ. These responses were numerically coded from 1 to 6 for statistical analyses, 1 being strongly disagree and 6 being strongly agree; the other options were disagree, somewhat disagree, somewhat agree, and agree.

MCII instruction was given to the four treatment classes on a day following the administration of the pre-SASIQ. The presentation focused on the benefits of social networks (e.g. linguistic and emotional), and a clear application of MCII was delivered using materials created by Oettingen.[2] These materials elicited each step of MCII using WOOP from the participants. The final step of the plan required an if-then statement. Students were encouraged to utilize MCII in their social network development throughout the semester.

It is important to note that all students in the intensive English program received some basic self-regulation training throughout the semester, such as how to be strategic learners, evaluate their efforts, and take care of themselves physically and mentally. This training was not done systematically across levels or teachers and was dependent on the instructors incorporating it into their classes.

After the initial MCII presentation, a writing exercise was done once a week within each of the treatment classes for the rest of the semester. These weekly ten-minute, timed-writing tasks required students to respond to predetermined prompts that asked them to articulate their use of MCII in regard to their social networks (prompts are outlined in the Materials section).

At the end of the semester, we reviewed the writing entries of the fifty-five students who had completed the MCII survey at the end of the semester, approximately 605 entries total. Entry length widely varied, ranging from 50 to 250 words, based on learner proficiency and motivation. We made four categories: new students who overall disagreed with the MCII survey prompts, returning students who overall disagreed, new students who overall agreed, and returning students who overall agreed. The constant comparative method was used (Glaser & Strauss, 1967) to identify emerging themes, commonalities, and patterns in both the agreeing and disagreeing participants. The process was cyclical and iterative, with all writing being revisited as new patterns became apparent. Given the quantity of data, we chose one student from each of the four categories whose responses were specifically illustrative of MCII use within social network development.

The quantitative findings from our data (the SASIQ and MCII survey) will first be presented, followed by the qualitative written responses of four students.

Results

SASIQ Data Results

The changes between the pre- and post-SASIQ for the control and treatment groups are reported in Table 8.2. Out of the five social network variables, there are no significant differences between the treatment and control groups. Summarizing the data, we see that both groups have positive changes in the social network measures of durability (frequency of English use) and intensity (closeness of the relationship); the MCII group has an overall larger change in both these variables, although this difference is small. The control group has positive changes in density (number of friends within social groups), whereas the treatment group shows negative changes. Both groups show a decrease in size (number of friends) and dispersion (number of social groups) by the end of the semester, with the control group having a higher negative change. The largest differences between these two groups are in measures of size (−0.421) and intensity (−0.364). Again, none of these differences were significant.

Although there are no significant differences between the control and treatment groups, it is important to point out that there does exist a significant interaction effect among the variables of size and intensity. This interaction effect means we cannot rely on the main effect data in Table 8.2 to understand what is occurring in the control and treatment groups; we must look at the effect of what a new versus returning student had on the control and treatment groups,

Table 8.2 Estimated Differences from Pre- to Post-SASIQ: Control vs. Experimental (MCII)

SN Measure	Estimated Change	SE	Partial Eta-Squared (Effect Size)	p	95% CI LL	UL
Size	−0.421	0.860	0.002	0.626	−2.127	1.285
Control	−0.428					
MCII	−0.007					
Durability	−0.123	0.150	0.003	0.416	−0.422	0.176
Control	0.043					
MCII	0.166					
Intensity	−0.364	0.245	0.021	0.141	−0.850	0.122
Control	0.083					
MCII	0.447					
Density	0.075	0.407	0.007	0.855	−0.734	0.884
Control	0.007					
MCII	−0.068					
Dispersion	−0.060	0.235	0.000	0.799	−0.526	0.406
Control	−0.065					
MCII	−0.005					

Note: SN = social network; CI = confidence interval; LL = lower limit, UL = upper limit;

which we see in Table 8.3. Within the control group, there are no significant differences between new and returning students among any of the five social network measures. In contrast, the results for the MCII group reveal that the new students significantly outgained the returning students in terms of size and intensity of their networks. Among these variables, the largest difference between new and returning MCII participants can be seen in size, where the new students reported having nearly two more friends at the end of the semester than they started with, whereas returning students lost two friends. The intensity (closeness of relationship) between the MCII new and returning students shows that the new students reported an average of 1.3 points higher than the returning students, which is considerable since this variable was measured on an eight-point Likert scale.

MCII Survey Results

We used MCII survey to evaluate the students' overall perceptions toward this self-regulation technique. First, the six Likert scale statements about MCII gave us quantitative insights concerning the students' attitudes and perceptions toward their implementation of MCII. Table 8.4 shows the

Table 8.3 Estimated Differences from Pre- to Post-SASIQ: MCII New vs. Returning Students

SN Measure	Estimated Change	SE	Partial Eta-Squared (Effect Size)	p	95% CI LL	95% CI UL
MCII Size	3.994	1.491	0.047	0.004	0.994	1.285
New	1.990	1.274		1.000	−3.380	3.273
Returning	−2.004					
Control Size	−0.054					
Control N	−0.456					
Control R	−0.401					
MCII Durability	−0.114	0.217	0.000	0.952	−0.680	0.451
New	0.094	0.243		0.994	−0.572	0.700
Returning	0.209					
Control Durability	0.064					
New	0.093					
Returning	0.029					
MCII Intensity	1.257	0.328	0.085	0.001	0.401	2.113
New	1.076	0.361		0.988	−0.824	1.059
Returning	−0.182					
Control Intensity	0.112					
New	0.142					
Returning	0.024					
MCII Density	1.201	0.534	0.016	0.118	−0.196	2.599
New	0.533	0.600		0.989	−1.761	1.378
Returning	−0.668					
Control Density	−0.192					
New	−0.089					
Returning	0.103					
MCII Dispersion	0.484	0.344	0.010	0.497	−0.414	1.382
New	0.277	0.378		1.000	−0.947	1.028
Returning	−0.208					
Control Dispersion	0.040					
New	−0.089					
Returning	−0.129					

Note: SN = social network; CI = confidence interval; LL = lower limit, UL = upper limit; R = returning student; N = new student.

percentages of students who agreed or disagreed to each of the six Likert scale questions (see Materials section for complete questions). For example, in response to the first question, "WOOP [MCII] helped me to meet more English-speakers (native and nonnative)," 69 percent of all treatment students indicated some degree of agreement, whether that was somewhat agree, agree, or strongly agree. Looking at each of the six questions, we see that most students agreed with each of the statements to at least some extent,

Table 8.4 Percentage of MCII Students Indicating Degree of Agreement to MCII Survey Questions

Variable	Meet People	Close Friends	Overcome Obstacles	Speak More	Continue WOOP	Used Weekly
% Agree	69	67	73	71	69	69
% Disagree	31	33	27	29	31	31

indicating that most students had a positive perception of MCII throughout the semester. The percentage of new (eighteen) versus returning (thirty-seven) students who agreed and disagreed was also calculated. The differences were very small (ranging from 0.0 to 0.3) and none were significant. In other words, no significant difference was found between new and returning students in their overall perception of MCII.

MCII Writing Prompt Responses

While quantitative data can help us visualize overall trends in our study, it is through qualitative data that we gain a more comprehensive picture of what learners were thinking and feeling about MCII during the fourteen-week semester. We highlight the experience of four students in this section. First, we will look at one new and one returning student who did not agree that MCII was helpful (an average rating of 3 or less). Then, we will examine the entries of one new and one returning student who, on average, agreed that MCII was helpful (an average rating of 4 or more on the MCII survey).

New, Disagree. Damian[3] was one of the eighteen new students in the MCII treatment group. He was among the five new students who did not agree that MCII was helpful. He already had several close friends at the beginning of the semester, but his apparently diligent effort to use MCII did not enhance his social networks. His social network changes on the post-survey are all zero, indicating that Damian had no social network gains or losses. This does not seem to be due to lack of trying, for he details his self-regulation efforts in his writing and repeatedly emphasizes his desire to speak more English and put forth his best effort. In the first entry of the semester, he writes:

> I want to learn and memorize the 10 words in the "Vocabulary Packet." I will use that words in conversations with the parents of my girldfriend [sic]. I want to have more good feelings with my english because I need to feel more trusted with my English . . . I would like to have great conversation.

In addition to outlining his goals to speak English with the people around him, Damian clearly iterates some of his obstacles to speaking English and his plan to overcome them, stating,

> I think the most important obstacle is that I don't want to have mistakes speaking . . . I need to feel more comfortable with myself using the english. My plan is keep trying, keep practicing, keep speaking although I have a lot of mistake. My plan needs to include do not speak spanish with my family and with my girldfriend [*sic*]. Practicing is the only way to achieve my goals even though having mistakes.

Although Damian continued this pattern of recording goals, identifying obstacles, and making a plan to overcome them throughout the semester, he ultimately felt that MCII was not a helpful exercise for him. In his last entry of the semester, the prompt for which was "How did WOOP [MCII] help your social interaction last week?," he says:

> I'm goint [*sic*] to be honest. WOOP is not helpful for me because I only remember my goals here in class. I don't make sure this in my weeks. I have my personal goals in my life but I don't like to write my goals in a place. I think that I'm achieving my own goals or doing my own efforts without count or think what I need to do.

Damian's last entry informs us that his attempts to use MCII were only demonstrated during class and were not continued at home. This seems to be a combination of not remembering his resolutions as well as feeling that he was already achieving goals. His writing shows us that even though a student can follow all of the steps of MCII during class, that same pattern may not carry over into life outside of the classroom.

Returning, Disagree. Most of the returning students who, on average, reported that MCII was unhelpful, did not elaborate on anything specific in their writing entries. Several of these students wrote one-sentence responses such as "It does not help," "It was interesting," and "Well, it kept me to remind to apply the goals that I seted [*sic*]," but none went into any further detail, even though they were given seven minutes to write. A student who did write with more detail was Daniel. His average response to the MCII survey was "somewhat disagree" and his social network measures support his sentiments. His post-SASIQ changes show that he lost three friends, spoke English less, wasn't as close to his friends, and belonged to two fewer social groups than when he began the semester. Contradictorily, his results also show his friendship groups were larger.

Daniel's written entries show that he did make an effort to use MCII, despite his lack of results. Early in the semester, he makes a specific goal to improve his social networks, writing,

> My week goal is to talk with anyone at anytime. I mean, everytime I have a chance to talk with a stranger, I will take it.

Daniel continues writing his goals and accompanying obstacles throughout the semester, showing forth more effort than his peers who disagreed that MCII was helpful. He even writes a positive response in answer to the question "How did WOOP help your social interaction last week?":

> It really helped me a lot. Everyday, I tried to have a conversation with anyone. I did not feel fear after all. I think I made a lot of friends . . . I did not focus on my WOOP [MCII] goals, but I try my best, and all I can say is that I see the benefits of putting goals every week.

Although Daniel says that MCII really helped him, he also comments that he was more focused on trying his best than on his specific MCII goals. Perhaps, like Damian, he did not remember his goals while outside of the classroom, even though he thought the practice of weekly goal setting was beneficial.

Daniel wrote that he made a lot of friends and responded "somewhat agree" to the survey item, "WOOP [MCII] helped me make more friends." However, his social network measure of size (number of friends) went down by three at the end of the semester. This contrasting result could be a case of inaccurate self-report data, or perhaps he would have lost more friends had he not utilized MCII.

New, Agree. Mahiro is a new student to the English program who utilized MCII. By the end of the semester, all of her social network measures had increased. She made nine more friends, had closer relationships, joined one new social group, and had larger social groups. Her smallest change is in durability (frequency of English use), which is quite small, but is a gain.

Similarly to Damian and Daniel, Mahiro elaborates weekly on her goals and obstacles throughout the semester. During the first half of the semester, she identifies the following goal and obstacle:

> My goal for this weekend is to talk to native speaker, and make friends. I usually talk to native speaker in my family, and I have really good time with them. But I want to make friends from this country, and speak English fluently . . . I am so shy, so I will try to overcome my obstacle, and change better person than before.

Mahiro followed the same weekly pattern of goal setting, identifying obstacles, and making plans that Damian and Daniel did, but she experienced much more social network success than them. Later in the semester, Mahiro iterates that MCII (WOOP) was key in helping her achieve social interaction in English:

> Woop helped me to be better using English ... I tried to use English better, and speak English with my friends, families, teachers and so on. I really like to using WOOP. WOOP help me to find my obstacle and overcome it. I really love my way of thinking right now. I have positively thinking, and I have a lot of friends right now.

From this entry, we can infer that Mahiro made MCII part of her life outside of the classroom and let it influence her thinking, whereas Damian and Daniel seemed to keep the exercise an in-class only activity. Perhaps Mahiro possessed higher motivation to become friends with native speakers than her counterparts, which helped her to remember her goals.

Returning, Agree. Camila reported MCII as an overall helpful tool for her, and kept her writing entries focused on goals, obstacles, and plans concerning her English-speaking social networks. However, the quantitative data do not paint the same picture. According to the SASIQ data, she did not make any more friends, did not speak English more frequently, or have stronger relationships by the end of the semester. She did report belonging to one more social group, but also recorded that her social groups had fewer people in them. As we can see from her writing entries, these results are not from lack of trying. She writes her goals at the beginning of the semester:

> My WOOP social interaction goal for this week is talking more with my friends, and meet more people. For that, I will talk with all my coworkers, I will spend more time with my roommates, and I will do an activity like going camping.

Camila writes about her goals, specific obstacles (living with nonnative English speakers), and plans (insisting on English only in the apartment), and reports that MCII assisted her in these efforts. She says:

> WOOP [MCII] helped me last week with my interaction by giving me the courage that I needed to overcome my obstacles ... It is amazing how WOOP helped me and also helped other people.

Despite not having any social network gains, Camila felt that MCII helped her social efforts. Without this tool, she might have lost friends or spoken less English, but with MCII she actively pursued her goals and at least maintained her social networks. Both her and Daniel's experience suggests that MCII may help give people positive social experiences, even if they do not see numeric social network gains from it.

It is feasible that the students who benefitted the most from MCII were already highly self-regulated to begin with. Sevincer, Mehl, and Oettingen (2017) found that naturally self-regulated people utilize mental contrasting without specifically being taught it. Perhaps the more self-regulated individuals among our study were the ones who benefited most from MCII because they were already using it in some form, and the in-class presentation of MCII and weekly timed-writing prompts enhanced their preexisting self-regulation skills by providing consistency and clarity.

Discussion

Students that have close relationships during study abroad can benefit linguistically, socially, and emotionally. To illustrate, intensity has been shown to be a predictor of language proficiency development in several studies (Baker-Smemoe et al., 2014; Dewey, Belnap, and Hillstrom, 2013), possibly because closer friendships often lead to a greater degree of social and linguistic opportunities than mere acquaintances. For example, deeper relationships often involve language that moves beyond small talk and into more complex structures. In addition to linguistic benefits, these friendships allow learners to feel integrated with the L2 culture and socially supported, feel higher motivation to learn the language, experience enhanced attitudes toward the culture, and experience a sense of increased well-being (Dörnyei, 2003; Isabelli-García, 2006; Scott, 2017).

Research has shown that new students are more prone to have high points of L2 contact early on in their study abroad program, but as time goes by, they experience a drop in this number (McManus, Mitchell, & Tracy-Ventura, 2014). As social network size declines over time, the remaining relationships tend to increase in intensity (Granovetter, 1973; Hillstrom, 2011). The only participants in our study that somewhat followed this trend were the new MCII students, who had both higher and more intense social networks by the end of the semester. Perhaps the gains we see in both size and intensity in the new MCII students can be attributed to the fact that these students more fully utilized MCII because it helped them to overcome acculturation challenges, which are typically present while adjusting to a new environment (Berry, 1980). It is possible that MCII assisted them throughout the various phases of acculturation (Burnett & Gardner, 2006), therefore helping them to establish larger and closer social relationships.

High hopes for native speaker interaction often accompany language learners at the beginning of study abroad, but as time goes on, a student may experience a reality contrary to their initial expectations of social interaction and become discouraged. Perhaps this is the case with the returning students in our study, who had already made attempts to build their social networks during their first semester of the program but became frustrated with a lack of progress. Even after the MCII returning students were introduced to a tool that could assist them, it is possible they did not see how MCII might address their concerns. Thus, they had a decline in both the size and the intensity of their relationships. New control students were likely eager to make friends and use their English skills with the people around them, but without self-regulation support, they too had a decrease in social network measures. Only the new MCII students significantly increased in social network size and intensity. This suggests that MCII may be most beneficial when it is implemented at the onset of a study abroad program, since it combines the high motivation of new students with a clear strategy.

Pedagogical Application

Individual differences and diverse sociocultural contexts make it impossible to find a "one size fits all" solution to effectively build social networks, and self-regulation strategies are no different. Although MCII was perceived as helpful for many students, it was not for others. Introducing MCII as one of many self-regulation strategies in the classroom could allow students to choose what technique suits them best, instead of just focusing on one method. That being said, it can be difficult for any individual to consistently remember and apply the strategies he or she has endeavored to utilize. As discussed earlier, Damian wrote that he did not strictly use the technique but did appreciate the reminder to set goals. Although the writing assignments were not favorably viewed by all students, we feel that using some class time to focus on MCII gave students a consistent, structured form to practice self-regulation. Whether or not teachers choose to offer MCII or other techniques as part of their curriculum, taking time during class to help students understand what self-regulation is and how to develop it can pay off in dividends outside of the classroom, as we saw in Mahiro's experience.

Teacher-led discussions of social network goals and MCII application could provide students an avenue to support and encourage each other. The writing prompts in our study were not shared among classmates, but it could be beneficial to take a few minutes each week to write and/or discuss social network and MCII successes and failures. This exercise would give the teacher and classmates a chance to brainstorm together about how to overcome obstacles and would reinforce students' goals and perhaps motivation.

Limitations and Suggestions for Future Research

One major limitation of this study is the use of self-report data. Self-report data are notorious for being inaccurate, yet with something as complex as measuring social networks, they are often utilized in efforts to capture students' perceptions and social interaction trends. Using both quantitative and qualitative sources helped us to triangulate the data, thus giving us a more complete understanding of students' experiences with MCII. Having additional ways to capture social network trends, such as through interviews or speaking with the participants' friends, could provide further insights. For instance, following a handful of students and interviewing them every week could provide a more in-depth look at how students incorporate MCII into their social interaction or language learning goals, challenges, and successes.

Conclusion

This study investigated the impact that MCII had on English language learners' social networks. The quantitative analysis found that most results were nonsignificant, although students who were new to the program and utilized MCII experienced significant social network gains in terms of size (number of friends) and intensity (closeness of the relationship). MCII positively impacted new students' social networks the most, and the majority of MCII participants reported that this self-regulation technique helped them to meet more English speakers, speak more English, develop closer relationships, and overcome obstacles to forming social networks. Insights from students' written responses showed us that MCII is a useful self-regulatory tool to consider in helping learners build their social networks while abroad.

Self-regulation research shows promise from motivational perspectives, which focus on perseverance toward goals, and cognitive perspectives, which focus largely on cognitive strategies for coping with challenges, for building belief in one's self-regulatory resources, and reframing one's identity. Identity reframing is particularly relevant in study abroad settings, given that "access to social networks" during study abroad "must be negotiated within the context of inequitable power structures, and this often requires learners to exercise considerable agency to reframe their relationship to their interlocutors and thereby resist marginalization" (Tullock, 2018: 262) (cf. Durbidge, Chapter 10, this volume). Additional studies connecting cognitive approaches to self-regulation with identity, social network development, and related variables associated with study abroad are in order, in particular given the promising findings of the present study and the clear importance of both agency and social network development during study abroad (c.f. Tullock, 2018; Ryan & Mercer, 2011).

Notes

1 All materials can be obtained electronically by contacting the first author at hannah_brown@byu.edu.
2 These materials can be found at http://woopmylife.org.
3 All students' names are pseudonyms.

References

Allwright, D. (1984). Why don't learners learn what teachers teach? The interaction hypothesis. In D. M. Singleton and D. G. Little (Eds.), *Language learning in formal and informal contexts* (pp. 3–18). Dublin: Irish Association for Applied Linguistics.

American Council on the Teaching of Foreign Languages. (2012). ACTFL Proficiency Guidelines 2012. Retrieved from https://www.actfl.org/publications/guidelines-and-manuals/actfl-proficiency-guidelines-2012

Baker-Smemoe, W., Dewey, D. P., Bown, J., & Martinsen, R. A. (2014). Variables affecting L2 gains during study abroad. *Foreign Language Annals*, 47(3), 464–86.

Berry, J. (1980). Acculturation as varieties of adaptation. In A. Padilla (Ed.), *Acculturation: Theory, models and some new findings* (pp. 9–25). Washington, DC: AAAS.

Bown, J., Dewey, D. P., & Belnap, R. K. (2015). Student interactions during study abroad in Jordan. In R. F. Mitchell, K. McManus, & N. T. Ventura (Eds.), *Social interaction, identity and language learning during residence abroad* (pp. 199–222). Essex: Eurosla Monograph Series Four.

Burnett, C., & Gardner, J. (2006). The one less traveled by . . .: The experience of Chinese Students in a UK University. In P. M. Byram & D. A. Feng (Eds.), *Living and studying abroad: Research and practice* (pp. 64–90). Retrieved from https://ebookcentral.proquest.com

DeKeyser, R. (2010). Monitoring processes in Spanish as a second language during a study abroad program. *Foreign Language Annals, 43*(1), 80–92.

Dewey, D. P., Belnap, R. K., & Hillstrom, R. (2013). Social network development, language use, and language acquisition during study abroad: Arabic language learners' perspectives. *Frontiers: The Interdisciplinary Journal of Study Abroad, 22*, 84–110.

Dewey, D. P., Bown, J., Baker Smemoe, W., Martinsen, R. A., Gold, C., & Eggett, D. (2014). Language use in six study abroad programs: An exploratory analysis of possible predictors. *Language Learning, 64*(1), 36–71. doi:10.1111/lang.12031

Dewey, D. P., Bown, J., & Eggett, D. (2012). Japanese language proficiency, social networking, and language use during study abroad: Learners' perspectives. *Canadian Modern Language Review, 68*(2), 111–37. doi:10.3138/cmlr.68.2.111

Dewey, D. P., Ring, S., Gardner, D., & Belnap, R. K. (2013). Social network formation and development during study abroad in the Middle East. *System: An International Journal of Educational Technology and Applied Linguistics, 41*(2), 269–82. doi:10.1016/j.system.2013.02.004

Dörnyei, Z. (2003). Attitudes, orientations, and motivations in language learning: Advances in theory, research, and applications. *Language Learning, 53*, 3–32.

Fraser, C. C. (2002). Study abroad: An attempt to measure the gains. *German as a Foreign Language Journal, 1*, 45–65.

Freed, B. F. (1995). Language learning and study abroad. In B. F. Freed (Ed.), *Second language acquisition in a study abroad context* (pp. 3–33). Amsterdam: John Benjamins Publishing Co.

Glaser, B. G., & Strauss, A. L. (1967). *The discovery of grounded theory: Strategies for qualitative research*. Chicago: Aldine Publishing Company.

Gollwitzer, P. M., & Sheeran, P. (2006). Implementation intentions and goal achievement: A meta- analysis of effects and processes. *Advances in Experimental Social Psychology, 38*, 69–119.

Granovetter, M. S. (1973). The strength of weak ties. *American Journal of Sociology, 78*, 1360–80.

Hillstrom, R. (2011). *Social networks, language acquisition, and time on task while studying abroad in Jordan*. Unpublished master's thesis, Brigham Young University, Utah.

Houssais, S., Oettingen, G., & Mayer, D. (2013). Using mental contrasting with implementation intentions to self-regulate insecurity-based behaviors in relationships. *Motivation and Emotion, 37*(2), 224–33. doi:10.1007/s11031-012-9307-4

Isabelli-García, C. L. (2006). Study abroad social networks, motivation and attitudes: Implications for second language acquisition. In M. A. DuFon & E. Churchill (Eds.), *Language learners in study abroad contexts* (pp. 231–58). Tonawanda, NY: Multilingual Matters Ltd.

Johnson, K., & Johnson, H. (Eds.). (1999). Interaction hypothesis. In Keith Johnson and Helen Johnson (Eds.), *Encyclopedic dictionary of applied linguistics: A handbook for language teaching* (p. 174). Oxford: Blackwell Publishers.

Kirk, D., Oettingen, G., & Gollwitzer, P. M. (2013). Promoting integrative bargaining: Mental contrasting with implementation intentions. *International Journal of Conflict Management, 24*(2), 148–65.

Lantolf, J. P., & Pavlenko, A. (2001). (S)econd (L)anguage (A)ctivity theory: Understanding second language learners as people. In M. Breen (Ed.), *Learner contributions to language learning: New directions in research* (pp. 141–58). London: Longman.

Lee, V., Dewey, D. P., Trimble, H., & Belnap, R. K. (2018). Mental contrasting with implementation intentions, social networking and second language development. In J. Mynard & I. Brady (Eds.), *Stretching boundaries: Papers from the third International Psychology of Language Learning conference, Tokyo, Japan 7–10 June, 2018.* Tokyo: International Association of the Psychology of Language Learning (IAPLL).

Macaro, E. (2001). *Learning strategies in foreign and second language classrooms.* London: Continuum.

McManus, K., Mitchell, R., & Tracy-Ventura, N. (2014). Understanding insertion and integration in a study abroad context: The case of English-speaking sojourners in France. *Revue française de linguistique appliquée, 19*(2), 97–116.

Mendelson, V. G. (2004). 'Hindsight is 20/20': Student perceptions of language learning and the study abroad experience. *Frontiers: The Interdisciplinary Journal of Study Abroad, 10,* 43–63.

Milroy, L. (1980). *Language and social networks.* Oxford: Basil Blackwell Publisher.

Oettingen, G. (2000). Expectancy effects on behavior depend on self-regulatory thought. *Social Cognition, 18*(2), 101–29. http://dx.doi.org.erl.lib.byu.edu/10.1521/soco.2000.18.2.101

Oettingen, G. (2012). Future thought and behaviour change. *European Review of Social Psychology, 23*(1), 1–63.

Ortega, L. (2013). *Understanding second language acquisition.* New York: Routledge.

Oxford, R. L. (2011). *Teaching and researching language learning strategies.* Harlow: Pearson Education.

Pérez-Vidal, C., & Juan-Garau, M. (2011). The effect of context and input conditions on oral and written development: A study abroad perspective. *IRAL: International Review of Applied Linguistics in Language Teaching, 49*(2), 157–85.

Ring, S. A., Gardner, D., & Dewey, D. P. (2013). Social network development during study abroad in Japan. In K. Kondo- Brown, Y. Saito-Abbott, S. Satsutani, M. Tsutsui, &

A. Wehmeyer (Eds.), *New perspectives on Japanese language learning, linguistics, and culture* (pp. 95–122). Honolulu: University of Hawai'i, National Foreign Language Resource Center.

Ryan, S., & Mercer, S. (2011). Natural talent, natural acquisition and abroad: Learner attributions of agency in language learning. In T. Lamb, X. Gao, & G. Murray (Eds.), *Identity, motivation and autonomy in language learning* (pp. 105–16). Bristol: Multilingual Matters.

Savignon, S. J. (1997). *Communicative competence: Theory and classroom practice: Texts and contexts in second language learning.* New York: McGraw-Hill.

Scott, J. (2017). *Social network analysis.* London: Sage Publications.

Segalowitz, N., & Ryder, A. (2006). *Montreal Index of Linguistic Integration (MILI).* Unpublished questionnaire, Concordia University, Montreal, Quebec.

Sevincer, A. T., Mehl, P. J., & Oettingen, G. (2017). Well self-regulated people use mental contrasting. *Social Psychology, 48,* 348–64.

Trentman, E. (2012). *Study abroad in Egypt: Identity, access, and Arabic language learning.* Unpublished doctoral dissertation, Michigan State University, East Lansing, Michigan.

Tullock, B. (2018). Identity and study abroad. In Cristina Sanz and Alfonso Morales-Front (Eds.), *The Routledge handbook of study abroad research and practice* (pp. 262–74). New York: Routledge.

Wen-Ta Tseng, Dörnyei, Z., & Schmitt, N. (2006). A new approach to assessing strategic learning: The case of self-regulation in vocabulary acquisition. *Applied Linguistics, 27*(1), 78–102.

Wilkinson, S. (1998). Study abroad from the participants' perspective: A challenge to common beliefs. *Foreign Language Annals, 31*(1), 23–39.

Zimmerman, B. J. (1990). Self-regulated learning and academic achievement: An overview. *Educational Psychologist, 25*(1), 3–17.

Appendix

MCII Survey and Writing Prompts

MCII Survey

Instructions: Please select how much you agree or disagree with each statement. Options include strongly disagree, disagree, somewhat disagree, somewhat agree, agree, and strongly agree.

"WOOP helped me to meet more English-speakers (native and nonnative)"
"WOOP helped me to develop close English-speaking friends"
"WOOP helped me to overcome my obstacles to speaking English with people"
"WOOP helped me to speak more English"

"I will continue using WOOP to make social goals"
"I used WOOP every week"

Writing Prompts

Students were timed for ten minutes in class to respond to the following prompts every week during class. The prompts were cycled through and repeated two to three times throughout the fourteen-week semester.

1. "What WOOP social interaction goal do you have this week? For example, speak English to someone new everyday, or have a conversation with your roommates, etc."
2. "What is an outcome you expect from speaking English with other people?"
3. "What is an obstacle that stops you from interacting with others in English? Remember, the obstacle needs to be in your control"
4. "What is your plan to overcome this obstacle?"
5. "How did using WOOP help your social interaction last week?"

Developing Friendship or Practicing Japanese?
Differential Impacts of Language Pledge on Study Abroad Students

Atsushi Hasegawa

Introduction

Over the past decades, study abroad has become an integral part of the educational experience of many university students across the world. In particular, short-term study abroad has now become the most popular choice (Institute of International Education, 2018), rather than a semester or a year abroad, which used to be regarded as the major type of study abroad (Gore, 2005). Research on study abroad and its impacts on language development have also thrived over the decades, but there is a general sense of dissatisfaction about the inconclusive findings reported by the earlier research due to its excessive emphasis on a fixed and unidimensional view of study abroad contexts and on the outcomes rather than the processes of learner experience (Kinginger, 2009, 2013). Since Kinginger's (2009) seminal call for a process-oriented approach, we have witnessed an increase in qualitative research that examined students' various and detailed experiences during study abroad (Wolcott, 2016).

Interpersonal relationships that sojourners develop while abroad are considered to be crucial for second language (L2) development (e.g., Coleman, 2013, 2015; Dewey, Bown, & Eggett, 2012; Durbidge, Chapter 10, this volume; Isabelli-García, 2006; Kinginger, Wu, Lee, & Tan, 2016; Shively, 2018; Trimble-Brown et al., Chapter 8, this volume). Indeed, Baker-Smemoe, Dewey, Bown, & Martinsen (2014) examined various factors that potentially affect L2 gains during study abroad and identified cultural sensitivity and social network to be the most responsible predictors for L2 development. Recognizing the importance of interpersonal relationship while abroad, however, detailed accounts of ways in which such connections—with fellow students and local people alike—develop (or not) have yet to be explored with empirical data and a suitable analytical framework. This study aims to fill this gap by investigating the formation and transformation process of interpersonal connections of short-term study abroad participants in Japan through social network analysis. The program examined in this study has a strict language policy, called the "language pledge," requiring its participants to use Japanese all the time while prohibiting the use of English. Consequently, the study's analytical focus is directed on the dilemma experienced by the participants who face challenges in choosing between the building of friendship, on the one hand, and the use of Japanese, on the other. Through the close examination of how sojourners' relational configurations impact, and are impacted by, their engagement in social interaction and hence opportunities for language use, this study contributes to a better understanding of language socialization in a study abroad setting.

Background

As a popular way to enhance social experience and increase exposure to the target language during study abroad, homestay has been widely accepted and often emphasized as a housing option believed to be conducive to language development, which is also reflected in the abundance of research in this context (Allen, 2010; Dewey, Ring, Gardner, & Belnap, 2013; Shiri, 2015). However, recent studies have also started investigating various processes of peer socialization, which apparently expose different facets of study abroad experience (e.g., Diao, 2016). For example, unlike homestay, where daily interaction with a host family is generally presumed and expected, what appears to be crucial for peer socialization is, first and foremost, to create opportunities to meet and get acquainted with local students. Building relationships with locals has been repeatedly discussed as a challenge for many sojourners, especially in short-term programs (e.g., Shiri, 2015).

In addition, typical short-term programs are configured as an *island* or *enclave* type (Goodwin & Nacht, 1988), in which a cohort of students from the same country study together (and live together) often in isolation from the local university functions. Consequently, participants in such programs do not have to take courses and mingle with local students. In such a setting, peer socialization primarily develops among fellow compatriots. Coleman (2013, 2015) tried to capture this social process with a concentric circle model, comprised of conationals (i.e., compatriots) in the innermost circle, followed by other outsiders (e.g., foreign students from other countries) in the middle circle, and finally, locals in the outermost circle. Coleman argues that study abroad participants' friendship process proceeds from inner to outer circles. This tendency, indeed, coincides with the design feature of typical island programs.

Although Coleman's concentric model makes intuitive sense and it represents the very nature of island programs, actual social networks are rather intricately formed and transformed. First of all, a dichotomous distinction between locals and compatriots appears to be precarious and simplistic, which runs the risk of obscuring complexity in interpersonal relationships and linguistic diversity. Second, details of social processes within each circle—missing in Coleman's model—are of great importance for a better understanding of socialization during study abroad. Social networks should be regarded both as a consequence of and a cause for sojourners' social activities. This duality of social network is what makes the process of socialization intricate and significant for examining language development. Past research has primarily focused on one or the other (the majority of past SLA research treated social network as an independent variable for L2 gains), neglecting the duality.

In this study, I closely examine how social networks are formed and transformed in an eight-week language-intensive program in Japan. Students face the challenge of balancing rapport building with program participants (American classmates) and becoming friends with local students in addition to the challenge of creating constant opportunities to use the target language. These challenges are intertwined by a strict language policy imposed through the language pledge. Therefore, this study also delves into the effects of language pledge on students' social experience, which has been largely under-researched (cf., Muramatsu, 2018).

I employ social network analysis as a main analytical framework for this study. Social network analysis was born in sociology and has since been developed into an interdisciplinary, multidimensional research paradigm (Carrigan & Scott, 2011). Although social network analysis has recently gained growing attention in L2 research (e.g., Isabelli-García, 2006; Kurata, 2010, 2011; Zappa-Holman & Duff, 2015), most studies have focused exclusively on egocentric networks, rather than sociocentric networks. Egocentric networks, or personal networks, are measured and analyzed around one focal individual. That is, an egocentric network is always configured with one person in the center (i.e., ego), surrounded by his/her connections (i.e., alters). In contrast, sociocentric networks, or whole networks, are the agglutination of personal networks of all individuals who make up a definable social group. Therefore, the positioning of actors in a sociocentric network (i.e., centrality) is always relative to and reflective of all members' connections, or lack thereof, with each other. Island/enclave programs are well suited for the examination of whole networks because there is presumably a definable boundary with clear membership (cf., Kibler et al., Chapter 3, this volume). In this study, I analyze the whole network of a short-term study abroad program, as well as focal students' personal networks and their detailed social processes, in order to highlight the complex interplays of contextual elements, individual dispositions and orientations, and social processes.

The Study

The goals of this study are twofold. First, with the visualization method of social network analysis, I describe how the program network is configured and changed over the eight-week period. A close description of the network is crucial for understanding of the social processes that give rise to language development. In addition, I examine peer socialization processes of three individuals vis-à-vis their various handling of the language pledge over the program period. Each focal student orients to the different—and sometimes opposing—goals of building interpersonal relationships, on the one hand, and using and learning Japanese, on the other. My analysis was guided by the following three questions.

1. How was the social network of a short-term study abroad program formed and transformed over the program period?
2. How did focal students build connections with other American students, as well as with local Japanese students?
3. What was the role of the language pledge in focal students' experiences creating opportunities to use Japanese and simultaneously making friends in this program?

Program Context

I collected data from an eight-week program run by a US-based organization and hosted at a small private university in an urban region of Japan. According to the program website, various measures were taken to overcome the typical problems associated with short-term island programs, including the paucity of naturalistic language use outside the classroom walls and the challenges of making local friends. The campus was located in a residential area of the city, which provided easy access to city amenities while simultaneously creating a quiet and somewhat enclosed environment for students. The program enforced a twenty-four-hour language pledge, whereby students promised to communicate constantly in Japanese on and off the campus. To ensure students' use of Japanese outside of classes, local students were recruited and assigned as roommates. These Japanese students too signed the language pledge so that they would not speak English with their American roommates. Moreover, local student-members of the Japanese chat club—a student organization managed by the program—regularly joined the lunch-hour gathering in a designated lounge space in the classroom building.

The program rented fourteen apartments for student housing. Some apartments were within walking distance while others were a train ride away. The locations of these residences are schematically shown in Figure 9.1.

This program included thirty students in total. They came from various types of colleges in different states (e.g., large state universities, small liberal arts colleges, and Ivy League universities). Four Japanese levels—2nd year, 2.5th year, 3rd year, 4th year—were offered, and the students' Japanese levels varied roughly from novice-high to advanced-mid (ACTFL, 2012). Classes met four hours a

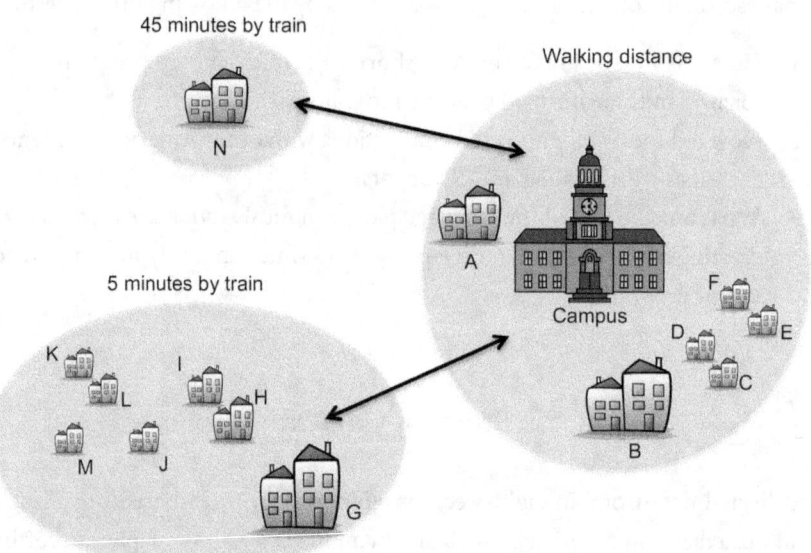

Figure 9.1 Student housing.

day on Monday through Friday. On weekends, a variety of extracurricular/cultural activities, such as temple visits and karaoke parties, were organized by the program or planned by the students.

Data

In order to closely describe the formation and transformation of interpersonal relationships, I collected data through the following methods: (a) social network surveys, (b) interviews, (c) activity logs, and (d) participant observation.[1] I invited all thirty students (fifteen males, fifteen females, age range: eighteen to thirty, age median: twenty) to participate in the study, all of whom gave consent. I designed the social network surveys based on the standard method laid out by Borgatti, Everett, & Johnson (2013) with a program roster. The questionnaire asked three questions concerning relational elements (i.e., friendship, closeness, and interaction), which were expected to elicit respondents' connections with one another and beyond the program. This study draws its analysis primarily from the closeness question:[2] "How close do you feel with this person?" The students were instructed to rate the closeness level of each individual on the roster with a sliding scale of 0 (distant), 1 (less than close), 2 (close), and 3 (very close). They were also asked to add other individuals that they interacted with (e.g., local students) and to rate their closeness levels in the same manner. The questionnaire was administered in the beginning (Week 1) and the end (Week 8) of the program. Based on the initial survey, I selected five students to examine closely their social experiences because their responses demonstrated particularly noticeable interpersonal behaviors (i.e., many ties, few ties, etc.). I asked focal students to keep track of their social activities using activity logs and conducted three interviews to discuss their experiences. Finally, throughout the program, I observed the students' activities during recess between classes, lunchtime, and after school as much as possible (i.e., one to eight hours per day, two to five days a week). Most of these observations took place in the lounge spaces in the classroom building.

Focal Students

In this study, I closely examine the cases of three focal students, Lily, Rose, and Joey,[3] all of whom showed distinct processes of socialization in the initial survey.

Lily is a twenty-year-old Korean American student, majoring in East Asian Studies at a private university in the Midwest. While she was born in Chicago, she lived and studied in international schools abroad, including Cambodia and Korea. Hence, she was raised bilingual in Korean and English. She started studying Japanese when she was in junior high school in Korea (two years) and continued in college (two-quarters = about twenty weeks). She was placed into Level 4, the highest level of the program. She lives in House H with an American and two Japanese, including her roommate, Yuka.

Rose is a 27-year-old English Education major at a regional state university in New England. Prior to the program, she self-taught Japanese and then took courses for two semesters in a community college. She then transferred to her current university, where no Japanese courses are offered. She continued self-education and organized a Japanese-English conversation table at her university, which allowed her to interact with Japanese speakers on a regular basis. She was placed into Level 2.5. Rose lives in House D with her Japanese roommate, Nana.

Joey is a 21-year-old Psychology major at a large state university in Texas. He had previously taken Japanese for one year at the university. His ethnic background is Chinese (his parents were from Taiwan), but he is unable to speak Chinese and is unfamiliar with Chinese characters. He was placed into Level 2, the lowest level in the program. Joey lives in House E with his Japanese roommate, Koji.

Social Network Formation and Transformation in the Program

This section presents the analysis of a network formed in this program. One of the premises of social network analysis includes visualization of complex relational configurations, which, otherwise, may not be easily observable. Based on the survey responses collected from the thirty program participants in Week 1, a graph was generated using a free software *Gephi* (Bastian, Heymann, & Jacomy, 2009), which is shown in Figure 9.2.

Each circle (i.e., node) represents an individual (i.e., actor), who is either a program participant (labeled with pseudonyms), a roommate (labeled as "R"), a chat club member (labeled as "C"), or other (labeled as "O"). The individuals enclosed with a circle (Lily, Joey, and Rose) are the focal participants of this study, whose interpersonal processes I closely describe in the next section. The lines (i.e., ties) indicate the connections between actors with directionality

Developing Friendship or Practicing Japanese?

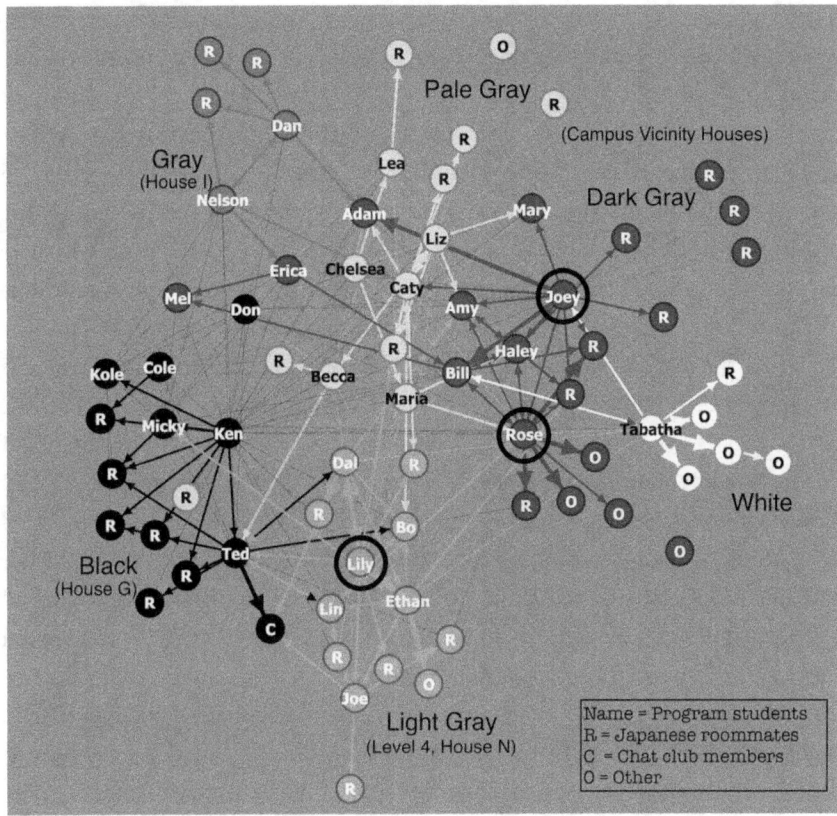

Figure 9.2 Whole program network in Week 1.

denoted by arrows. The thicker the line is, the stronger the connection is. In the present case, the relationships expressed as "very close" have the thickest line, followed by "close" and "less than close," respectively. Those relationships expressed as "distant" do not show any line (i.e., no connection).

The nodes in this graph are organized according to the layout algorithm "*Force Atlas*" (Jacomy, Venturini, Heymann, & Bastian, 2014), which aims to place related nodes close together while positioning unrelated nodes apart from each other. This layout also minimizes the overall number of line crossings. Therefore, Figure 9.2 shows a least entangled, hence most clearly partitioned, state of this network graph. Moreover, a modularity analysis (Blondel, Guillaume, Lambiotte, & Lefebvre, 2008) was conducted in order to examine the substructure of this network. The modularity analysis identified six subgroups of relatively denser connections among individuals. The groups are color-coded as black, dark gray, gray, light gray, pale gray, and white.

Overall, this is a well-connected group with many ties; however, mostly weak connections among actors. Nonetheless, we can also clearly identify distinct groups existing in this network. One indication is the positioning of the nodes—based on the Force Atlas layout—that illuminates areas with denser/stronger connections. The nodes positioned closely together correspond to the color-coded groups generated by the modularity analysis. Although the modularity analysis is only one of many different ways to identify substructures of a network, the boundaries of each color-coded group are clearly discernible in this graph. If we look closely at the details of nodes grouped together, it is clear that the institutional arrangements of the program are contributing to the emergence of these groups. For example, *Black* has the members of House G while *Gray* is based on the House I residents. *Light Gray* has the residents of House N or the students in Level 4. Most members of *Dark Gray*, *Pale Gray*, and *White* are living in the campus vicinity location and/or are taking either Level 2 or Level 2.5. Lily—one of the focal students—is grouped together with her classmates, Joe, Ethan, and Dal, in Level 4. Similarly, Joey and Rose are grouped together with other students living in the campus vicinity. Clearly, this program network is influenced by the institutional settings, such as housing assignments and class placements. As McPherson, Smith-Lovin, and Cook (2001) discussed, "geographic propinquity, families, organizations, and isomorphic positions in social systems all create contexts in which homophilous relations form" (p. 415). In the current case, the institutional settings created the propinquity, which led to the development of interpersonal relationships in this program. Students in a short-term program, like the current case, seldom have other social groups to connect with. In such a situation, a network arranged by the program would likely become their only social life.

However, relationships built on institutional arrangements may not necessarily coincide with personal preferences or dispositions. In fact, some notable changes occurred in the configurations of the network from Week 1 to Week 8. Figure 9.3 shows the program network in Week 8. First of all, a clear increase in the number of ties (355→813) and the density (0.068→0.099) is observed in this graph. The students developed stronger connections among themselves over the eight-week period. Second, although the modularity analysis generated similar groupings from Week 1 to Week 8, the boundaries of the groups are less delineable due to the overall mingling of people beyond the groups. Moreover, changes in membership occurred in some groups. For example, *Black* attracted significantly more people from other groups, while *Pale Gray* lost some members. As explained earlier, *Black* was primarily based

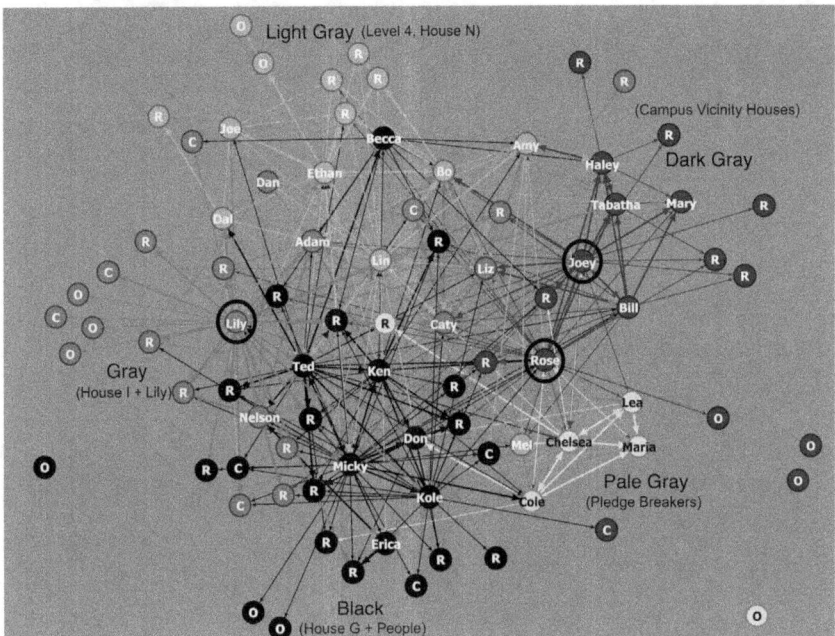

Figure 9.3 Program network in Week 8.

on the residents of House G. With twelve residents (i.e., six American male students and six Japanese male students), House G was the largest residence of the program and served as a "party house" where people—both American and Japanese students—gathered nightly for various activities. By contrast, *Pale Gray* now has only four program participants (i.e., Lea, Maria, Chelsea, and Cole). These four students made a collective decision to break the language pledge and started using English around Week 3. The pledge breaking eventually spread to other students, but these four students are the initial "oath-breakers." As I will explain in the following section, because of the social proximity to these students, Rose and Joey, who both remained in the same group, were some of the students most strongly affected by the pledge breaking. Moreover, Lily moved from *Light Gray* to *Gray*, which was initially based on the residents of House I. This group attracted Japanese students from other houses. Being surrounded by many Japanese students, Lily remained unaffected by the pledge breaking until the end.

In order to examine a clearer structure of this network, a graph was recreated only with the strong ties ("very close") as illustrated in Figure 9.4. With only strong connections, the structure of this network is more evident. There is a group of four students on the left side (in rectangular), who broke the pledge and

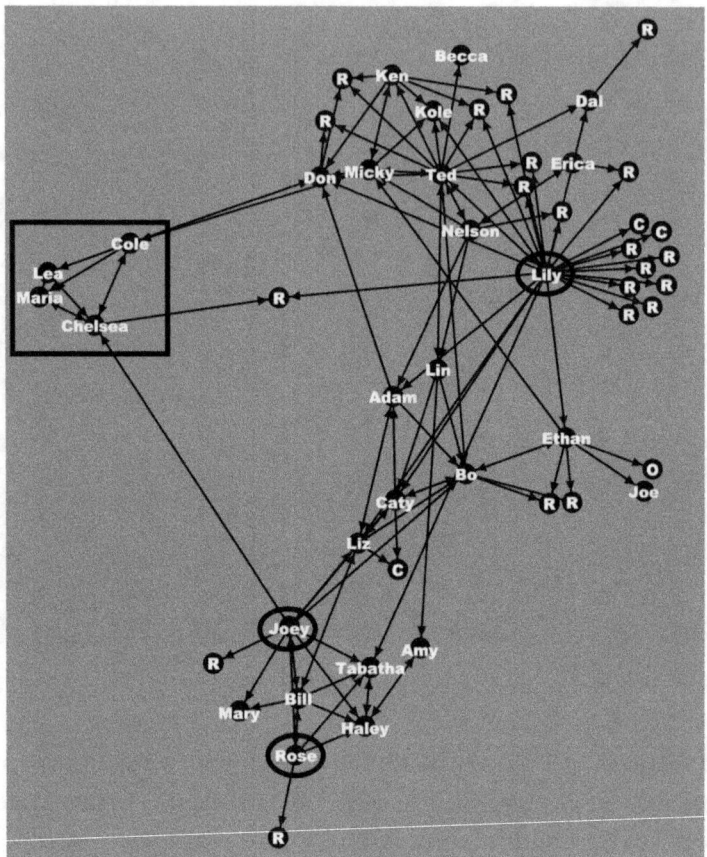

Figure 9.4 Program network in Week 8 (only "very close" ties).

started using English together around Week 3. They are not well connected with the rest of the program. Lily is part of a group of students congregated together on the upper-right corner. These are the groups of House G and House I. Rose and Joey belong to the group clustered at the bottom. And then, there is a loosely bound group of students who appear to be anchoring the upper and bottom groups. Note that there are many Japanese students ("R" and "C") involved in the upper group while the group on the bottom does not have many strong relationships with Japanese students. Therefore, although this whole network appears to be well connected on the surface level ("close" or "less than close"), when it comes to the strong connections ("very close"), it shows a different picture; the program is largely divided into groups of those who are closely related with local Japanese students, those who are not, and the oath-breakers.

In looking at the entire network configurations and how changes occurred, many questions arise as to what happened to each individual in this network. For example, how did Lily move from the original group to a different group and make many Japanese friends? Why did Rose and Joey stay in the original group and not develop close connections with Japanese? Did Rose and Joey go through similar experiences as they were in the same group? What are the effects of the language pledge and its breaking on these students? The next section will explore these issues by focusing on the three cases.

Interpersonal Processes of the Focal Students

Lily and Her Close Relationship with Japanese Students

As mentioned earlier, Lily's interpersonal relationships—immediate circles of people she was associated with—changed over the program period. At first, she had ties with those taking the same class (Level 4), but she gradually became closer with the people living in House I—the house adjacent to her own apartment. In the final questionnaire, she indicated that the Japanese students who gathered nightly in House I were her close friends.

She decided to participate in this program because she wanted to increase her confidence in speaking Japanese. Based on the placement test, she was initially assessed as Level 5, one level higher than Level 4, which, however, was not offered because she was the only student. Also, she had already passed the Level 2 (N2) of Japanese language proficiency test (JLPT),[4] which was, in fact, the target goal of the Level 4 class. Despite her relative proficiency, she repeatedly emphasized that she was not confident with her Japanese. In the interview, she alluded to a possible cause for this:

> I don't have any confidence. It is not that I continued studying Japanese for a long time, so I was not sure where my Japanese level stood because I didn't have chances to speak with Japanese people. When I went back to Korea, my Japanese teacher told me that my Japanese sounded like American. That was interesting.
>
> [July 27, 2016, original in Japanese]

She uses the word "interesting" here, but she recounted this episode as a somewhat negative and traumatic experience. This experience motivated her, at least partially, to participate in this program and to immerse herself in the environment where only Japanese was spoken. This orientation is shown in the following comment she made in response to my question about the reason why she often hung out with Japanese students:

> I feel more comfortable interacting with Japanese students [than American students]. That is because if I speak with Americans, my pronunciation [of Japanese] becomes like theirs, and I can meet American people anytime [in America].
>
> [July 27, 2016, original in Japanese]

Thus, she was actively seeking to interact with Japanese students in this program. As shown in Figure 9.3, her connections with local Japanese students living in House I grew over the period. At first, Lily apparently started going to House I because of her roommate, Yuka, who was friends with the Japanese residents of House I (all male house). House I was located adjacent to Lily and Yuka's apartment (see Figure 9.1). In addition, House I had a dining area large enough to hold several people. Therefore, she visited House I almost every night to study and see the Japanese students.

> I go to House I normally to study there because Japanese people are there. If I go there, I have chances to see Japanese students, so it's like "killing two birds with one stone."
>
> [July 27, 2016, original in Japanese]

It is remarkable that Lily's immediate social circle consisted exclusively of Japanese students (her roommate, Yuka, the male Japanese students living in House I, and their Japanese friends). According to Lily, the three American students living in House I were not interested in hanging out with the Japanese students. As such, Lily was regularly the only non-Japanese person at the nightly gathering. Lily shared her observation of this situation:

> I have invited Maria, but [she did not come because] her Japanese level is low, and she went for an easier choice than a challenge. Partners are not interested in helping [American students], either. They do not have motivation to help [American students]. They do what they enjoy. Japanese students enjoy hanging out with other Japanese students.
>
> [July 27, 2016, original in Japanese]

Maria is Lily's housemate in House H and was one of the four students that decided to break the pledge. Maria was uninterested in interacting with Japanese students, according to Lily's comment here, much like the American students living in House I.

To summarize Lily's interpersonal relationships, a graph of her egocentric network in Week 8 with only strong ties ("very close") is shown in Figure 9.5. Lily made the largest personal network involving many Japanese students, among the three focal students. It is clear that her motivation to interact with Japanese students and practice Japanese with friends helped form her social circle. Additionally, she was introduced to a group of Japanese students through her roommate, which helped her to belong to this group easily. To Lily, the language pledge was neither an issue nor necessary because she was able to achieve both language practice and friendship building with or without it. She even stated that she did not know about the collective pledge breaking by other students until a few weeks before the program ended, despite the fact that her housemate, Maria, was one of the catalysts for it. However, Lily's experience was rather special, which will be demonstrated in further examples.

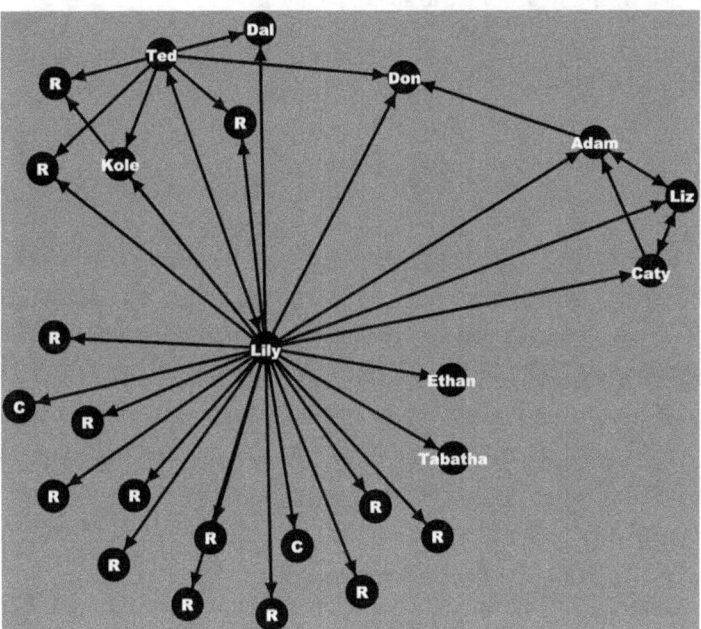

Figure 9.5 Lily's egocentric network in Week 8 (only "very close" ties).

Rose and Her Changing Relationships with Everyone

Rose participated in this program to improve her speaking skills. At her college, she organized a conversation exchange group with Japanese students and American students. Through this experience, she accumulated frustration with her inability to speak Japanese. According to her, she was able to comprehend but unable to speak Japanese in face-to-face conversations.

> I want to be able to speak Japanese. Up until now, when it comes to speaking Japanese, I have anxiety. Up until now, [I spoke Japanese] only over the phone. I was not able to [speak Japanese] directly. I was very nervous. I always only listened to people. My speaking ability and listening ability have a large gap.
>
> [June 23, 2016, original in Japanese]

She emphasized that she would like to be able to use "normal Japanese" by interacting with local Japanese students [June 23, 2016, original in Japanese]. In this regard, her initial motivation is somewhat comparable with Lily's—with a strong focus on speaking natural/normal Japanese with friends. Although the program is challenging to her, Rose apparently enjoys it because she is surrounded by many people who speak Japanese.

> Very very challenging every day it's challenging. Struggle to communicate every day just to do anything. That is great for me. Most people don't like challenge. I'm glad that I picked this program, because there are so many people around. Everyone is so friendly, invested in this program.
>
> [June 23, 2016]

Her social standing in this program was remarkable from the beginning. According to the social network survey, she had the highest in-degree centrality in Week 1, which means that she received the largest number of closeness ties from other participants in the program. In-degree centrality can be seen as the sign of prominence or popularity in the network. Her social standing was observable from her active demeanor. She was always found in the lounge space during recess, lunch, and after school, interacting with a variety of people. In the interviews, she also named many students—both Japanese and American—with whom she interacted on a regular basis.

However, Rose's behavior and comments gradually started to change around the midpoint. In particular, the relationship with her roommate, Nana, became increasingly adverse.

> Talking to her has become difficult sometimes. It's always been a little bit. Explaining things to her, she's uh- we have a personality difference, I like Nana, but often when I want to explain something to her and she already has a certain idea about it, I can't explain or convince her of anything.
>
> [July 8, 2016]

Moreover, around the same time, the language pledge was broken in her immediate circle. The four students who decided to speak English were all in her social circle. As such, she was apparently one of the first people to hear about this news from these students.

> But, everyone wanted to build more relationships, so that's why they made that decision together. "Let's break the pledge together so we can become better friends." Cole told me this yesterday, two days ago. "I can't make relationships. I can't." This is what he said. "I don't feel like I can make relationships if I have to speak Japanese all the time." He said "I wouldn't know y'all very well if I couldn't speak English with you."
>
> [July 8, 2016, original partly in Japanese]

At first, she was not very sympathetic about the situation. She felt it was not necessary for her to build relationships using English.

> I'm used to language barrier being there and building relationships despite it, overcoming that, I'm used to that. I love that. That's so cool for me. I'm really interested in cultural exchange and stuff. But, for the other students, they have expressed a lot of frustration like they have an issue with their roommate, they can't communicate well... They want to know people more, but they don't know the questions to ask or how to ask them. They don't feel super close with the other students.
>
> [July 8, 2016]

By contrasting "I" and "they" in this statement, she emphasizes that she is different from those who broke the pledge. However, in fact, her stance toward the use of English is not consistent or fixed. She is torn between her desire to improve her Japanese and her growing need to build relationships with people (American students).

> [I feel close with more] Americans. Bill, Tabatha, Joey are pretty much (close). It's because of the way they interact with me that I feel mutual closeness there. The Japanese tend to be a step apart, and they don't come to me necessarily with problems. There're certain things we talk about, and that's probably due to language barriers, or perceived language barriers, to certain extent, but like I was saying, I'm closest with certain, like, American students, because they have talked to me about certain things that are important to me as well, and things that I can tell are important to them they wanted to come to me with, and for the most part, we probably have done that in English. There's a certain level of that language barrier, like limiting my ability to become closer with them.
>
> [July 8, 2016]

Improving Japanese, her original reason for participation in the program, is conflicting with her inevitable social needs. Toward the end of the program, Rose came to understand that the use of English is justifiable for the sake of getting closer with her American friends. In the end, she perceived her relationships with Japanese to be dissimilar to the relationships with American students.

> I'm glad that I have made the friendships that I have with the American students. But, there's an edge to it. I noticed though a lot of people making friendships with American students comes at the cost making friendships with Japanese students. A lot of people were isolated and lonely. It was really impacting mental health.
> [August 1, 2016]

Rose's experience in the program started off as consistent with her initial motivation. She was making herself available to people in the program, which made her popular. She focused on making friends with everyone, but she started valuing deeper connections with her American friends more and more with the use of English. In the end, Rose did not develop a large network, as shown in her ego network of closeness relationships (Figure 9.6).

Rose's network is, in fact, the smallest of the three focal students despite her active and sociable demeanor in the beginning and throughout the program. This is because Rose's connections were mostly "less than close" or "close." In this regard, her interpersonal process can be labeled as "broad yet not-so-close" (Hasegawa, 2019). However, her network (except for "R") is a tight-knit exclusive group, forming a five-vertex clique.[5] Clique is a subgroup, where its every member has direct ties with every other member (Hanneman & Riddle, 2011). She formed this small yet close group with the help of English.

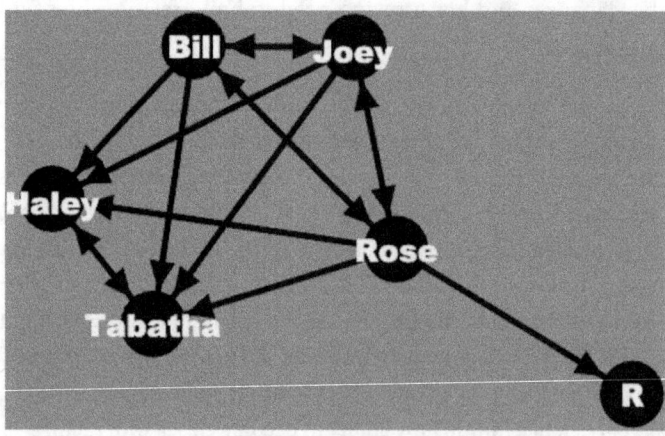

Figure 9.6 Rose's egocentric network in Week 8 (only "very close" ties).

Joey and His Gradual Expansion of Circle

Joey's experience resembles Rose's in that he started out by following the pledge faithfully in the beginning, but once his friends decided to break the pledge, he started using more English. However, in contrast to Rose's bitter ending, Joey sounds very positive about his experience, which is attributable to his expectations for the program, the language pledge, and the Japanese students.

> With the pledge, I'm glad that I broke it. Because there's things you can't express in Japanese when it's not your first language to other people. And if you're speaking English to people, there's more that you can express and that helps people get closer together.
>
> [July 29, 2016]

In fact, he says he was looking forward to using English before the pledge was broken.

> I don't want to be the first one to break the pledge, I kind of waited for other people to break it, because I don't want to be the first. I don't want to be the one to blame.
>
> [July 12, 2016]

In thinking about the contrast between Rose's experience and Joey's experience, a striking difference is found in their purposes for joining the program and expectation for the language pledge and the Japanese students. Rose sought a program that had a language pledge that forced her to use Japanese all the time, but Joey's reasons were not solely focused on the improvement of his speaking abilities per se.

> [My motivation is] credits. Because I am minoring in Japanese, I can earn credits [to satisfy my minor requirements]. My major is psychology, and my minor is Japanese. I want to be able to speak [Japanese] fluently in the future.
>
> [June 16, 2016, original in Japanese]

Obviously, it is naïve to presume that students have one clear purpose for studying abroad. However, comparing Joey's response with Rose's (and even Lily's) shows a notable difference. Rose was clearly counting on this study abroad experience to overcome her fear of speaking Japanese, but for Joey one of the great motivations for participating in this program is fulfilling requirements for his minor (Japanese). Unlike Rose, who was active from the beginning making connections with everyone in the program, including local Japanese students,

Joey's interaction with American students was more frequently observed than with Japanese students in the first few weeks into the program.

His relationship with his roommate, Koji, was not very strong but not clearly bad either, and it remained more or less the same from the beginning to the end, which also limited Joey's access to other Japanese students.

> My relationship with Koji hasn't changed a lot. I don't think we're like super close nor super distant from each other, but in terms of homework, I don't really ask, like, him for help that much because I feel like I can do a lot of it by myself. Although I feel like I should ask him because you learn better.
>
> [July 12, 2016]

Without support provided by his roommate in making connections with Japanese students, nonetheless, Joey gradually explored connections within the program on his own, and his social circle became increasingly larger and more diverse over time. His activity logs show that he went out with friends (both Japanese and American) almost every day from around midway toward the end of the program.

> It's kind of weird, but over the past week, my learning curve has gone up quite a lot. Actually, since last Friday, because I've been hanging out with a lot of the Japanese students. Like Saturday I hung out with Nana and Yuri. On Sunday, I hung out with Yuri, Caty, Liz, Yuri. To Nara. Saturday, Caty, Liz, Bo.
>
> [July 12, 2016]

As stated here, Joey thinks his Japanese is greatly improving despite the fact that he started using English.

> I don't think it's interfering with my Japanese because I'm still going to class. I'm still interacting with Japanese students. And sometimes from time to time, we'll mix up some English and Japanese with *ryuugakusee* [international students], so as long as I'm having that interaction with people being able to speak Japanese, I think speaking English is fine. I think I just use English to interact with people. Other than that, I don't think it's been interfering with my Japanese.
>
> [July 28, 2016]

His understanding of and attitude toward the use of English is very different from Rose's. Joey thinks that English is merely an additional tool to facilitate good communication, whereas Rose thinks that the allowance of English will constrain her opportunities to use Japanese. Joey's comments also show that he does not solely rely on Japanese students as opportunities for language practice

Developing Friendship or Practicing Japanese?

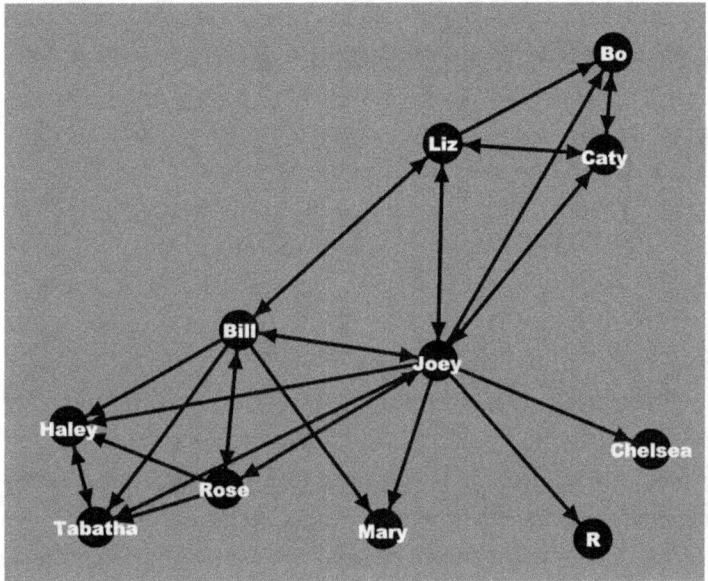

Figure 9.7 Joey's egocentric network in Week 8 (only "very close" ties).

and development, which is contrastive to Rose's heavy reliance on Japanese students in this regard.

Figure 9.7 shows his ego network in Week 8 with only strong connections shown. Interestingly, Joey is part of Rose's clique (Figure 9.6), but his egocentric network contains other individuals as well. In fact, he is part of three other cliques, one with Bill and Liz, another with Bill and Mary, and the other with Bo, Liz, and Caty. In this regard, Joey's social experience is more diverse than Rose's. This also points to his expectations for the use of English; Joey did not have any reservation about using English with his friends, which apparently helped expand his circle freely with program participants.

Discussion and Implications for Teaching and Learning

In this study, I have illustrated the formation and transformation of interpersonal connections observed in a college-level study abroad program. I have also examined individuals' distinctive social experiences and their different handling of the language pledge. Essentially, the common problems found in island study abroad programs, such as the lack of opportunities to use the target language and the challenges of making local friends, cannot be solved entirely by the enforcement of a strict language policy and the accommodation arrangements with Japanese-speaking roommates. Desire to feel connected with others and to nurture strong relationships is a fundamental need of many students which should not be overlooked in the programming. This study clearly showed that relationships with compatriots (i.e., American students) bear immediate importance to many students (Coleman, 2013, 2015). Pitts (2009) discussed in her study on the stress coping mechanism of short-term American sojourners in France: "within the co-national network, everyday talk provides sojourners the agency to make the cognitive, behavioral, and affective adjustments necessary to succeed abroad" (p. 459). Strict enforcement of the program's language pledge would have resulted in the impediment of such basic needs and support.

Interpersonal connections in this program were highly influenced by the institutional setting, such as the housing and class placement, especially in the beginning. The changes observed in social network formation from Week 1 to Week 8, then, indicate how homophily based on individuals' preferences and dispositions may override such program arrangements. In this regard, social network is a dynamic process entailing individuals' agency and histories, environmental affordances and constraints, and intricate social impetuses, all intertwined therein. Homophily, an overwhelming propensity of people developing close connections with similar others (McPherson et al., 2001), is demonstrated variously in the current data. Sharing similarities can be accomplished on different levels and in different degrees, but short-term study abroad programs are inevitably limited in this respect because of the obvious time restriction and a lack of expansive networks for most sojourners. In addition, having a clear role distinction between study abroad students as language learners/guests and local Japanese students as volunteer language supporters/hosts, inherent in the program arrangements, may also become an obstacle for constructing homophilous groups on the basis of personal preferences and dispositions. Rose's comment on the difficulty of breaking the barrier with the Japanese students alludes to this point. Given the shortage of time available for sojourners, strategic matching of study abroad participants with Japanese locals in program functions, such as housing, extracurricular activities, and even curricular activities, according to their personal similarities, is one important aspect of promoting rapport building within the program. Program activities should also encourage students—both study abroad and local—to overcome the imagined wall between them and explore common ground. In this sense, intercultural training that focuses on similarities rather than differences may promote such an awareness.

Further, the collective breaking of the language pledge, which happened midway in the program, impacted each individual differently, according to their positions in the network. For example, Rose and Joey were susceptive to the influence due to their social proximity to the oath-breakers, while Lily and other students who were remotely positioned from the oath-breakers were less impacted. In addition, there were other elements, such as language ability, motivation, and personality that differentiated how the pledge breaking affected each student. Thus, even those who were in a similar social position, for example, like Rose and Joey, were affected differently. As Joey indicated in his final interview, mixing English and Japanese to communicate effectively for the purpose of relationship building—translanguaging (Wei, 2018) or translingual practice (Canagarajah, 2018)—appears to benefit many students without sacrificing the opportunities for language use (cf., Durbidge, Chapter 10, this volume). An increasing volume of recent applied linguistics literature has discussed the virtue of "trans-" perspectives (Hawkins & Mori, 2018) as a way to destabilize boundaries that traditionally created discrete categories and labels. There is a need for pre-study abroad training and preparation that becomes crucial for nurturing "trans-" perspectives and making fuller advantage of study abroad experience. Mori and Sanuth (2018), for example, discussed the importance of critical analysis of actual language use in context, which helps raise awareness of language speakers. This kind of training should be incorporated in language instruction to prepare students to develop "trans-" perspectives before sojourn.

As a final note, I would like to highlight the utility of social network analysis as a strong analytical framework to investigate detailed processes of interpersonal relationships. As this study revealed, social experiences of study abroad are diverse and dynamic, which cannot be simply summarized with the apprenticeship model. More future research should look into such intricate processes with the social network analytic framework.

Notes

1 This study is part of a larger project. For details of data collection, see Hasegawa (2019).
2 Compared with the other indexes (i.e., friendship and interaction), the closeness index yielded the most robust contrasts and trends among individuals.
3 All names in this chapter are pseudonyms.

4   This test is administered by the Japanese Ministry of Education, Culture, Sports, Science and Technology (MEXT) and the Japan Foundation and considered to be one of the most widely recognized tests of Japanese language. N2 is the second highest level after N1.
5   The directionality of ties is disregarded in this case.

References

ACTFL. (2012). *ACTFL Proficiency guidelines.* New York: The American Council on the Teaching of Foreign Languages.

Allen, H. W. (2010). What shapes short-term study abroad experiences? A comparative case study of students' motives and goals. *Journal of Studies in International Education, 14*(5), 452–70.

Baker-Smemoe, W., Dewey, D. P., Bown, J., & Martinsen, R. A. (2014). Variables affecting L2 gains during study abroad. *Foreign Language Annals, 47*(3), 464–86.

Bastian, M., Heymann, S., & Jacomy, M. (2009). *Gephi: An open source software for exploring and manipulating networks.* International AAAI Conference on Weblogs and Social Media.

Blondel, V. D., Guillaume, J. L., Lambiotte, R., & Lefebvre, E. (2008). Fast unfolding of communities in large networks. *Journal of Statistical Mechanics: Theory and Experiment, 10*, 1–12.

Borgatti, S. P., Everett, M. G., & Johnson, J. C. (2013). *Analyzing social networks.* Thousand Oaks, CA: SAGE.

Canagarajah, S. (2018). Translingual practice as spatial repertoires: Expanding the paradigm beyond structuralist orientations. *Applied Linguistics, 39*(1), 31–54.

Carrington, P. J., & Scott, J. (2011). Introduction. In J. Scott & P. J. Carrington (Eds.), *The SAGE handbook of social network analysis* (pp. 1–8). London: SAGE.

Coleman, J. A. (2013). Researching whole people and whole lives. In C. Kinginger (Ed.), *Social and cultural aspects of language learning in study abroad* (pp. 17–44). Amsterdam: John Benjamins.

Coleman, J. A. (2015). Social circles during residence abroad: What students do, and who with. In R. Mitchell, N. Tracy-Ventura, & K. McManus (Eds.), *EuroSLA monograph series 4: Social interaction, identity and language learning during residence abroad* (pp. 33–52). Amsterdam: The European Second Language Association.

Dewey, D. P., Bown, J., & Eggett, D. (2012). Japanese language proficiency, social networking, and language use during study abroad: Learners' perspectives. *Canadian Modern Language Review, 68*, 111–37.

Dewey, D. P., Ring, S., Gardner, D., & Belnap, R. K. (2013). Social network formation and development during study abroad in the Middle East. *System: An International Journal of Educational Technology and Applied Linguistics, 41*, 269–82.

Diao, W. (2016). Peer socialization into gendered L2 mandarin practices in a study abroad context: Talk in the dorm. *Applied Linguistics, 37*(5) 599–620.

Goodwin, C. D., & Nacht, M. (1988). *Abroad and beyond: Patterns in American overseas education*. New York: Cambridge University Press.

Gore, J. E. (2005). *Dominant beliefs and alternative voices: Discourse, belief, and gender in American study abroad*. New York: Routledge.

Hanneman, R. A., & Riddle, M. (2011). A brief introduction to analyzing social network data. In J. Scott & P. J. Carrington (Eds.), *The SAGE handbook of social network analysis* (pp. 331–9). London: SAGE.

Hasegawa, A. (2019). *The social lives of study abroad: Understanding second language learners' experiences through social network analysis and conversation analysis*. New York: Routledge.

Hawkins, M. R., & Mori, J. (2018). Considering "trans-" perspectives in language theories and practices. *Applied Linguistics, 39*(1), 1–8.

Institute for International Education. (2018). Open doors online: Report on international educational exchange. Retrieved July 20, 2018 from https://www.iie.org/Research-and-Insights/Open-Doors/

Isabelli-García, C. (2006). Study abroad social networks, motivation and attitudes: Implications for second language acquisition. In M. DuFon & E. Churchill (Eds.), *Language learners in study abroad contexts* (pp. 231–58). Clevedon: Multilingual Matters.

Jacomy, M., Venturini, T., Heymann, S., & Bastian, M. (2014). ForceAtlas2, a continuous graph layout algorithm for handy network visualization designed for the Gephi software. *PLOS One, 9*(6), e98679.

Kinginger, C. (2009). *Language learning and study abroad: A critical reading of research*. Basingstoke: Palgrave Macmillan.

Kinginger, C. (Ed.). (2013). *Social and cultural aspects of language learning in study abroad*. Amsterdam: John Benjamins.

Kinginger, C., Wu, Q., Lee, S.-H., & Tan, D. (2016). The short-term homestay as a context for language learning: Three case studies of high school students and host families. *Study Abroad Research in Second Language Acquisition and International Education, 1*(1), 34–60.

Kurata, N. (2010). Opportunities for foreign language learning and use within a learner's informal social networks. *Mind, Culture, and Activity, 17*(4), 382–96.

Kurata, N. (2011). *Foreign language learning and use: Interaction in informal social networks*. London: Continuum.

McPherson, M., Smith-Lovin, L., & Cook, J. M. (2001). Birds of a feather: Homophily in social networks. *Annual Review of Sociology, 27*, 415–44.

Mori, J., & Sanuth, K. K. (2018). Navigating between a monolingual utopia and translingual realities: Experiences of American learners of Yorùbá as an additional language. *Applied Linguistics, 39*(1), 78–98.

Muramatsu, C. (2018). *Portraits of second language learners: An L2 learner agency perspective*. Bristol: Multilingual Matters.

Pitts, M. J. (2009). Identity and the role of expectations, stress, and talk in short-term student sojourner adjustment: An application of the integrative theory of communication and cross-cultural adaptation. *International Journal of Intercultural Relations, 33*, 450–62.

Shiri, S. (2015). The homestay in intensive language study abroad: Social networks, language socialization, and developing intercultural competence. *Foreign Language Annals, 48*(1), 5–25.

Shively, R. L. (2018). Language socialization during study abroad: Researching social interaction outside the classroom. In S. Coffey & U. Wingate (Eds.), *New directions for research in foreign language education* (pp. 97–112). New York: Routledge.

Wei, L. (2018). Translanguaging as a practical theory of language. *Applied Linguistics, 39*(1), 9–30.

Wolcott, T. (2016). Introduction to the special issue: Study abroad in the twenty-first century. *L2 Journal, 8*(2), 3–11.

Zappa-Hollman, S., & Duff, P. (2015). Academic English socialization through individual networks of practice. *TESOL Quarterly, 49*(2), 333–68.

10

Social Network Development and Language Learning in Multilingual Study Abroad Contexts

Case Studies of Japanese Adolescents

Levi Durbidge

Introduction

Traveling abroad to live and study in a new community can be both an exciting and anxiety-inducing experience. One of the biggest challenges can be finding a place in the community while simultaneously attempting to navigate new ways of being and communicating. As global academic mobility has increased over the past several decades, so too has interest in investigating how studying and living abroad contribute to linguistic development. Language learning during study abroad is a deeply social practice, situated in an ecology of individual connections, sociocultural institutions, and wider ideological structures (The Douglas Fir Group, 2016). For this reason, theories of language acquisition that view learning as socially situated and a "struggle for participation" (Pavlenko & Lantolf, 2000: 155) have been particularly fruitful in uncovering links between social interaction and linguistic development.

Increased recognition of the linguistic diversity found in many peoples' lived realities is now reshaping how researchers approach language learning (The Douglas Fir Group, 2016), including the contexts of study abroad. Previously, research on language learning abroad had focused on the acquisition of a single variety of language in a location conventionally associated with that variety. While recent research has begun uncovering the linguistic complexity of the social contexts of study abroad (e.g., Mitchell, Tracy-Ventura, & McManus, 2017), more research is needed on how sojourners, particularly those from outside the Anglosphere, navigate this complexity.

In what follows, I will look at how the relationships and social networks of Japanese adolescents were formed and developed during a year abroad in multilingual contexts. Tracing the evolution of the informants' social connections in the host community over time, the results highlight the importance of certain individuals at different stages of their time abroad. The support and opportunities for interaction these individuals provided were vital for the informants' linguistic development. The results also show that while the informants' initial relationships were a function of circumstance, improved linguistic competence later in the stay allowed the informants to more agentively negotiate and diversify their social networks. This chapter concludes with reflections on the implications of these results for language teaching.

Study Abroad, Social Connections, and Language Learning

Social networks have proven to be an effective concept for examining how the social connections an individual makes during study abroad contribute to their linguistic development. The interrelation of a sojourner's social networks with their investment in learning language was affirmed in pioneering work by Kurata (2004) and Isabelli-García (2006). More recently, studies by Dewey, Belnap, and Hillstrom (2013), Shiri (2015), and Mitchell et al. (2017) have demonstrated the importance of locals in sojourners' social networks in respect to their linguistic development. Other key findings of research on the effects of social networks in study abroad include the power of network size (Dewey et al., 2014), multiplex relations (Isabelli-García, 2006; Zappa-Hollman & Duff, 2015), and intensity in individual relationships (Dewey et al., 2013) in promoting linguistic development. While this research has been productive in revealing the holistic effects of social networks on language learning, there remains a need to look qualitatively at how they form and develop during time abroad (Dewey et al., 2013; Mitchell et al., 2017; Zappa-Hollman & Duff, 2015).

Qualitative research on language learning in study abroad has also revealed a range of complex individual and contextual factors that can affect the formation and development of social connections in the host community. Japanese sojourners in Ayano (2006) complained that local students at a British university only interacted with them to practice their Japanese and were not interested in friendships. A study on international students at a Japanese university by Morita (2012) found that discrimination toward Chinese students meant that local students avoided interacting with them, preferring to engage with those from Western counties.

The qualitative literature has also underscored how sojourners' desire to interact with locals can be negatively impacted by a variety of factors including harassment (Polanyi, 1995), anxiety when encountering unfamiliar communicative practices (Durbidge, 2017), and a preference for interactions with conationals (Mikal, Yang, & Lewis, 2015; Tanaka 2007). The formation and development of social networks is a dialogic process that requires conditions conducive for both sojourners and members of the host community to engage in repeated, reciprocal interaction.

One of the most consistent sites for observing the type of reciprocal interaction that leads to strong connections has been the homestay. As Dewey et al. (2013) found in their study of homestays in Morocco and Jordan, the largest and most important social group in sojourners' social networks was the host family. In Knight and Schmidt-Rinehart's (2002) study of host families in Spain and Mexico, they argued that the dynamic of the homestay offered participants opportunities for interaction with members of the host community that were more difficult to obtain elsewhere. Turning toward the effect homestays have on the development of participants' social networks outside the host family, some studies have stressed their ability to provide opportunities for interaction across a range of settings (Shiri, 2015) and connections with those in the wider community (Isabelli-García, 2006). Overall though, the homestay may not be a panacea for developing strong connections in the host community, as some university-aged participants often report that homestays limit their independence (Mitchell et al., 2017; Schmidt-Rinehart & Knight, 2004) or that the arrangement is more transactional than personal (Kinginger, 2008; Wilkinson, 1998).

One thing all of these studies have in common is that they deal with the experiences of emergent adults from English-speaking backgrounds, particularly the United States, an ongoing limitation of study abroad research more broadly (Durbidge, 2017). While often unacknowledged, circumstances which define the social lives of emerging adults may not be present in other populations. Adolescent sojourners often lack the legal and financial independence of their older peers which can shape their expectations of, and dependence on, the host family. Depending on the current stage of their psychosocial development, their social and emotional needs may differ (Erikson & Erikson, 1998) and they may be "more willing to accept the constraints of host family life" (Tan & Kinginger, 2013: 174). Furthermore, Duerden et al. (2018) found that for adolescent participants, "the familial and parental frameworks of home life extended into the lens with which they interpreted much of their study abroad experience" (26), making the unit of family central to their understandings of community and identity.

In terms of the effect homestay settings may have on sojourners' social network development, findings suggest that relationships in the host family inform how and if connections are pursued outside of that setting. In a study by Yashima, Zenuk-Nishide and Shimizu (2004) of fifty-seven Japanese high school students on year-long sojourns to the United States, participants who had positive, communicative relationships with their host family also appeared to experience less difficulties making friends outside of the host family. Grieve's (2015) study of German high school students in Australia also found that a positive relationship with members of the host family was critical in gaining access to the linguistic and material support required for increased interaction with teenagers outside of the host family.

Research which looks at how adolescents' social connections are formed beyond the homestay is, however, highly limited. Perhaps the best example is Spenader's (2011) study of American adolescents who attend a Swedish high school. One key finding to emerge from this study was that participants who were outgoing and actively engaged in interaction were largely successful in forming social connections with their Swedish-speaking peers. This engagement though appeared dependent on the participants' initial levels of linguistic competence, and, as the participant "Elsa" reported, their own ability to insert themselves into social activities. The case of "Max" demonstrates the other side of this phenomenon, since he lacked the linguistic competence and assertiveness of the other participants and did not develop relationships with his Swedish peers. Instead, he disengaged from classroom learning and became more connected to the marginalized English-speaking immigrant community at the school.

Overall, the research does highlight the variability of sojourners' experiences and the diversity of factors which can contribute to their ability to form meaningful social connections, it does suggest that host families are a vital source of connection. Furthermore, the qualitative literature on the role social connections play in language learning abroad, particularly in the experiences of adolescents, suggests that what occurs within the homestay may contribute to sojourners' ability to develop their social networks elsewhere. For this reason, this chapter will explore how social connections both inside and beyond the host family were formed and evolved, and their role in linguistic development.

Theoretical Approach

The cases presented in this chapter are drawn from a larger, longitudinal, mixed-methods study that examined the linguistic developmental of Japanese high school students who studied abroad. In order to explore the role social connections played in informants' sojourns, I adopted an approach that identified and traced the formation and evolution of their connections with individuals and communities over the course of their time abroad, in particular noting the nature of interactions and support offered.

Informing this approach was Zappa-Hollman and Duff's (2015) understanding of social connections as Individual Networks of Practice (INoP). INoP extends the notions of Community of Practice (Lave & Wenger, 1991) and social network theory (Milroy, 1987) to conceptualize "the multifaceted social dimensions and relationships that underpin learning" (Zappa-Hollman & Duff, 2015: 339). While this investigation does not adopt the analytical tools developed by Zappa-Hollman and Duff (2015), their conceptualization of an individual's social connections and the support they offer for language learning provided the framework for investigating the data presented in this chapter. Importantly, INoP accounts for the agency of the individual in the development of social connections and the influence of the wider social contexts in which they are embedded, emphasizing connections both within social groups (communities) and extending outside those groups. Crucially, an individuals' social connections in an INoP are not conceptualized as static or equally beneficial; instead, their characteristics relate to the investment of those involved and are subject to change over time.

Looking at the characteristics influenced by an individual's investment in their social connections, the typology of Garton, Haythornthwaite, and Wellman (1997) offers a useful point of reference. Garton et al. view individual connections as characterized by the following features: *content*, or the resource which is being transferred including the type of information; *direction*, the symmetry of the relation and the extent to which each party is committed to or initiates; and *strength*, the frequency of contact and the ascribed value of what is being transferred. From a multilingual perspective, alternations in language varieties also form an important consideration. Direction is key in understanding questions of power, agency, and strategy in the development of social networks, while the notion of strength is important for establishing the degree to which the connection provides interpersonal interaction "in regularly occurring and recurring contexts of use" (The Douglas Fir Group, 2016: 27), essential for language learning.

The strength of a connection also has ramifications for the extent to which it can function as a support resource when the individual encounters stressful situations. Drawing on the work of psychologists Cohen and Wills (1985), this support can be classified in four ways. *Affective support* is provided when the individual can confide in and be comforted by another. *Informational support* comes in the form of advice which helps the individual to understand and manage their situation. *Embedded support* (also described as social companionship or belongingness) emphasizes the positive feeling associated with having a clear, recognized role when in the company of others. Finally, *instrumental support* involves supplying resources and services to aid an individual. Drawing on these conceptions, I will illustrate the nature and development of the informants' social networks detailed in the following section.

Drawing on the literature and theory described earlier, I propose to address the following questions:

1. What role do social connections in the host family play in supporting informants' linguistic development and social participation?
2. How do the informants form and develop social connections outside the host family?
3. What role do these connections outside the host family play in supporting informants' linguistic development and social participation?

Research Context

The Japanese adolescents whose experiences are described in this chapter participated in year-long homestays organized through the nongovernment organization *AFS Intercultural Programs Japan* between 2016 and 2017. Participants in Japan-originating AFS programs are recruited nationwide and must pass a selection process to be accepted. Primarily, the objective of the program is to foster intercultural communication between participants and the receiving communities; however, language learning often emerges as a pivotal part of that experience. Competence in host language varieties is only needed for predominately English-speaking destinations, such as the United States, and most respondents in this study reported limited or no competence in host varieties before departing.

AFS exchanges typically last ten to eleven months, timed to align with the school calendar of their destination. As a result, participants drawn from all over the world arrive in the destination country around the same time and undergo a multiday orientation session together before traveling to meet and live with a local family. There are general expectations in AFS programs that the exchange student will participate and be recognized as a member of the hosting family. This was reflected in the informants' accounts as they referred to hosting family members using terms such as "host mother" or "host sister." Contact with the host family is generally established through email several months prior to departure; however, informants indicated that this was often limited to exchanges of greetings and requests for information about the host community. Participants in AFS programs predominately live with the same host family and attend a local secondary school throughout their stay, and each of the informants in this study followed this pattern. While several of the informants in this study reported having other exchange students living in their local area, all reported being the only Japanese participant in that area. Participants also attend occasional events with other local AFS participants during their year abroad and are supported by volunteers from the host community; however, the frequency and quality of this support was reported by informants to be highly variable.

The results presented in this chapter focus on four informants who spent around eleven months abroad between August 2016 and July 2017. These informants were selected for analysis for this chapter from a larger group of fourteen, based on the following criteria: (1) they each traveled to destinations where the host language was not considered to be English; (2) they were highly engaged in the data collection process, making themselves available for extended interview sessions, providing access to semi-private social media accounts, and responding to follow-up questions via email; (3) using results from a questionnaire conducted with a larger cohort (N=100) the informants were drawn from, hierarchical cluster analyses (Norušis, 2009) showed that these informants' responses to multi-item scales on (a) reasons to study abroad and (b) perceived outcomes were representative of more than 50 percent of that cohort; (4) the informants were evenly distributed between male and female, the only genders in the cohort. These informants are detailed in Table 10.1.

Methods

Data was drawn from a number of sources. Each informant initially completed a nineteen-item questionnaire, during which they indicated interest in being interviewed for the project. They then participated in two sessions of retrospective interviews, with each session lasting from one to

Table 10.1 Demographic, Background, and Study Abroad Data

Name	Gender	High School Year at Departure	Previous Experience Traveling Abroad	Previous Experience Living Abroad	Languages Previously Studied	Destination Country	Languages Spoken Abroad (in Order of Usage)	Host Family Members
Nagisa	F	1	Brazil, the United States, Singapore, Hong Kong, Malaysia, Korea	(None)	English, Portuguese	Brazil	Portuguese, English	Mother, father, sister
Raiken	M	2	Canada, Indonesia	(None)	English	Finland	Finnish, English	Mother, father, two brothers
Manabu	M	2	(None)	(None)	English	Canada (Quebec)	French, English	Mother, father, sister
Nikko	F	2	England, France	Two-week exchange to England	English	Hungary	English, Hungarian	Mother, sister

three hours. The interviews were conducted and recorded through *Zoom* VoIP software. The first session occurred approximately one to two months after returning to Japan, and the other approximately one year after returning. The first session of interviews focused on the events leading up to, during, and immediately after their exchange. The second session focused on the year that had followed and their ongoing perceptions of their time abroad. Informants were able to use both Japanese and English in the interviews. Follow-up questions were sent by email when clarification was required or further questions emerged. The informants also agreed to provide access to their Instagram account from which photos and accompanying comments were extracted.

In order to account for the multimodal nature of the data and develop a holistic picture of the informants' experiences, I adopted a multistranded approach to analysis. As part of the analysis for the larger project, data collected from interviews was subjected to attribute coding (Saldaña, 2012) through which important social relations were identified through a set of nested codes. Following are the codes which emerged most frequently: (1) host family, of which the subcodes host mother and host sibling were most prominent; (2) host community, which primarily consisted of the host community friends subcode; (3) family in Japan; (4) friends in Japan; and (5) AFS. Social connections were also analyzed by reviewing comments by visitors to the informants' Instagram accounts based on their frequency, content, and whether the informant responded to them. The large majority of comments could be attributed to either (2) host community friends or (4) friends in Japan.

Narratives of the informants' experiences were then reconstructed using narrative analysis (Barkhuizen, Benson, & Chik, 2013) based on individual questionnaire responses, interview, and Instagram data. Given the focus in this chapter on social connections in the host community, narratives for each of the cases in Table 10.1 were analyzed to determine at which points communities and relations corresponding to codes (1), (2), and (5) were most prominent. A comparative cross-case analysis (Duff, 2008) was then performed to determine points of similarity and difference in the development of, and support offered by, the informants' social connections.

Due to limitations of space, extracts from the informants' data are all presented in English. Both Raiken and Nikko predominately communicated in English and their extracts are presented as is. Extracts from Nagisa and Manabu are my translations of their responses in Japanese.

Results

Arrival and Host Families

Upon arriving in the destination country, each of the informants attended a multiday orientation session in English, run by AFS. This initial encounter became a source of anxiety for the informants as they found their linguistic competence limited in comparison to other exchange students.

> **Manabu:** I was the only Japanese ((mm)). People who had come from other countries, there were more than twenty from places like Italy. There were so many, but because both my English ability and French ability were low, I didn't really have friends in AFS. At the start, I didn't have any. That was hard.

Manabu went on to explain how perceptions of his linguistic competence meant that he was dismissed by other exchange students during AFS events, reporting that they said things like "That Japanese can't speak, I don't like him" and "Just go over there [away from us]."

While Manabu's experience was the most explicit example, a sense of distance or isolation stemming from limited English competence emerged across the informants' accounts of these initial orientation sessions. As Kurata (Chapter 5, this volume) has pointed out, those with limited competence in a language can struggle to create opportunities for interaction, particularly in the informal settings commonly encountered during study abroad. This struggle was apparent throughout the informants' first months as they focused on navigating the new social, linguistic, and geographical topographies of life in the host community. School in particular was a source of anxiety, as the informants found the content of classes largely unintelligible, and social interaction with peers was highly limited.

During these initial weeks and months, the host family was a vital source of learning, support, and inclusion. For the informants in this chapter, communication with family members was often collaborative, multilingual, and negotiated around the proficiencies of each member involved.

> **Levi:** Did you always have conversations with [your host family] in Hungarian?
>
> **Nikko:** [. . .] with my host sister, she speaks English and a little bit Japanese, so we usually talk in English and then sometimes Hungarian or Japanese. But my host mum doesn't speak English so we only spoke in Hungarian. Like at the beginning I was really bad at Hungarian, so I couldn't really have conversation with my host Mum then. But there [was] my host sister, so she could translate what I'm saying and she could translate what my host mum said to me.

As this extract shows, host siblings were crucial in mediating communication between informants and the host parents during the first few months. This included interpreting between the host varieties and English, or Japanese in Manabu's case, and acting as a conduit for initial connection between the host parents and the informants. Host siblings also served as guides to the unfamiliar geographical and social environments the informants found themselves in, and acted as the first point of contact with the social networks of their host school. Host siblings were therefore a key source of informational and instrumental support across the contexts of both home and school, while also acting as a link between them.

Even as host siblings were providing a range of support, informants reported a strong desire to contribute more fully to family life and be seen as members of the family.

> **Raiken:** [The host family] said like, "you [are] my guest" or like that. But because I became the member of the host family [. . .] I felt I should do something, for like [the] family.

As Pavlenko and Lantolf (2000) have noted, the desire for membership and participation in language communities is critical to linguistic development, and informants typically spent several hours each evening investing in the linguistic practices of the host family, including self-study, consuming media, and interacting with host family members, particularly host mothers.

Highly valued by the informants, the almost nightly episodes of interaction with host mothers were crucial to their language development, particularly during the first several months. This was exemplified in Nikko's narrative. Around three months into her sojourn, Nikko's host sister left to study abroad in Japan and Nikko realized that she needed to improve her competence in Hungarian to better communicate with her host mother. Nikko decided to write diary entries in Hungarian to share with her host mother each evening. Her host mother would correct the entry, which would then serve as a basis for conversation. This multimodal learning strategy not only improved her Hungarian but also strengthened their shared connection. Nikko even credited this practice with helping to mend their relationship after they had a misunderstanding over Nikko staying overnight at a friend's house.

Host mothers were also a key source of affective and informational support for the informants, giving them advice, affirmation, and explaining language and cultural norms. During Manabu's struggles with language and the subsequent difficulties making friends described earlier, his host mother's reassurances were important in shaping his attitudes and motivation.

> **Manabu:** When I said how hard that was, [My host mother] told me that things would get better, that for the Italians and others [. . .] languages like Italian and Spanish were really close to French. They could learn to speak French much faster and that's just how it is. [She told me] "You can't compare yourself to them."

Perhaps the most significant thing that host mothers did to support the informants was to make themselves approachable and available and allow them to share in the quotidian aspects of family life. The availability and willingness of Nagisa's host mother to engage with her on familiar terms provided crucial opportunities to experience the communicative practices of home life in Brazil.

> **Nagisa:** We would be talking and she would complain about her work, talk about things that were bothering her, also about her mother, she would tell me about things like that. We made a habit of spending our time together this way from the time I got home from school until I studied and went to bed.

Sharing these types of details on a daily basis would increase the strength, and emphasize the symmetry of the relationship between informants and host mothers. Furthermore, like the participants in Shiri (2015), the ongoing accumulation these regular interactions socialized informants into the linguistic practices of the host family and was a vital part of becoming part of the "ingroup" (21). While the informants often spoke of difficulties negotiating and communicating with others in their host families, the relationship with their host mother was characterized by stability, affection, and mutuality.

Like the *señoras* in Knight and Schmidt-Rinehart's (2002) study, host mothers were valuable sources of affirmation and feedback on the progress of the informants' linguistic development, as Nikko's use of the diary demonstrated. The close relationship Nagisa shared with her host mother also functioned in this way, allowing her to check her comprehension when conversations took place between other family members.

> **Nagisa:** I would be listening intently to what [host family members] said and repeating it in my head. Then, when I understood something, I would ask [my host] Mum, "Did they say this thing?", and she would praise me by saying like, "Ah! You just understand that Nagisa!" That made me so happy.

In addition to supporting the informants' linguistic development, the clearly defined parent-child roles which underpinned the relationship with host mothers provided embedded support throughout the informants' stay, which was vital during the stressful first few months when the range and strength of peer networks was highly limited.

Forming Connections Outside the Host Family

While relations with the host family played an important role during the first months abroad, connections at high school took longer to emerge. In some cases, the informants initially spent time with their host siblings' friends at school; however, participation in these groups appears to have been limited and transitory. Instead, the first meaningful connections with peers were often born of interaction initiated outside these groups.

> **Raiken:** One friend, he was interest[ed] in Japanese culture ((ok)), so like first [??] he was approaching me like, "Where you from are you from? Japan?" like that, [...] and then we talked about culture, [...] like anime and manga, and like, Japanese temple and like, how to use chopsticks and like, downhill ski.

Raiken and his friend took several of the same classes and used the same bus to travel to and from home, the shared social contexts allowing for regular, unplanned interactions to take place and leading to the development of a friendship.

Manabu too described how connections to two communities at his school were initiated by members of those groups. First, a largely English-speaking "immigrant" group, identifying Manabu as a new arrival at the school who didn't speak French, invited him to eat lunch with them, which became a regular routine. His contact with a Francophone group came several months later, when another student sitting next to him had, unprompted, helped Manabu understand when he was struggling in a maths class. Like Raiken, regular and unplanned contact during shared classes and catching the same bus home led to a friendship. Through this relationship, Manabu began spending time and developing connections with others in his new friend's social network.

The informants' accounts also demonstrate that these regularly recurring contexts of interaction which lead to stronger social connections were not limited to copresent interaction. Each of the informants described how online communication platforms including Snapchat, Facebook Messenger, WhatsApp, and Instagram were a vital part of their interactions at school. Nikko explained that the relationship she had with members of her class in Hungary evolved after they took the relatively simple action of inviting her to connect with them on the messaging service WhatsApp.

> **Nikko:** [...] at the beginning I wasn't really close to my classmates, but they sent me like WhatsApp, then we were talking.

What is noteworthy about each of the cases described is the way that contact was initiated by the actions of a local peer, perhaps responding to an interest or perceived need in the sojourner. Further recurring opportunities for interaction, essential for developing the strength of social connections (Boissevain, 1974) as well as linguistic competence, took place through shared social contexts, including online spaces.

Negotiating the Nature of Peer Networks

As the informants' competence in the linguistic and social practices of the host community developed, so too did their ability to exert greater agency over the nature of their social networks. This was particularly salient when the informants became dissatisfied with their social situation. In both Nagisa and Nikko's cases, issues emerged which affected their ability and desire to maintain the strength of the relationship they had with their host sister. While Nagisa had initially been supported by her host sister's knowledge of English, her developing competence in Portuguese allowed her to use it as her main language of interaction around three months in to her stay. In addition to this, the behavior of Nagisa's host sister and her boyfriend, emblemized in Nagisa's discovery of a used condom left on the floor after arriving home from school one afternoon, led her to seek out new friendships as she explained:

> **Nagisa:** At the start I spent time with my host sister's friends, her boyfriend, people like that, but gradually I realised that they weren't very good people. When there was a new school semester, [. . .] I started spending time with different friends and I made more friends.

Nikko also began to reconsider the nature of the relationship with her host sister when she perceived her host sister's responsibility for taking care of her was becoming a point of tension. Accessing the social network she was developing with her classmates for support and advice, she connected with another exchange student from Estonia, Kristel.

> **Nikko:** I said to [my classmates] that "I'm having kind of bad relationship with my host sister, I don't know what to do" or something like that. Then Kristel [. . .] told me I shouldn't care about that much and I should live my life. [. . .] so I decided to take a distance with my host sister and I started to spend more time with Kristel at school, then that made our relationship more stronger.

This encounter began a realignment in Nikko's peer networks, with Kristel becoming a significant part of Nikko's social life and source of affective support.

Their shared role as exchange students with English and Hungarian as second languages allowed them to develop a strong, reciprocal relationship. Nikko and Kristel began studying Hungarian together, which eventually led to them supporting each other as they switched the main language of interaction with their classmates from English to Hungarian.

Manabu too recalled a specific moment when he took an active role in negotiating the language of interaction in one of his social networks.

> **Manabu:** At first we spoke in English but there was this time I said, "Let's change to French." Every now and then English would be mixed in [our conversations] but I was determined to not speak anything but French, so I just talked to them in French from that point on.

Raiken too described how he gradually switched to Finnish in interactions with friends, both in person and in instant messages. In contrast to Manabu however, he was more willing to accept the integration of English in Finnish interactions, particularly in cases where his linguistic competence was limited.

Taken together, these examples demonstrate how competence in the linguistic and social practices of the host community afforded the informants greater agency to determine who they interacted with and how these interactions took place. By renegotiating the nature of their social networks, the informants were also negotiating the types of support available to them and therefore the ability to further invest in the linguistic practices of their peers in the host community.

Diversification of Peer Networks

Heading into the later stages of the informants' time abroad, the options and possibilities for social interaction increased, supported by the linguistic and social resources they had developed. This allowed the informants to begin actively expanding the range of their social networks. Nikko described how several months into her stay, a community of exchange students in her city would often gather at a park or coffee shop after school. She explained that through these regular ongoing meetings everybody's English ability improved and "we were making fun of each other or just sometime have a deep conversation," leading to stronger social ties. This community grew quickly as the members shared connections and invited other members from their individual networks.

> **Nikko:** My friend is Kristel, then Kristel could get to know AFS people. She was [a] student [of another organisation] and I was AFS student [...] then she could

get to know AFS people from me. So I mean like in this way, I could also get new friends and I could get confident to speak in English.

In Nikko's case, there was a reciprocity in participating in this community, as members benefitted from each other's networks and were mutually able to increase the range of their own network. While Nikko reported that her participation in this community contributed to the development of her English competence, there was also evidence that this community's shared linguistic repertoire also began to reflect the diversity of its members and the surrounding linguistic context. Later in her account, Nikko described how the exchange students would intersperse their English with swear words from Hungarian as a sign of informality, solidarity, and knowledge of youth culture in Hungary, while interactions on Nikko's Instagram with other exchange students contained elements of English, Hungarian, Portuguese, and Mandarin.

For the other informants, extracurricular activities provided opportunities to diversify their networks. Nagisa was an active food and design Instagrammer, and developed relationships with staff at the stores she frequented as well as local university students who participated in cosplay events. These relations continued online and consequently Portuguese began appearing in comment exchanges on Nagisa's Instagram posts. Raiken and Manabu described sporting activities as important sources of social connection, emphasized by images of their participation posted to Instagram. Manabu's networks were of particular interest since he played Flag Football with a primarily English-speaking group and Ice Hockey with French speakers. Fascinatingly, several comments made by members of these groups on his Instagram posts used romanized Japanese, suggesting that reciprocal nature of their relations had influenced the linguistic repertoires of both Manabu and his peer networks.

Toward the end of their stays, some respondents reported that opportunities for romantic interaction occurred, often linked to interest in their Japanese identities (cf. Inaba, Chapter 7, this volume). While Nagisa was uninterested in having a romantic relationship with a local, she described how being Japanese elicited romantic attention, particularly from boys who were interested in Japanese *otaku* culture, such as anime and video games. Nikko too found her Japanese identity highlighted late in her stay when, while out one evening with friends, she was approached by a local boy who was interested in Japan. At the time they connected on Facebook and continued messaging each other during the following week. The following weekend they met in person again and, at that point, "he told me that he liked me, then I also started to kinda like him," demonstrating the role of communications technology in facilitating the development of social connections, including opportunities to reconnect after a first encounter. Raiken also described how a romantic relationship was initiated by a local who expressed an interest in Japan.

> **Levi:** How did the relationship start for you? Was it just friends or?
>
> **Raiken:** Yeah, [. . .] it was just friends, like, she was interest[ed] in Japanese culture so it was the most biggest things maybe. And then we talked about that and then [. . .] she approached me and then, yeah, like, I don't know, like she was really like, active, you know?
>
> **Levi:** Active?
>
> **Raiken:** Active, yeah [. . .] then I just followed her and it was kind of fun.

Importantly, all of these romantic interactions, wanted or otherwise, were initiated by locals rather than the informants. While both Raiken and Nikko spoke of how these connections provided them with opportunities to experience romantic interaction firsthand, Raiken lamented that his competence in this area limited his ability fully express his feelings to his partner. The role of linguistic competence in pursuing romantic interactions was also apparent in Manabu's account as he described being interested in a girl while in Canada, but lacking the ability to flirt confidently with her. This again highlights the interrelatedness of linguistic proficiency with the ability to initiate, forge, and participate in new roles that go beyond those of family and friend.

Discussion

This study set out to investigate the nature of adolescents' social networks during study abroad and their role in supporting linguistic development and social participation. While aspects of the informant's development were idiosyncratic to their linguistic competencies, experiences, and the unique nature of the environments and communities they traveled to, similarities emerged. One of these was the importance that specific connections had in providing various types of support, summarized in Table 10.2.

Embedded Support in Host Families

Viewing the development of the informants' individual networks chronologically, relations with the host family were most salient in the informants' narratives over the first months of their stay. Predominantly, early participation in host family

Table 10.2 Support Offered by Informants' Social Contacts at Different Stages of their Sojourn

Relationship	Type of Support	Examples of Support	Approximate Months of Sojourn when Relationship was Most Salient in Informants' Accounts
Host sibling	Informational support	Advice on local school and transportation	2–3
	Instrumental support	Interpreting, social networks	
Host mother	Affective support	Reassurance during stressful periods, praise for linguistic development	4–8
	Informational support	Cultural and linguistic explanations	
	Instrumental support	Housing, food, transportation	
	Embedded support	Parent-child role, recurring interactional opportunities in home language	
Host community friend	Affective support	Reassurance during stressful periods,	4–10
	Instrumental support	Interpreting, social networks	
	Informational support	Advice during class, cultural and linguistic explanations	
	Embedded support	Friendship, recurring multilingual interactional opportunities	
Romantic interest	Embedded support	Recurring romantic interactional opportunities	8–11

life was meditated by informants' multilingual host siblings. Acting as *language brokers* (Morales & Hanson, 2005), host siblings provided instrumental support through interpretation and strengthened the connection between the informant and their host parent by facilitating communication and understanding. While in some cases informants' relationship with the host sibling became strained over time, the initial support they offered as interpreters and guides appear pivotal to the informants' adaption to their new social environment.

Quite quickly though, the informants sought greater participation in the host family, and host mothers emerged as important sources of affective, embedded, and informational support, similar to the *señoras* in Knight and Schmidt-Rinehart's (2002) study. As Kinginger (2015) has suggested, the willingness of the informants to take on the role of child in the host family may have assisted the development of this relationship. The sense of stability that subsequently emerged and ongoing support this relationship provided could help to explain why Yashima et al. (2004) and Grieve (2015) also found having positive relations with the host family contributed to developing relations with adolescents in the wider host community. Furthermore, while multiplex relations in study abroad have been highlighted for the language learning opportunities they provide (Isabelli-García, 2006; Zappa-Hollman & Duff, 2015), the informants' relations with their host mothers demonstrate that certain strong uniplex relations can also be decisive in fostering linguistic development.

One interesting observation to come out of my analysis was that while the informants described the mediating role their host siblings played, they did not explicitly link this relationship to their language learning. While interactions between host siblings and the informants would have undoubtedly contributed to linguistic development, the nature of these relationships would have been qualitatively different to those shared with host mothers. The emergence of tension in the relationships Nikko and Nagisa had with their host sisters suggests that these relationships can be more unstable than those with host mothers. Especially since, as Knight and Schmidt-Rinehart (2002) note, the decision to host a sojourner ultimately rests with the host parents and siblings may resent the change to their home life.

Looking at the reported evolution of language use in the host family during the year abroad, while the language of interaction was initially negotiated on the basis of shared competencies, it appears there was a trend toward exclusive use of non-English varieties of the host language over time. This is perhaps a function of the informants' desire to participate and be perceived as full members of the host family, performed through an increasing attunement to the family's normative linguistic practices, as Shiri (2015) also found.

Overall, these results emphasize how the support offered by various members of the host family can contribute to sojourners' integration and linguistic development. Moreover, it adds to a body of work which is highlighting the central role that host families can play in adolescent study abroad (Grieve, 2015; Kinginger, 2015; Tan & Kinginger, 2013, Yashima et al., 2004).

Developing Peer Networks Abroad

Establishing meaningful social connections outside of the host family can be a challenging aspect of study abroad and is not something all sojourners achieve (e.g., Dewey et al., 2013). As the accounts of the informants demonstrate, their ability to initiate and participate in informal interactions is contingent on their linguistic competence and how that competence was perceived and accommodated for by others.

An important finding was the presence of certain key individuals whose friendship provided the informants with various forms of support, especially when peer networks were initially very limited. One important role these key individuals played was to act as links to wider networks of peers. An example of this process can be found in a study by Tomiya (1997) of non-Japanese women who married Japanese men. Tomiya found that the social networks of her participants were vastly expanded though specific individuals who shared their connections with the newcomers. In much the same way, close contact with a key individual, such as Manabu's Francophone friend, allowed the informants to increase the range of peer networks (cf. Kurata, Chapter 5, this volume; Carhill-Poza, Chapter 2, this volume).

Friendships with these key individuals also provided informants with affective and informational support in contexts outside of host family settings, such as the reassurance Nikko received on the relationship with her host sister or the assistance Manabu received while struggling in maths class. This follows Murphy-Lejeune's (2002) findings that relationships with certain key individuals can help sojourners to navigate the complexities of the host community. The significance of the support this relationship offered was made more so by the fact that informants' networks, and therefore access to other avenues of support, were very limited until the later parts of their time abroad.

Diversification in the range, composition, and languages of informants' social networks did appear tied to the informants' linguistic competencies. Importantly, increases in their competencies afforded the informants greater agency to determine how and with who they communicated. This was exemplified in

Nagisa's ability to distance herself from her host sister's friends and develop her own social network at school and in Manabu's declaration to his friends that he wished to speak French rather than English. Importantly, the informants' accounts show how linguistic competence can be used to reshape an individual's social networks to align with the identities they aspire toward.

Peer networks took on an ever-greater importance as the year abroad progressed, with the informants' Instagram accounts increasingly focused on activities they did with groups of friends, while their interviews highlighted the importance of peer connections to the multilingual identities they were developing. In contrast to the contexts of homestays, the main language of interaction for these peer networks was initially English, but through renegotiations and increasing diversity in member composition there was a shift toward increased linguistic diversity. Increasingly, the languages of interaction used in informants' peer networks were dynamically negotiated based on the competencies, identities, and conventions of its members and reflected an ability to "choose across their languages and/or varieties and registers in response to local demands for social action" (The Douglas Fir Group, 2016: 26).

Implications for Language Teaching

The accounts of the informants in this study are a valuable reminder of the link between language and participation, and the way language learning can be part of "the process of becoming a member of a certain community" (Sfard, 1998: 6). Reflecting on my own practice as a language teacher, I am aware of how easy it can be to lose sight of this link when language is constantly, and perhaps exclusively, encountered in the confines of the classroom or end of semester exam. The results of this study highlight the need to connect classroom practice with the process of becoming and belonging.

The results of this study illustrate how the informants' ability to initiate and negotiate social connections in the host community is a function of their linguistic competencies. Without the repertoires to initiate or pursue interactions with others, their ability to participate is determined by those in the host community who are willing to help and accommodate them. If we wish to grant learners and users of language in our classrooms the power to shape and negotiate the types of social connections they can pursue, then we need to ensure they have the functional language for, and practical experience of, doing this. If classroom practices and assessment do not reflect the actual contexts that learners will encounter, then the value of what is taught is diminished.

The experiences of the informants also demonstrate that interaction in multilingual contexts can be negotiated based on the competencies of all participants. The ability to strategically draw on multiple varieties to enable communication was an essential part of their participation. In some cases, such as the use of Hungarian among Nikko's English-speaking exchange student community, it also indexed identity and belonging. These experiences sit in contrast to the "concurrent negative language ideologies of monolingualism and nativespeakerism, which posit that learners should develop the pure competence of two monolinguals in one head" (The Douglas Fir Group, 2016: 35) that permeate many language classrooms. Language teaching should seek to draw on the full range of learners' linguistic competencies and demonstrate the strategic and social benefits of multilingualism.

References

Ayano, M. (2006). Japanese students in Britain. In M. Byram & A. Feng (Eds.), *Living and studying abroad: Research and practice* (pp. 11–37). Bristol: Multilingual Matters.

Barkhuizen, G., Benson, P., & Chik, A. (2013). *Narrative inquiry in language teaching and learning research*. New York: Routledge.

Boissevain, J. (1974). *Friends of friends: Networks, manipulators and coalitions*. Oxford: Blackwell.

Cohen, S., & Wills, T. A. (1985). Stress, social support, and the buffering hypothesis. *Psychological Bulletin*, 98(2), 310–57. https://doi.org/10.1037/0033-2909.98.2.310

Dewey, D. P., Belnap, R. K., & Hillstrom, R. (2013). Social network development, language use, and language acquisition during study abroad: Arabic language learners' perspectives. *Frontiers: The Interdisciplinary Journal of Study Abroad*, 22, 84–110.

Dewey, D. P., Bown, J., Baker, W., Martinsen, R. A., Gold, C., & Eggett, D. (2014). Language use in six study abroad programs: An exploratory analysis of possible predictors. *Language Learning*, 64(1), 36–71. https://doi.org/10.1111/lang.12031

Duerden, M. D., Layland, E., Petriello, M., Stronza, A., Dunn, M., & Adams, S. (2018). Understanding the unique nature of the adolescent study abroad experience. *Journal of Hospitality, Leisure, Sport & Tourism Education*, 23, 18–28. https://doi.org/10.1016/j.jhlste.2018.04.004

Duff, P. A. (2008). *Case study research in Applied Linguistics*. New York: Routledge.

Durbidge, L. (2017). Duty, desire and Japaneseness: A case study of Japanese high school study abroad. *Study Abroad Research in Second Language Acquisition and International Education, 2*(2), 206–39.

Erikson, E. H., & Erikson, J. M. (1998). *The life cycle completed (extended version)*. New York: W. W. Norton & Company.

Garton, L., Haythornthwaite, C., & Wellman, B. (1997). Studying online social networks. *Journal of Computer-Mediated Communication, 3*(1). https://doi.org/10.1111/j.1083-6101.1997.tb00062.x

Grieve, A. M. (2015). The impact of host family relations and length of stay on adolescent identity expression during study abroad. *Multilingua, 34*(5), 623–57. https://doi.org/10.1515/multi-2014-0089

Isabelli-García, C. (2006). Study abroad social networks, motivation and attitudes: Implications for second language acquisition. In R. Ellis & M. A. DuFon (Eds.), *Language learners in study abroad contexts* (pp. 231–58). Clevedon: Multilingual Matters.

Kinginger, C. (2008). Language learning in study abroad: Case studies of Americans in France. *The Modern Language Journal, 92*(s1), 1–124. https://doi.org/10.1111/j.1540-4781.2008.00821.x

Kinginger, C. (2015). Language socialization in the homestay: American high school students in China. In R. Mitchell, N. Tracy-Ventura, & K. McManus (Eds.), *Social interaction, identity and language learning during residence abroad* (pp. 53–74). Amsterdam: The European Second Language Association.

Knight, S. M., & Schmidt-Rinehart, B. C. (2002). Enhancing the homestay: Study abroad from the host family's perspective. *Foreign Language Annals, 35*(2), 190–201. https://doi.org/10.1111/j.1944-9720.2002.tb03154.x

Kurata, N. (2004). Communication networks of Japanese language learners in their home country. *Journal of Asian Pacific Communication, 14*(1), 153–78.

Kurata, N. (2010). Opportunities for foreign language learning and use within a learner's informal social networks. *Mind, Culture, and Activity, 17*(4), 382–96.

Lave, J., & Wenger, E. (1991). *Situated learning: Legitimate peripheral participation*. Cambridge: Cambridge University Press.

Mikal, J. P., Yang, J., & Lewis, A. (2015). Surfing USA: How internet use prior to and during study abroad affects Chinese students' stress, integration, and cultural learning while in the United States. *Journal of Studies in International Education, 19*(3), 203–24. https://doi.org/10.1177/1028315314536990

Milroy, L. (1987). *Language and social networks* (2nd ed.). Oxford: Blackwell.

Mitchell, R., Tracy-Ventura, N., & McManus, K. (2017). *Anglophone students abroad: Identity, social relationships and language learning*. New York: Routledge.

Morales, A., & Hanson, W. E. (2005). Language brokering: An integrative review of the literature. *Hispanic Journal of Behavioral Sciences, 27*(4), 471–503. https://doi.org/10.1177/0739986305281333

Morita, L. (2012). Language, discrimination and internationalisation of a Japanese university. *Electronic Journal of Contemporary Japanese Studies, 12*(1). https://japanesestudies.org.uk/ejcjs/vol12/iss1/morita.html

Murphy-Lejeune, E. (2002). *Student mobility and narrative in Europe: The new strangers.* New York: Routledge.

Norušis, M. J. (2009). *PASW Statistics 18 statistical procedures companion.* Upper Saddle River, NJ: Prentice Hall.

Pavlenko, A., & Lantolf, J. P. (2000). Second language learning as participation and the (re) construction of selves. In J. P. Lantolf (Ed.), *Sociocultural theory and second language learning* (pp. 155–77). Oxford: Oxford University Press.

Polanyi, L. (1995). Language learning and living abroad. In B. F. Freed (Ed.), *Second language acquisition in a study abroad context* (pp. 271–37). Philadelphia, VA: John Benjamins.

Saldaña, J. (2012). *The coding manual for qualitative researchers.* London: Sage.

Schmidt-Rinehart, B. C., & Knight, S. M. (2004). The homestay component of study abroad: Three perspectives. *Foreign Language Annals, 37*(2), 254–62.

Sfard, A. (1998). On two metaphors for learning and the dangers of choosing just one. *Educational Researcher, 27*(2), 4–13. https://doi.org/10.3102/0013189X027002004

Shiri, S. (2015). The homestay in intensive language study abroad: Social networks, language socialization, and developing intercultural competence. *Foreign Language Annals, 48*(1), 5–25. https://doi.org/10.1111/flan.12127

Spenader, A. J. (2011). Language learning and acculturation: Lessons from high school and gap-year exchange students. *Foreign Language Annals, 44*(2), 381–98. https://doi.org/10.1111/j.1944-9720.2011.01134.x

Tan, D., & Kinginger, C. (2013). Exploring the potential of high school homestays as a context for local engagement and negotiation of difference. In C. Kinginger (Ed.), *Social and cultural aspects of language learning in study abroad* (pp. 155–77). Philadelphia, VA: John Benjamins.

Tanaka, K. (2007). Japanese students' contact with English outside the classroom during study abroad. *New Zealand Studies in Applied Linguistics, 13*(1), 36–54.

The Douglas Fir Group. (2016). A transdisciplinary framework for SLA in a multilingual world. *The Modern Language Journal, 100*(S1), 19–47. https://doi.org/10.1111/modl.12301

Tomiya, R. (1997). *Nihonjin to kekkonshita gaikokujin jyosei no nettowāku to nihonngo gakushū no katei [The networks of foreign women who married a Japanese and Japanese language learning processes]* (No. 4; pp. 74–93). Nihongo Kyouiku Gakkai.

Wilkinson, S. (1998). Study abroad from the participants' perspective: A challenge to common beliefs. *Foreign Language Annals, 31*(1), 23–39.

Yashima, T., Zenuk-Nishide, L., & Shimizu, K. (2004). The influence of attitudes and affect on willingness to communicate and second language communication. *Language Learning, 54*(1), 119–52.

Zappa-Hollman, S., & Duff, P. A. (2015). Academic English socialization through individual networks of practice. *TESOL Quarterly, 49*(2), 333–68. https://doi.org/10.1002/tesq.188

Appendix: Transcription Conventions

[ ]   insertion
[…]   omitted section
[??]   unclear utterance
(( ))   backchannelling

Concluding Discussion

11

A Social Network Perspective on Language Teaching

Avary Carhill-Poza and Naomi Kurata

Social network analysis offers language teachers an incredible tool for understanding the social support that their students access within and beyond the classroom. Relationships are an underutilized and often overlooked asset for language learning, an afterthought in most classrooms and programs. Current work with social networks in applied linguistics builds on our understanding of relational ties as the invisible framework that supports language learning in classrooms and other social spaces. Engaging this perspective to better understand language development can shift pedagogical focus toward facilitating of the social relationships that motivate and sustain language learning. Given the complexities of language teaching around the world, we believe that social network analysis offers precisely the kind of information teachers need now to understand student agency within the constraints and opportunities of classroom learning.

In this concluding chapter, we explore the teaching implications of social network research with language learners through the rich variety of contexts presented in the studies in this book. First, we present ideas that can transform practice, drawn from themes that span different age groups and settings in the collected research in this book. Then, we reflect on the implications of the work presented in this volume and propose a theory of social networks for language teaching and language learning. Finally, we imagine a research agenda for social network analysis that can clearly and persuasively inform language teaching.

Social Networks and Classroom Practice

One of the prevailing myths about language learning is that all you need to do is make friends with a native speaker. Most people believe that authentic communication with such a friend will propel language learning beyond what can be achieved in a classroom alone. Less clear is where the friendship with a native speaker will be initiated or which languages will be used in what ways to maintain the relationship. In addition to being vague about the mechanisms of language learning, this myth is also pernicious as it reifies the native speaker ideal (Leung, Harris, & Rampton, 1997) and presupposes that such relationships are widely available to any L2 learner who wants one. The myth of the native-speaking friend both limits the scope of classroom language learning and sets students up for failure.

To address the native-speaking friend myth, teachers need to first recognize that networks that support language learning do not occur easily or incidentally. The evidence gathered within the chapters of this book shows that language learners of all ages employ conscious and unconscious strategies to create opportunities for using the target language with others. Their agency is constrained by the social opportunity structures in their schools, language classrooms, and study abroad programs. And, the relationships that they do develop rarely display the symmetry we might expect of an ideal (native-speaking or otherwise) partnership. Take as an example, Emily, a college student studying Japanese as a foreign language in Australia (Kurata, Chapter 5, this volume). Neither her classroom nor her program provided enough structured social support for establishing and maintaining social networks in which she was exposed to Japanese. Over time, she reached out to the friends of her friends to develop a multiplex network that included both Japanese students and other Australian learners of Japanese. Her network provided her with opportunities to use and learn Japanese—primarily with other learners of Japanese—and relationships with Japanese native speakers that motivated her to identify with Japanese language and culture. This example and others throughout this volume show us the arduous pathway to developing and drawing on the resources of one's social network. These stories also show us that social networks that support language learning are more complicated and more interesting than the native-speaking friend myth.

Teachers can support their students' long-term language development in several ways: by raising awareness of social networks that support language learning, linking students to opportunities to cultivate those networks, setting clear and demystified expectations for building and maintaining relationships, and reflecting on language use and identity in students' social networks. Teachers can do this by directing students to peer social networks including online learning communities, L2 social clubs, extracurricular activities, and elective coursework. Teachers might arrange study groups and language exchange activities (Inaba, Chapter 7, this volume) or peer-tutoring, mentoring, and community-integrated activities (Carhill-Poza, Chapter 2, this volume). Teachers can explicitly frame these activities with realistic expectations, including the idea that relationships are long-term investments where language use does not always follow initial expectations. As Emily's case demonstrates, investment in L2-engaged communities can provide linguistic and affective affordances which in turn are conducive to the development of motivation and language learning over months and years. Much of the research in this volume also highlights the important role of other L2 learners in supporting long-term language and identity development—the cases of Melissa and Fredrik (Inaba, Chapter 7, this volume) are a good example of the very important role of emergent bilingual peers. Teachers can also guide students to reflect on the role of relationships in language learning and set goals for building networks that support students' motivation and language learning in line with their identity (Trimble-Brown et al., Chapter 8, this volume). We believe that this is essential work for language teachers with long-term benefits for students.

It is also important for teachers to understand the implications of school and program-level policies for social networks and to advocate for change when the development of social resources for language learning is impeded by unexamined or untrue assumptions. Sometimes the work of facilitating students' entry into L2-engaged communities aligns with the institutional agenda; at other times, a critical assessment of school or program policies reveals obstacles to developing and maintaining social networks that support language development. For example, Hasegawa (Chapter 9, this volume) describes a study abroad program in which a target language–only pledge limited students' ability to develop a diverse network with conationals (i.e., American students) and local Japanese students. By resisting the policy, students managed to construct social networks that drew on their multilingual repertoires and supported their language development. Carhill-Poza (Chapter 2, this volume) describes a set of school policies that segregated students who were learning English from bilingual and monolingual students who were more proficient. Although students in her study could draw on bilingual peers to support their language learning, neither school policy nor classroom practice valorized these relationships. While the policies both authors describe were designed to support language development by prioritizing use of the L2, these policies also undermined students' access to multilingual resources for learning and deterred students from developing diverse social networks that included bilingual and L2 learner peers. For teachers of immigrant and refugee populations in particular, when learning a new language is necessary for survival and long-term success, school policies need to engage the strengths that students bring to this herculean task—foremost their identities, experiences, and skills in their first language.

Valuing the multilingual resources students have access to through their peers, families, teachers, and others to support language learning is the first step to creating a pedagogical space where the language use of bilingual and multilingual individuals is noticed, understood, and leveraged for learning. Social network research in applied linguistics is foremost an account of the ways that the individuals a student knows influence their language use and language learning. Teachers can, for example, reassess the assumption that multilingual peer talk is off-topic or disruptive in the classroom, a misunderstanding of the rich multilingual space that relationships with bilingual peers provide for adolescent language learners (Carhill-Poza, Chapter 2, this volume). Teachers can envisage a central role for families in supporting L2 and heritage language development, an arena frequently overlooked by language teachers who focus on classroom learning (Oriyama, Chapter 4, this volume; Palfreyman, Chapter 6, this volume). For example, Durbidge (Chapter 10, this volume) reflects on the role of host mothers and host siblings as critical links to developing diverse, multilingual social networks.

After teachers rethink *who is the context of language learning*, the next step is shaping pedagogical activities to create spaces for language use and language learning in line with what our students are already doing. Multilingual approaches to language teaching that consciously draw on languaging (Swain, 2006) or translanguaging (Garcia & Wei, 2014) can guide teaching practice. A translanguaging approach builds classroom language practices around students' existing language practices, consciously unpacking the social, historical, and political inequalities that inform students' use of language. In all classrooms, valuing the multilingual resources of language learners (not just their skills in the target language) is essential to advancing students' social network development. Fundamentally, teachers facilitate relationships in their classrooms by understanding and valuing peer support. This often involves taking a step back from the front of the classroom in order to create interactive learning environments or allow space for student collaboration. Kibler et al. (Chapter 3, this volume) demonstrate that students benefit from concerted classroom-level support to develop "mutually reinforcing" social networks. In some classrooms, this may take the form of cross-linguistic relationships, while in others bilingual peers or other L2 learners may provide support for one another. But as Kibler et al. point out, students are better able to build strong peer relationships when teachers provide direct behavioral support, guiding students to interact with each other in ways that apprentice them into sustained friendships. Teachers who address issues of discrimination in the classroom and create an inclusive culture are building the foundation for mutually supportive relationships to flourish.

Social networks within our classrooms create powerful spaces for language learning, but technology also enables L2 learners to develop and maintain social networks that can support language development beyond the classroom. Inaba (Chapter 7, this volume) describes the linguistically rich interactions that students of Japanese as a foreign language in Australia and Sweden formed with other learners online. Palfreyman (Chapter 6, this volume), also, reflects on the affordances of online communication for a gender-segregated community of learners, noting that in many cases students were able to access resources beyond the university, which are often overlooked by educators. An important finding is that the growing role of technology in language learning is still mediated by human relationships. Melissa and Fredrik were both introduced to the online communities that they engaged with by a friend or family member (Inaba, Chapter 7, this volume). As several authors point out, the goals of online community engagement could be additional practice while studying a new language or continued language learning as students transition out of coursework. Teachers can facilitate student engagement with language learning online in the same ways that they support their in-class social network development: by raising awareness of the importance of relationships for language learning, connecting students to online networks when possible, setting reasonable expectations for the development and maintenance of social networks via technology, and facilitating reflection on the role of technology-dependent relationships in L2 learning.

Implications for Theory

Social network analysis in applied linguistics describes the relationships that support language learning therein providing a nuanced accounting of the balance between individual agency and the social contexts that structure learners' experiences and language development trajectories. The studies in this volume make a valuable contribution to understanding the resources language learners recruit, accrue, and access via their social networks in unique settings from around the world. This collection also foregrounds the complexity of language use in multilingual contexts, a reality that research and practice cannot afford to overlook.

Our collected work suggests connections between learner social networks, available support/affordances, and language learning careers/outcomes, shown in Figure 11.1. In contrast to models of social networks that constrain

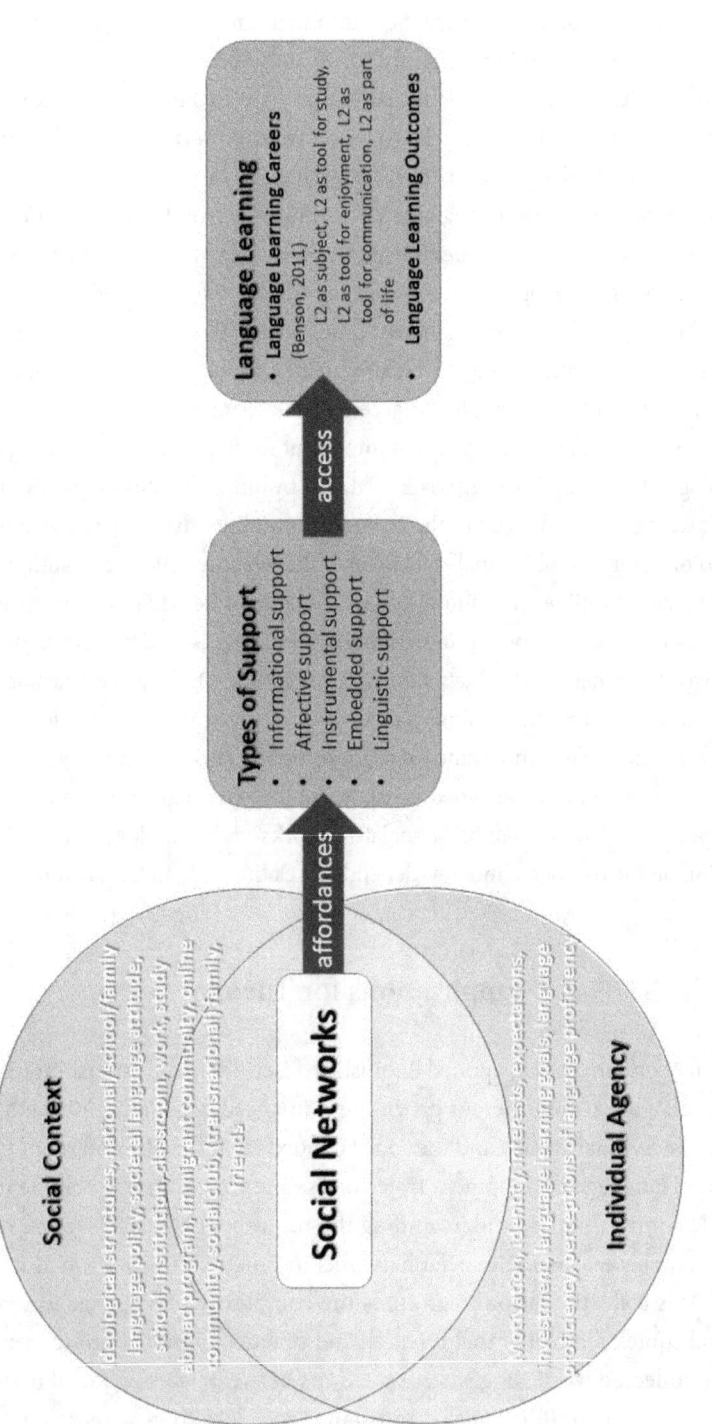

Figure 11.1 Language learners' social networks.

agency to a single directing force (e.g., a teacher-directed network or individually directed network), our model of social networks highlights the balance of sociocultural context and individual agency. Among others, Carhill-Poza (Chapter 2, this volume), Kibler et al. (Chapter 3, this volume), and Oriyama (Chapter 4, this volume) produce evidence of mediation between individual agency and the affordances of schools, classrooms, and family circles. In this model, social networks are formed through the constant push-pull of forces within and beyond the individual's control, and are interdependent constructs. Van Lier's (2004, 2008) concept of affordance, which is defined as the relationship between properties of the environment and the active learner, exists in this space. While classroom networks may be nominally directed by a teacher, the teacher works in tandem with other sociocultural factors, and students actively participate in creating networks for learning purposes. Importantly, classrooms are not viewed as the only contexts for learning or developing social networks. Individual agency is foregrounded in many accounts of social network development outside the classroom. For example, the university students of Japanese in Kurata's and Inaba's studies (Chapters 5 & 7, this volume) all sought membership in social networks—including online learning communities and conversation practice groups—for the purpose of cultivating a space to use and learn the L2. But here too, sociocultural factors shaped network formation, such as the availability of L2-related communities in the city where a learner resides (cf. Kurata, Chapter 5, this volume).

We draw on Benson's (2011) concept of language learning careers alongside other language learning outcomes to define a set of process-oriented language learning goals/outcomes that co-occur with "an ongoing process of developing an identity as a language learner" (Benson, 2011: 547). We argue that a crucial part of this process is derived from learners' social networks. Language learning trajectories encompass a wide variety of developmental outcomes and occur in contexts where different aspects of their learning align with situated research questions. For example, in a school setting, Carhill-Poza (Chapter 2, this volume) measured oral academic English proficiency, while Kurata (Chapter 5, this volume) captured changes in L2 identity over time. Given that many of our participants were not solely interested in achieving a particular L2 proficiency score, but in figuring out how to solve for the area of a triangle (Carhill-Poza, Chapter 2, this volume), gain cultural expertise (Inaba, Chapter 7, this volume), or make friends in a new country (Hasegawa, Chapter 9, this volume), language learning itself must be understood as variable.

The research we draw on in this volume captures a variety of resources that learners access through their social networks and connects this support to language learning experiences and outcomes. The most common types of support described in the extant literature and within this volume are (1) affective support, provided when a person trusts and is comforted by another, (2) informational support, which involves advice to help a person to understand and manage their situation, (3) embedded support (also described as social companionship or belongingness), which stresses a person's positive feeling related to having a recognized role when in the company of others, and (4) instrumental support, which includes supplying resources and services to assist a person (c.f. Cohen & Wills, 1985). In addition to affective, informational, embedded, and instrumental support, we add linguistic support, a multilingual and multimodal conceptualization of the interactions that a person engages in with others in their network. Throughout the work in this volume, multiple types of support are accessed by students alongside linguistic support through their networks. That is, linguistic support is always a component of the relationship, but it is not the only type of support accessible through one's social network.

At the heart of our work, we are interested in the ways that relationships create linguistic environments for learners. For example, social networks sustain the affordances of the L2 classroom, supporting language learning and identity development through multiple levels of support. A relationship of mutual trust between a teacher and students can lead to the provision of affective support. Teachers and peers can also provide students with learning materials (instrumental support) and concrete pathway knowledge to help them to manage their situation (informational support). Linguistic support could be accessed at the same time as other forms of support. And, students can generate positive feelings about themselves by being recognized and having a sense of belonging to classroom networks (embedded support). Embedded support is a type of support that may originate from peer relationships that are facilitated by teachers (e.g., Kibler et al., Chapter 3, this volume) or from peer relationships that are independent of teachers (e.g., Carhill-Poza, Chapter 2, this volume).

Another context that is prevalent in our collected work is peer groups. Peer social networks in which the L2 is widely used can be especially hard to establish (cf. Kurata, Chapter 5; Hasegawa, Chapter 9; Durbidge, Chapter 10, this volume), and a number of individual factors seem to be in play—including the learner's L2 competence, how they perceive themselves as L2 users, and how their L2 use is perceived and accommodated by other members of their networks. Meaningful interaction in peer social networks could provide students with all of five types of social support, such as advice and resources related to L2 (informational and instrumental support), encouragement or reassurance (affective support), and friendship or legitimate membership of the group/network (embedded support) at the same time as linguistic support. In particular, we highlight the importance of embedded support, which would facilitate the development of learner identity as multilingual and a competent user of L2.

While we do not propose a specific mechanism for accessing these various forms of support available to learners through their social networks, the researchers' and participants' understanding of social support in our collected work aligns with Benson's (2011) concept of language learning careers that we mentioned earlier. It is useful to think about accessing social support in four different ways: (1) phases, clearly defined periods such as the duration of a course or study abroad program, (2) processes, activities that were characteristic of particular phases (and often reported as being repetitive), (3) incidents, events that happened once, and (4) critical incidents, incidents recounted in order to account for a change of direction or a transition between phases. Much of the research in this volume defines available social resources in terms of phases. Although phases are often clearly defined within a specific time period, they are also determined by more subjective criteria including how learners conceptualize the target language. An example of a critical incident can be found in Kurata (Chapter 5, this volume) where Emily changed her conception of the target language from an academic subject to a tool for communication. Initially, Emily focused on learning an L2 as simply another subject at university, but as her language skills developed, she looked for and engaged in activities and interactions in the L2. This and other studies support an argument for different and changing mechanisms for understanding how L2 learners access the resources available to them through their social networks.

Another example can be found in research on online communities. Participants in online L2 communities (cf. Fredrick's case in Inaba, Chapter 7, Emily's case in Kurata, Chapter 5) shared an interest in the target language and culture with the online group as a whole while also initiating smaller groups focused on particular learning activities within their communities (such as aiming to pass a language proficiency test). Such groups exchange informational support (e.g., linguistic explanations and advice), instrumental support (e.g., L2 resources and learning strategies), and, of course, linguistic support. In the case of learners who have a strong interest in learning an L2 itself, their conceptualization of the L2 would become that of a tool for enjoyment rather than that as a subject, while those who enjoy pop culture could move from viewing the L2 as a subject to considering the L2 as a tool for enjoyment as well.

In sum, a model of learners' social networks needs to recognize the variety of support that students/L2 users draw on from their social networks, multiple processes and outcomes that relate to L2 learning, and the interdependence of social context and individual agency in developing and engaging social networks for language learning. Visualizing the plurality of resources for language learning available via one's social network is an especially important aspect of theorizing the role of social support in language teaching. It is also clear that "pure" linguistic support is not commonly offered on its own, but rather is intertwined with other types of support.

A Research Agenda for Social Networks in Language Teaching and Language Learning

In writing this book, we considered the state of our field at a time of challenge and opportunity. Social network analysis is in many ways tailored to this moment where language learning is defined by its complexity, mobility, and innovation within an ever-expanding set of transnational and multilingual learning contexts (The Douglas Fir Group, 2016). The transdisciplinary nature of research on social networks in language learning and language teaching is a strength as we seek to understand how languages are learned in life beyond the university classroom. The studies in this volume make a valuable contribution to understanding the multilingual resources students recruit, accrue, and access via their social networks in unique settings from around the world, but more work needs to be done.

Throughout this book project, we turned to our collaborators to better understand how the lens of social network analysis can guide policy and practice. We highlight three central considerations for social network analysis in language learning and language teaching moving forward. First, the recognition of the multilingual repertoires of learners is essential to understanding learners' identities, motivations, and agency in recruiting support for language learning. A multilingual perspective is also basic to an accurate understanding of the processes of language learning. Theories of languaging (Swain, 2006) and translanguaging (Garcia & Wei, 2014) must continue to be engaged to describe more realistic accounts of language use and linguistic resources. A multilingual perspective redefines who counts as a resource for language learning and is especially important in terms of school or program-level policy. For example, it is important to examine how learners/students initiate social interactions and establish social networks with L2 speakers, including peers. By utilizing their multilingual repertoires rather than focusing only on their L2 use with native speakers, we can learn how their identities and motivations are constructed across time and space in multilingual social networks.

Second, social network analysis can provide much-needed background for the interactions that we see in classrooms, friendship groups, and online communities. Without acknowledging the multiple layers of social support that networks of relationships provide, we can easily misunderstand the long-term investment that is manifest in a single interaction or set of interactions. We advocate a mixed-methods approach that pairs classroom observation or recordings of social interaction in natural settings with in-depth analysis of social networks through surveys and interviews to document the process of language learning in its relational context. We also encourage researchers to examine links between classroom learning and settings beyond the classroom through a relational lens, shifting the focus from a moment in time to a more complicated frame of human investment. These connections between micro- and macro-level foci has the potential to transform language teaching practice.

And finally, social networks develop and change over time, necessitating more longitudinal research and a continuing curiosity about language learning throughout the lifespan. Social network analysis has the potential to document the ways that structures enacted through policy and practice mutually reinforce the social networks that our participants develop, but this window of insight, if narrowly focused, can also lead to policies that fail to leverage the full potential of social support. Language learners recruit support from contexts that we may not think of as the ideal—online communities, other L2 learners, friends of friends, immigrant and transnational parents. And yet it is these relationships in changing formations over time that are the context of language learning. As L2 learners grow more confident, as identities shift, and as interests and investments change, so too do the goals of the language learning career and the social support sought. By richly detailing the interaction between social context and individual agency in the development and utilization of social networks among language learners, we hope that the many sources of support available to language learners will be acknowledged, understood, and engaged to support their learning in classrooms and throughout their lives.

References

Benson, P. (2011). Language learning careers as an object of narrative research in TESOL. *TESOL Quarterly, 45*(3), 545–53.

Cohen, S., & Wills, T. A. (1985). Stress, social support, and the buffering hypothesis. *Psychological Bulletin, 98*(2), 310–57.

Garcia, O., & Wei, L. (2014). *Tanslanguaging: Language, bilingualism and education.* New York: Palgrave Macmillan.

Leung, C., Harris, R., & Rampton, B. (1997). The idealised native speaker, reified ethnicities, and classroom realities. *TESOL Quarterly, 31*(3), 543–60.

Swain, M. (2006). Languaging, agency and collaboration in advanced language proficiency. In H. Byrnes (Ed.), *Advanced language learning: The contribution of Halliday and Vygotsky* (pp. 95–108). London: Continuum.

The Douglas Fir Group. (2016). A transdisciplinary framework for SLA in a multilingual world. *The Modern Language Journal, 16,* 19–47.

van Lier, L. (2004). *The ecology and semiotics of language learning: A sociocultural perspective.* Boston, MA: Springer.

van Lier, L. (2008). The ecology of language learning and sociocultural theory. In A. Creese, P. Martin, & N. H. Hornberger (Eds.), *Encyclopedia of language and education, vol. 9: Ecology of language* (pp. 53–65). New York: Springer.

Contributors

Sydney Cadogan (University of Virginia, USA)
Avary Carhill-Poza (University of Massachusetts Boston, USA)
Dan P. Dewey (Brigham Young University, USA)
Levi Durbidge (Monash University, Australia)
Dennis L. Eggett (Brigham Young University, USA)
Lauren Molloy Elreda (University of Virginia, USA)
Betina Fuentes (CIA International School, Cambodia)
Atsushi Hasegawa (University of Hawaii, USA)
Vonna Hemmler (University of Virginia, USA)
Miho Inaba (Cardiff University, UK)
Amanda Kibler (Oregon State University, USA)
Naomi Kurata (Monash University, Australia)
Vashti Lee (Georgetown University, USA)
Kaya Oriyama (Swinburn University of Technology, Australia)
David M. Palfreyman (Zayed University, United Arab Emirates)
Alexis Rutt (University of Virginia, USA)
Hannah Trimble-Brown (Brigham Young University, USA)

Author Index

Benson, P. 89, 90, 104, 106, 108, 109, 138, 141, 217, 243, 245
Bernstein, K. A. 2, 3, 91
Boissevain, J. 7, 93, 106, 222
Borgatti, S. P. 6, 189
Bourdieu, P. 5, 16, 67, 93, 109
Bown, J. 3, 91, 163, 166, 184

Carhill-Poza, A. 2–8, 15, 17, 18, 19, 26, 28–30, 37, 57, 91, 228, 239, 240, 243, 244
Carolan, B. 2, 6, 7, 139, 142, 155
Chik, A. 97, 139, 140, 217
Cohen, S. 213, 244
Coleman, J. S. 5, 16, 31, 33, 39
Cummins, J. 65, 66, 83

Dewey, D. P. 2, 3, 91, 92, 140, 161–3, 166, 176, 184, 185, 210, 211, 228
Donato, R. 17, 115
Dörnyei, Z. 90, 101, 146, 163, 176
Douglas Fir Group 209, 213, 229, 230, 246
Duff, P. A. 2, 41, 69, 91, 92, 93, 116, 140, 142, 186, 210, 213, 217, 227
Durbidge, L. 5–9, 133, 179, 184, 205, 211, 240, 244

Eggett, D. L. 2, 91, 163, 184

Faust, K. 2, 37, 139
Fishman, J. A. 65, 66

García, O. 32, 240, 246
Gest, S. D. 40, 45, 46, 57

Hasegawa, A. 2, 6, 7, 9, 91, 163, 200, 239, 244
Hillstrom, R. 176, 210

Inaba, M. 6, 7, 9, 91, 133, 138, 142, 152, 224, 239, 241, 243, 245
Isabelli-García, C. 2, 3, 91, 92, 105, 106, 140, 176, 186, 210, 211, 227

Kibler, A. 2, 3, 4, 5, 7, 8, 17, 18, 32, 40–3, 45, 46, 57–8, 187, 240, 243, 244
Kinginger, C. 3, 184, 211, 227, 228
Kurata, N. 2, 3, 5–8, 16, 58, 90, 91, 116, 117, 140, 155, 186, 210, 218, 228, 238, 243–5

Lantolf, J. P. 5, 17, 18, 92, 93, 139, 141, 163, 209, 219

McManus, K. 3, 116, 175, 209
Mercer, S. 117, 162, 179
Milroy, L. 2, 16, 67, 68, 89, 93, 100, 162, 213
Mitchell, R. 3, 116, 176, 209–11

Norton, B. 92, 93, 116

Oettingen, G. 161, 164, 168, 176
Oriyama, K. 6, 7, 8, 57, 64, 70, 73, 80, 240, 243
Ortega, L. 115, 163
Oxford, R. L. 100, 163

Palfreyman, D. M. 3, 5, 6, 8, 25, 103, 107, 113, 116–18, 132, 133, 134, 139, 140, 240, 241
Pavlenko, A. 92, 93, 163, 209, 219

Scott, J. 138, 143, 176
Shiri, S. 185, 210, 211, 220, 227
Smith, L. R. 2, 16, 91, 140
Suárez-Orozco, C. 16, 17
Swain, M. 17, 115, 240, 246

Tan, D.   184, 211
Thorne, S. L.   5, 18, 92, 139, 141
Trimble-Brown, H.   6, 7, 9, 184, 239

Valdés, G.   16, 42
van Lier, L.   5, 18, 32, 37–40, 92, 93, 243
Vygotsky, L.   17, 18, 115, 139, 141, 142

Wasserman, S.   2, 37, 139
Wei, L.   2, 16, 117, 205, 240, 246
Wenger, E.   68, 82, 213
Wiklund, I.   3, 16, 18, 91
Wilkinson, S.   162, 211
Wills, T. A.   213, 244

Zappa-Hollman, S.   2, 69, 91, 92, 116, 140, 142, 186, 210, 213, 227

Subject Index

academic language   17, 22, 27–8, 31, 32, 66
academic skills   17, 38, 47, 49, 50–2, 57, 123, 130, 134, 140, 163
academic support   2, 17, 21, 23, 24, 69, 242
Activity Theory   138–9, 141–2, 150, 151, 152, 154
adolescents   2, 8, 9, 17, 18, 22, 31, 33, 37–8, 40, 43, 57, 65, 68, 143, 210, 212, 214, 225, 227
advocacy   239, 247
affective support   2, 69, 99, 103, 105, 214, 222, 226, 244–5
affordance   4, 5, 6, 37, 39, 93, 99, 103, 108, 109, 115–17, 118, 123, 204, 239, 241, 243–4
afterschool program   20, 24, 29, 54–5, 80, 100, 101, 102, 106, 109, 113, 151, 152, 162, 163, 188, 189, 190, 204, 224, 238
agency   4, 15, 25, 31, 33–4, 57, 93, 116, 162–3, 179, 204, 213, 222–3, 228, 237, 238, 241–3, 246–7
agent   2, 25, 90, 105, 109, 141, 155, 163
Anime   95, 144, 148, 149–50, 221, 224
Arabic   44, 114, 129, 132, 163
Australia   8, 9, 64, 66, 70, 71, 73–5, 77–80, 91–5, 101–4, 139, 143–6, 152, 153, 212, 238, 241
awareness   3–4, 15, 18, 58, 78, 97, 100, 140, 204–5, 238, 241

bilingual/multilingual peers   2, 15, 17, 18, 19, 24, 26, 27–9, 30, 31, 32–3, 239, 240

centrality   7, 25, 187, 198
classroom context   4, 15, 32, 37–8, 39–41, 50–1, 56–7, 89, 108, 115, 156, 240
clusters   7, 69, 93, 100, 102, 194, 215

community   22, 33, 64, 68, 79–82, 97, 99, 103–5, 116–18, 139–40, 142–3, 165–6, 239
  classroom community   37–8, 56, 58, 99
  community member(s)   1, 33, 68, 97, 105, 109
  community school   70–1, 74–5, 77, 80, 83
  host community   210–11, 217, 222–3, 229
  online community   99, 103, 116, 153, 155–6, 238, 241, 243, 245, 247
Community of Practice   68–9, 134, 213
co-regulation of learning   115, 119, 123, 126
cross-linguistic relationships   3, 32, 240

data collection   6–7, 20–1, 45, 46, 93, 144, 145–6, 148, 150, 152, 205, 215
  case studies   6, 8, 28, 93, 109, 139, 144, 156
  diaries   7–8, 93–4, 96–7, 146, 149, 219–20
  ethnography   7, 19, 21, 134
  interviews   8, 19–21, 69, 73, 92–4, 102, 146, 153, 178, 189, 195, 215, 217, 229, 247
  observation   7, 21, 30, 45, 189, 247
  surveys   6, 7–8, 41, 43, 46, 69, 73, 109, 113, 118–20, 161, 166–7, 168–9, 189, 247
degree of connection   3, 7, 39, 91
density   6, 7, 16, 92, 93, 97, 100, 103, 164, 166, 169, 191, 192
dispersion   3, 164, 166, 169, 170, 171
Dubai   8, 113, 114, 119, 121, 127, 129
duration of interaction   7, 164, 166, 169, 174

ecological perspective   3, 5, 18, 32, 37–40, 43, 58, 134, 209
embedded support   214, 220, 225–7, 242, 244–5

emergent bilingual   15, 18, 19, 24, 25, 26, 29–33, 239
English as a lingua franca   114, 123, 153, 155
English as a Second Language (ESL)   19, 24, 29, 140–1, 155, 223
expectations   25, 31, 33, 49, 53, 66, 99, 118, 177, 201, 203, 211, 214, 238, 239, 241
   family expectations   66
   learner expectations   25, 53, 99, 177, 201, 203, 211, 239, 242
   setting expectations   31, 33, 214, 239
   teacher expectations   238, 239, 241
foreign language learning (FLL)   95, 139, 155, 156, 238, 241
frequency of interaction   2, 16, 50–1, 52, 57–8, 73, 122, 123, 127, 132, 213, 215, 217
funds of knowledge   115, 123, 133

Gulf-Arab   116

help   17, 20–3, 25, 27, 30, 37–41, 45, 46, 50, 75, 77, 81, 97, 99, 102, 115, 119, 120, 126–31, 132–4, 163–5, 167, 171–8, 196, 197, 202, 214, 221, 228, 229, 244
heritage language development   8, 65–6, 69, 73, 74, 76, 81, 82–3, 240
high school   9, 20, 30, 148, 190, 212, 221
home-country settings   3, 8, 33, 65–6, 82, 91–2, 94, 106, 108–9, 145, 149, 153
homestay   185, 211–12, 214, 229
homophily   192, 204
host-country settings   3, 65–6, 185, 214, 218
host family   185, 211–12, 214, 215, 217, 218–20, 225, 227–8
hypersegregation   29

identity   6, 65–9, 76, 89–90, 93, 99, 107–8, 143, 179, 224, 229–30, 238–40, 243–7
   cultural identity   8, 66, 67–9, 73, 78–80, 81–3, 114
   L2 user identity   1, 4, 8, 89–90, 104, 108, 243, 245
immigrants/immigration   3, 6, 8, 15, 16–17, 18, 19–22, 23–5, 26, 28–9, 30–1, 33–4, 37, 40, 43, 57, 65–6, 91, 114, 140, 212, 221, 239, 247
informational support   214, 219, 226, 228, 242, 244, 245
instrumental support   214, 219, 226, 227, 242, 244, 245
integration   3, 8, 9, 39, 40–1, 43, 44, 45, 46, 47, 48, 49, 50, 51, 56, 57, 58, 166, 223, 228
interaction   2–4, 7, 16, 18, 31–2, 39, 40–3, 91–2, 93, 94, 102–4, 105, 107, 109, 115–16, 162, 166, 169, 178, 222–5, 228–9, 240, 244–5, 247
   multilingual interactions   30, 196, 202, 223, 224, 227, 229, 230, 244
   off-task interaction   46, 48, 240
   peer interactions   18, 26, 27, 30, 40–3, 46–7, 48, 54–6, 58, 89, 102–4, 107, 109, 115, 140, 175, 190, 198, 202, 210, 212, 218, 221–2, 224–5, 229, 240–1, 244, 247
   small talk   42, 57, 176
   teacher-student interactions   41–3, 46–7, 48, 51–4, 115, 123
interdisciplinary perspectives   1, 2, 186
interpersonal connections/ relationships   1, 31, 67, 184–7, 189, 195, 197, 200, 203–5

Japan   66, 70, 71, 74, 75, 80, 82, 94, 100, 101, 102, 104, 106, 145, 151, 152, 153, 185, 214, 219
Japanese   3, 8–9, 66, 69, 70, 73, 74–80, 81–2, 90–1, 93–4, 95–104, 105–8, 109, 117, 138–9, 140–1, 142–3, 144–5, 147–54, 155–6, 165, 185, 187, 188, 190, 193–4, 195–203, 204–5, 210, 212, 214–15, 217, 218–19, 221, 224–5, 228, 238–9, 241, 243

K-12 education   4, 6, 15, 19, 40, 43, 70, 75–7, 79–80, 82, 94, 125, 143, 215

L2 development   25–6, 28–9, 33, 37, 97, 114, 140, 184, 224, 240
Language attitudes (societal)   64, 76, 78, 82, 140, 176, 242
language change   2, 16, 65, 73, 74, 76, 77, 79, 81, 82

language learning careers 106–7, 108–9, 243, 245, 247
language learning outcomes 4, 5, 6, 18, 241, 242, 243, 245
language maintenance 16, 64–6, 68–9, 74, 76, 81–3
language pledge 185, 188, 193, 196–7, 199, 205
language policy 15, 16, 18, 30, 64, 185, 186, 204, 239, 246–7
  education policy 16, 18, 25, 31, 185, 186, 204, 239, 246–7
  family language policy 64
language proficiency 2, 19, 20, 21, 22, 26, 28, 29, 31, 38, 40, 41, 42, 52, 66, 76, 99, 108, 118, 132, 140, 151, 153, 162, 166, 167, 169, 176, 195, 218, 225, 242, 243, 245
language socialization 4, 7, 69, 73–5, 78, 80, 81–83
languaging 115, 240, 246
learner attitudes 3, 64, 68, 76–8, 82, 89, 118, 133, 140, 166, 170, 176, 202, 219
learner characteristics 3, 6, 7, 8, 19, 21, 26, 53–4, 55–6, 70, 71, 75, 80, 81, 95, 113–22, 124, 126, 127, 129, 130, 132–4, 140, 141, 162, 165, 189, 190, 193, 196, 212, 215, 216, 220, 223, 225, 227, 241, 244
  educational background 21, 70, 75, 80, 95, 116, 117, 118, 119, 121, 124, 141, 190, 212
  gender 3, 6, 8, 19, 26, 70, 71, 113, 114, 115, 116, 117, 118, 119, 120, 122, 126, 127, 129, 130, 132, 133, 134, 140, 162, 165, 189, 193, 196, 215, 216, 241
  perceived expertise 3, 57, 103
  social roles 3, 52, 53–4, 55–6, 81, 116, 119, 220, 223, 225, 227, 244
learner reflection 25, 77, 90, 146
linguistic competence/competencies 210, 212, 218, 222–3, 225, 228–30
linguistic integration 39–40, 43, 50, 56–9, 166
linguistic repertoire(s) 16, 30, 224
linguistic resources 2, 5, 8, 18, 22, 26, 33, 246

linguistic support 18, 21, 22, 24, 29, 33, 97, 99, 103, 105, 204, 242, 244, 245, 246
literacy 64, 66–7, 70, 73, 75–9, 81–2, 132
longitudinal research 6–7, 8, 93, 105, 156, 212, 247

mediation 1, 3–4, 16, 18, 40, 41, 92, 134, 141–3, 154, 219, 227, 241, 243
membership(s) 24, 65, 74, 99, 102, 105, 117, 187, 192, 219, 243–4
mental contrasting 9, 161, 164, 176
methods (of SNA) 6–8, 37, 45, 93, 118, 161, 184, 189, 210, 246–7
  ethnographic methods 7, 19, 21, 29, 30, 31, 134
  mixed-methods 7, 18, 20, 43, 165–9, 189, 212, 247
  qualitative methods 21, 45, 46, 70, 93, 145, 168, 169, 172, 184, 210–12
  quantitative methods 7, 20, 22, 41, 90, 118, 134, 161, 166–7
motivation 3, 64, 89–92, 94–9, 101, 105–9, 141, 151, 156, 164, 175–9, 201, 205, 239, 246
  ideal L2 self 90, 101, 104, 106
  instrumental motivation 90, 104
  integrative motivation 90, 91, 95, 99
  intrinsic motivation 90, 94–5, 97, 105, 107
motive(s) 90, 142, 144–5, 149–55
multilingual settings 4, 19, 43, 70, 144–5, 165, 187–8, 214–15
multiplexity 2, 7, 16, 93, 100, 102, 103, 106, 109, 210, 227, 238
myths about language learning 237–8

narrative(s) 130, 133, 217, 219, 225
native speaker 94, 97, 99, 102, 103, 105, 106, 108, 109, 132, 134, 140, 144, 147, 151, 152, 153, 155, 156, 161, 162, 163, 167, 170, 174, 175, 177, 230, 237, 238, 247
natural setting(s) 93, 99, 101, 105, 247
network development 3–4, 17, 81, 100, 162–4, 167–9, 179, 212, 240–1, 243
Network of Practice 67, 69, 116, 213

network size   7, 21, 25, 93, 100, 102, 164, 166, 169, 170, 174, 176, 177, 178, 210
network types   5, 6, 7, 37, 38, 41, 43, 44, 45, 186, 187–9, 197, 200, 203
    classroom peer network   37, 38, 41
    complete networks   6, 7, 43–5, 187–9
    egocentric networks   5, 37, 43, 186, 197, 200, 203
    sociocentric networks   37, 43, 186
newcomer(s)   18, 20–2, 25–6, 28–9, 33, 228

online resources   89, 96–7, 99, 102–3, 105, 109, 116, 121–2, 126, 129, 130, 133, 134, 140, 147, 152, 153–4, 155, 156, 224, 238, 241, 243, 245, 247
oral language development   3, 4, 99, 140
out-of-class contexts   97, 109, 138–9, 140, 141–3, 144, 145–6, 147, 149–50, 154, 155, 156, 162

parents   16, 22–5, 33, 66, 118, 220, 240
participation   8, 26, 38–40, 41–3, 46–7, 48–53, 55, 56, 57, 58, 68–9, 76, 78, 106, 209, 214, 221, 224, 225, 227, 229
    active participation   39, 47, 48–50, 57, 78, 99, 105, 107–8, 140, 163, 196, 212, 243
    participation schemata   221
pedagogical implications   28, 32, 58, 81–2, 108, 133, 154–5, 177, 203, 229, 237–41
peer(s)   17, 20, 25–9, 32, 37, 38, 42, 58, 73, 109, 238, 240, 244
peer mentoring   24, 162, 165, 239
peer network linguistic integration   8, 39, 40–1, 43, 45–6, 47, 48–50, 51, 52, 56, 57, 58, 166
peer social network   4, 8, 9, 25–30, 46, 109, 238, 244–5
percent of L2 users   2
perception of L2 proficiency   96, 132, 218, 228, 242, 244
pop culture   53, 101, 102, 104, 107, 139, 140, 144, 147–8, 149–50, 154–5, 246
positive thinking   18, 57, 64, 68, 140, 172, 175, 201

practice   1, 75, 80, 97, 100, 104, 115, 116, 122, 142, 151, 152, 153, 164, 197, 202, 210, 241, 243
primary/elementary school   75–6, 77, 94

reciprocity   5, 211, 223, 224
relationships   16, 17, 21, 22, 23, 24, 25–9, 31–3, 37, 38, 42, 57, 58, 66, 73, 77, 78, 107, 109, 118, 148–9, 154, 155, 220, 238–9, 240, 244
role   3, 16, 21, 22, 23, 33, 52, 53–56, 81, 115, 116, 119, 149, 153, 204, 214, 220, 223, 225, 227, 240, 244

school adult(s)   15, 18, 22–5, 29, 33
secondary school   4, 15, 19, 43, 70, 75–7, 79–80, 82, 94, 143, 215
segregation   17, 25, 29, 46
self-regulation   9, 115, 161, 163–4, 166, 168, 170, 172, 176, 177, 178–9
siblings   16, 77, 78, 118, 148–9
significant others   103, 138–9, 143, 147, 154–5
social capital   5, 16, 25, 31, 33, 33, 93, 106, 108, 109, 115
social context   5, 17, 39, 90, 115, 117, 142, 209, 213, 221, 222, 241, 242, 246, 247
social interaction(s)   1, 5, 58, 105, 109, 162, 166–7, 173–5, 177–9, 185, 209, 218, 223, 247
socialization   2, 4, 9, 25, 64, 65, 66–7, 68, 69, 73, 74–5, 77, 78–81, 82–3, 116, 140, 185–6, 187, 189, 220
social media   73, 117, 215
social network approaches   6–7, 18, 37–8, 186–7, 237
social network models   93, 142, 146, 185–6, 242–3, 245
social opportunity structure   9, 17, 238
social resources   3, 4, 5, 8, 9, 15, 17–18, 25, 27, 31, 33, 127, 134, 141, 223, 239, 245
social support   2, 4, 16, 18, 237, 238, 245, 246–7
sociocentric network   37, 43, 186–7
sociocultural context(s)   67, 81, 243
sociocultural theory/perspective   5, 17–18, 92, 139, 141–3

sociolinguistics   1, 2, 139
sociology   2, 5, 139, 143, 186
sojourn   65, 66, 184, 185, 186, 204, 205, 209, 210, 211, 212, 213, 219, 222, 226, 227, 228
Spanish   19, 20, 21, 23–30, 32, 44, 68, 91, 165, 173, 220
stages of language learning journey   6, 78, 105, 226
strength of ties   3, 16, 22, 24, 53, 69, 118, 133, 175, 191, 192, 193, 194, 197, 202, 203, 204, 211, 213, 219–23, 227, 240
   close ties   2, 7, 16, 190–1, 192, 193, 194, 197, 198, 200, 203, 223
   strong ties   16, 53, 175, 191–4, 197, 202–4, 211, 221, 223, 227, 240
   weak ties   16, 133, 192
structural inequality   4, 179, 240
study abroad   3, 7, 9, 65, 91, 105, 106, 140, 161, 162–4, 166, 176, 177, 179, 184, 185–7, 201, 203, 204, 205, 209, 210–11, 215, 216, 218, 219, 225, 227, 228, 238, 239, 245
Sweden   8, 9, 139, 143, 144, 145, 146, 241
Swedish   145, 151, 212

teachers   16, 21, 22–5, 42, 57, 58, 109, 155, 238–9
teaching practices   4, 9, 16, 18, 19, 31, 32, 41, 52, 55, 57–8, 229–30, 237–41, 247
   address discrimination   58, 241
   collaborative teaching practices   3, 29, 45, 83, 109, 240
   reflection   24, 229, 238, 239, 241
   strengths-based teaching practices   15, 33, 125, 133, 239
technology/technologies   64, 89, 114, 116–17, 130, 133, 138, 224, 241
ties   2, 7, 16, 64, 69, 106, 118, 189, 192–4, 197–8, 200, 203, 223, 237
transactional content   7, 93
transition   42, 106, 156, 241, 245
translanguaging   30, 205, 240, 246
transnational youth   8, 65, 66, 69, 70, 72, 73, 78–83

United Arab Eremites   3, 8, 113, 114, 116, 117, 124, 133, 134, 140
United States   8, 9, 15, 17, 19, 26, 43, 114, 161, 164, 165, 211, 212, 214

work   17, 20, 22, 25, 70, 75, 80, 101, 104, 114, 118, 119, 121, 123–7, 132, 150, 152, 163, 166, 220, 242

www.ingramcontent.com/pod-product-compliance
Lightning Source LLC
Chambersburg PA
CBHW072136290426
44111CB00012B/1890